D0686640

Hearing Voices

Embodiment and Experience

Lisa Blackman

FREE ASSOCIATION BOOKS / LONDON / NEW YORK

First published in Great Britain 2001 by
Free Association Books
57 Warren Street
London W1T 5NR

ISBN 1 85343 534 1 hbk; 1 85343 533 3 pbk

A CIP catalogue record for this book is available from the British Library

10	09	08	07	06	05	04	03	02	01
10	9	8	7	6	5	4	3	2	1

Designed and produced for Free Association Books by
Chase Publishing Services, Fortescue, Sidmouth, EX10 9QG
Printed in the European Union by Antony Rowe, Chippenham

Contents

Acknowledgements

There are numerous thanks and acknowledgements to make throughout the long gestation of this project. The research developed in this book was conducted mainly from 1990–94 under the supervision of Professor Nikolas Rose at Goldsmiths College, London. I would like to thank Nikolas for all his support during and after this period and his friendship thereafter. The research was funded by the ESRC who I would like to thank for supporting the interdisciplinary focus of the research. This research however would not have been possible without the support and encouragement of friends and mentors at the University of East London, Psychology Department. I would like to extend thanks to Professor Mary Boyle who encouraged me to develop these ideas beyond an undergraduate dissertation. Professor Harriette Marshall, Dr Kate Gleeson and Professor Celia Kitzinger gave me my first foray into critical psychology providing relief from statistics and experiments. I would like to thank the friends I made during this time, especially Jane Roscoe, Emma Finn, Sonita Singh and all those at Windsor Road! During the research period Pam Alldred, Sulma Mansuri, Nigelle De Bar, Sabine Peris, Heidi Bezzant, Petra Nienaber, Helen Lucey and Ian Hodges gave much support and encouragement. The development of these ideas into a book has taken place over a relatively short period of time. I would like to thank friends and significant others who have given support during this time, particularly Ain Bailey for music, love and laughter, Dr Sarah Kember and Dr Alan White for intellectual and emotional support, Alan Grier for pointing me in the right direction, and my family, Myra, Bob, Chris, Charlotte and Leon. A big thank you to my good friend and mentor Professor Valerie Walkerdine for continually encouraging and supporting my research. Thank you to all the students and colleagues in the Media Department at Goldsmiths College who have supported my ideas and research, particularly graduate students Stuart Fincham, Martha Michailidou and Garth Rennie, students on the 'Embodiment and Experience' course, and David Dibosa for his energy and enthusiasm. Heartfelt thanks go out to the Hearing Voices Network who embraced me with such warmth when I initially approached them and have supported my research since, especially Ron Coleman and all those at the Manchester office including Mickey and Sharon DeValda. Lastly, a thank you to David Stonestreet who commissioned this book and has given much encouragement.

This book is dedicated to all those who support the Hearing Voices Network and want radical transformation of the psychiatric system.

Introduction

Unravelling the mystery of schizophrenia

This book is about ways in which we might begin to understand the relationship between phenomena understood as 'biological' and/or 'psychological' in nature, and those disciplines which claim a special status for their knowledge and practice in relation to these phenomena. These disciplines, such as the 'psy' disciplines[1] use particular knowledges of these processes to intervene in aspects of thought and conduct, which are understood as symptomatic of disease and illness. The phenomenon of hearing voices is an exemplary example, although appearing across a range of psychiatric syndromes; it primarily appears as a diagnostic measure of schizophrenia. Schizophrenia, although itself a contested category (Boyle 1990), is a syndrome seen to include a range of other 'positive' and 'negative' symptoms which represent an underlying biochemical or neurological deficit or disorder. With the advent of new biotechnologies, associated more with the life sciences than the human sciences, psychiatry is increasingly turning its attention to those aspects of our biology which we carry in the molecular structures of our bodies.

A cursory glance at a journal such as the *British Journal of Psychiatry*, will reveal the extent to which psychiatry invests in practices such as genomic techniques to identify those genetic and molecular markers seen to predispose a person to particular forms of thought and conduct, such as hallucinations, delusions, flattened affect and so forth. Schizophrenia, despite concerns about its validity and reliability as a syndrome (Bentall 1990), is ultimately conceived as having a neurochemical basis, which these new technologies will render visible to the naked eye. It is hoped that these new techniques will also allow psychiatry a more sophisticated understanding of the complex psychopharmacology of some of the new anti-psychotics offered to cure and relieve such distressing symptoms (Kerwin et al. 1999). On the one hand then, there is evidence to suggest that psychiatry is becoming more 'biological', and will partner with the biomedical industry to pioneer cures

1

which will eventually alleviate the symptoms of mental distress, or at least make them more amenable to intervention.

However, alongside these developments, there are studies and research projects concerned with what some have termed the 'softer' side of psychiatry (Miller 1986). Running alongside the 'harder', biologically oriented research studies, are those which evaluate and advocate more psychologically oriented techniques, concerned less with biochemistry, and more with understanding and listening to the symptoms of mental distress. These studies to a certain extent recuperate many of the criticisms of psychiatry[2] where the patient simply becomes a signifier of disease and illness, rather than a person with a meaningful life history, which can be utilised in the understanding of the content of symptoms. In the context of the disproportionate number of black people incarcerated within the psychiatric system (Harrison et al. 1999), studies are beginning to address the ways in which possible misdiagnoses take place through 'miscommunications' between the doctor and patient (Goater et al. 1999, Hickling et al. 1999). These studies are open to many criticisms, as we will see in Chapter 2, because they rely on a particular way of understanding the relationship between culture and ethnicity (cf. Mercer 1986).

What is clear for the purposes of this book, is that psychiatry is not a homogeneous and unified discipline. It is a loosely assembled set of practices (Miller 1986), ranging from hard biological techniques to softer, more psychologically oriented practices that target the person in different ways. However, neither are the psychologically oriented techniques simply unproblematic alternatives. They have particular histories of emergence and combine with biological techniques in specific ways, in most instances complementing rather than radically destabilising some of the presumptions of the biomedical model. As an example, cognitive behavioural techniques are increasingly used in relation to psychotic symptoms. The distinction between the neurotic and psychotic, although of recent historical invention as we shall see in Chapter 6, has played an important role in policing the parameters of what kinds of thought and conduct are viewed as amenable to psychological intervention.

The orthodoxy within mid-nineteenth- to late twentieth-century psychiatry, was that the psychoses were directly linked to structural dysfunction(s) within the brain, often viewed as progressive, which produced symptoms which could only be addressed through biological processes. In the last decade of psychiatric practice the gaps and contradictions within this viewpoint have come to light. In a recent editorial in the *British Journal of Psychiatry* (Byrne 1999:1), the effects of stigma on a person receiving a psychiatric diagnosis, as well as on the practice of psychiatry itself, is raised as an important object for clinical reflection. On the one hand, it has been well documented, especially through the campaigns of service users, and radical magazines such as *Asylum*, that the conferring of a psychiatric diagnosis operates like a mark of shame. There is also more of a recognition amongst psychiatrists that 'difficult patients', those who are euphemistically referred to in the practice as 'heart-sink' patients (ibid.:1), are less likely to be listened to.

There is more attention to 'emotional processes' which affect the dynamics of psychoses, from the 'family burden' of those caring for a person with mental distress (Jenkins et al. 1999), to the role of 'expressed emotion' in the production of psychosis itself (ibid.). Psychiatrists are urged to be more mindful of the kinds of emotional responses brought up by patients in the course of a psychiatric encounter, and the dangers of simply turning the patient into a medical object (Hinshelwood 1999). It is within the interstices of what are considered the social dimensions of psychiatry, that psychological techniques have their place. As mentioned earlier, cognitive behavioural techniques (CBT), once tied to the province of the strictly neurotic, are now being advocated for the psychoses (Haddock and Slade 1996, Jones et al. 1998). The main presumptions underlying these techniques are that it is important to listen and attempt to make sense of patients' symptoms and problems. There is an acknowledgement that the symptoms may also have a meaning and function in the context of a person's life. Particular techniques have been developed on the basis of this set of relational dynamics and their specific focus on a person's symptoms, which will be discussed in more detail in Chapters 2 and 7.

When symptoms persist

Some researchers in this area claim that psychiatry is undergoing a major shift in outlook (Haddock and Slade 1996), moving towards a more holistic rather than strictly biomedical approach. One of the main arguments which this book will explore is the extent to which this supposed shift can be viewed as a move towards the psychological, and how the 'psychological' becomes reconfigured within these techniques. The use of CBT has emerged in relation to very specific problems, mainly to do with 'treatment resistant' symptoms,[3] the acknowledgement that drug regimes can produce severe side effects (Barnes and McPhilips 1999), and lastly the issue that has received most public and media attention – non-compliance.

The issue of non-compliance has haunted the public imagination, and contributed to the perceived failure of psychiatry to provide techniques of cure, which will allow the person to return safely to the community. The case of Christopher Clunis in 1992 highlighted the gap between a knowledge of biological processes which the interventions of anti-psychotic drugs are based on, and the individuals' willingness or ability to maintain their own drug regime upon discharge. Clunis had stopped taking his drugs, although his psychiatrists prior to this point had considered him well and able to live outside the hospital. He had gone on to stab and murder Jonathon Zito. Media reports at this time, in line with the repeated way in which mental health signifies within the broadsheets and tabloid press, brought into play an associated set of signifiers which constitute 'mental illness' as sick; dangerous; a risk; a timebomb waiting to go off (Blackman and Walkerdine 2001, Philo 1994, 1996). These signifiers were hung around an image of Clunis as a large black man who had killed a young, white, recently married man.

Aside from the racist connotations, which also underpinned this reporting, the case highlighted the ways in which it was relatively easy for a person with a prior psychiatric history to slip through the net. As Rose (1996b) suggests, the main plight being that psychiatry as an apparatus was now spread across a range of practices, involving a team made up of representatives from each site. The community mental health team comprises professionals from social work, community psychiatric nursing, psychiatrists, housing workers, psychologists, occupational therapists, GPs and so forth. With so many locales and people involved in one case, the mismanagement of beaurocracy and administration of risk is manifold. Despite the sensationalist press reporting, the government inquiry highlighted that Clunis was as much 'a victim of the mental health system as the young man he killed' (ibid.:2).

It is within this problematisation of the mental health system, that 'softer', more psychologically oriented techniques are increasingly being used to target 'treatment resistant' symptoms and non-compliance (Jones et al. 1998). For those 5–25 per cent of people who continue to experience symptoms in spite of medication (Davis and Casper 1997), CBT is viewed as a 'valuable adjunct'. CBT is considered a valuable tool for effecting the kinds of changed relations to psychotic symptoms which may help the person to not feel so at mercy, and take up a more self-determining position in relation to voices, delusions and so forth. Drug regimes are viewed as part of the package, allowing individuals to identify symptoms, monitor themselves and administer the drugs as an on-going pro-phylactic. It is for this reason that pharmaceutical companies, one of the biggest funders of biomedical research, are also funding research looking at the durability of the effects of CBT outside the immediate therapeutic context (Tarnier et al. 1999). It is obviously in the interests of all authorities concerned to facilitate 'drug-based self-management' (Blackman and Walkerdine 2001), if the bio-medical industry is to maintain its privileged position.

Empowering people who hear voices

In a book entitled *Cognitive-Behavioural Interventions and Psychotic Disorders* (Haddock and Slade 1996), the authors highlight that it is only a small number of researchers who are pioneering these tech-niques in relation to the psychoses. Most of the chapters offer a kind of 'technical know-how', reviewing different techniques used to enable a person to take up a more self-determining position. However, one chapter by Marius Romme and Sandra Escher talks about the different 'survival strategies' that voice-hearers use to cope with their voices. Survival is not a term which is part of the lexicon of psychiatric terminology; more at home in the campaigns of service users than professional practice. What is interesting for the purposes of this book, is that Romme and Escher have been adopted by user groups who are attempting to radically change the status of voice-hearing in the wider society. These campaigns are significant as a recent editorial of the BJP suggests that 'increasingly these user organisations will be demanding a major voice in policy decisions, in clinical governance, and in the training of psychia-trists' (Eisenberg 2000:8).

The case study at the heart of this book will concentrate on the practices of the Hearing Voices Network, an international group of voice-hearers who are challenging the notion that voices must be lived and experienced purely as signs of disease and illness. The history of their emergence will be discussed in Chapter 7, but their impact on professional practice and understandings is undenied.

This has led some psychiatrists to even claim the HVN as the new 'science of hearing voices' and to align themselves with the increasing number of professionals who are converted by their 'success stories'. Romme and Escher, for example, regularly speak at their international conferences, have been willing to listen to voice-hearers and challenge some of the bases of their own professional practice (Romme and Escher 2000). They have also produced a range of publications, which tell of their collaborations with voice-hearers within and outside the mental health system (Romme and Escher 1993, 1996).

Many cognitive psychologists at international voice-hearing conferences I have attended have argued that the practices of thé HVN are continuous with cognitive techniques underpinning CBT. This assertion is one which will be challenged throughout this book. Cognitive psychology, as a way of conceptualising psychological processes, although focusing on, rather than denying the voices, is modelled on a number of internal cognitive mechanisms, which are considered lacking, in deficit, or biased (Bentall 1996, Slade and Bentall 1988). As Bentall (1996) suggests, their success is in 'the design of cognitive behavioural interventions that accurately target those cognitive abnormalities which underlie particular symptoms' (ibid.:21). This way of figuring the psychological is one which the kind of 'critical psychology' developed in this book thoroughly refuses. The aim of this book is to develop a 'critical psychology' which can engage with the biological and the social, and the ways in which they have combined historically, within and with other concepts, to make the phenomenon of hearing voices intelligible and amenable to certain sorts of intervention.

Doing critical psychology

Critical psychology is a broad umbrella term for a range of psychological approaches, which have more affinity with social and cultural theory than with traditional psychology. The continuities and disparities between these approaches will be considered in Chapter 3. For the purposes of this introduction they can be summarised as a move from an inner world of psychological processes, to a concern with how the 'psychological' is constructed through the workings of language, discourse and social and historical processes. They share a commitment to moving away from understandings of individual psychology based upon models of depth and interiority. Metaphors of depth and interiority, used to invoke the psychological, are based on an essentialist approach to the question of 'what makes us human'. The psychiatric and psychological approaches broadly considered in this introduction all subscribe to such a view, where the psychological, and even the biological, are viewed as part of human nature, pure and untainted by historical and cultural processes, contained beyond the envelope of the skin.

Constructionist approaches, which broadly characterise 'critical psychology', reject the notion that a changeless and ahistorical set of biological and psychological processes can explain social and psychological life. Rather than going on a voyage ever inwards, with the aid of more and more refined techniques, constructionists argue that everything we know and understand about ourselves, our bodies, our psychology, is the product of social and historical processes. This is an interesting move and, as we shall see, is largely a reaction to the notion that the subject-matter of the 'psy' disciplines is indeed an object which can be studied in laboratory settings, where the supposed influence of the social is bracketed and held at bay.[4] However, in the context of the present investigation of the phenomenon of hearing voices, the eschewal or rejection of biology altogether does not seem a satisfactory alternative.

Both Diana Fuss (1989) and Denise Riley (1983) have warned of the perils of simply moving from essentialism to constructionism, without offering anything in its place. Both are forms of determinism and leave the dualisms of the biological and the social in place, favouring one or other side of the pendulum. This is important, as if we, as cultural theorists, do not engage with the biological, other than dismissing it as reductionist, or a reactionary biologism, we leave its theorisation to the life and human sciences which can equally dismiss our arguments as deterministic. As we have already seen, in relation to psychiatry, the apparatus is made up of both 'hard' and 'soft' approaches, which combine the biological and social in particular ways. It is this interaction or combination which needs critical attention, as it is within this intersection that a particular way of thinking about the biological, the psychological and the social is made possible.

This book will not therefore follow a great many 'critical psychological' studies, which have opted to analyse psychological phenomena purely through the operation of language and discourse. It is not enough to say that everything we experience and understand about ourselves is a product of the language at our disposal (cf. Potter and Wetherell 1987). There are good historical reasons for rejecting the biological, a version of which underpinned intelligence testing, eugenics and other strategies which sought to understand psychological and social life on the basis of an under-lying inherited predisposition to rational thinking. However within this rejection, the biological remains a stable, enduring, changeless entity, rather than fully being understood as a historical phenome-non. By simply rejecting the biological, we are rejecting the ways in which the biological has been made to signify, and come to be lived out in a social form by individuals and social bodies.

Rather than asking whether the phenomenon of hearing voices is rooted in nature (biology, biochemistry, neurology, genes etc.), or is a socially constructed phenomenon, I wish to explore how it is that a particular way of figuring the biological and psychological within the 'psy' disciplines has come into being. How do these explanations, and the particular combining of the biological, social and psychological produce specific psychiatric and psychological understandings? How have these understandings shifted and changed since the inception of the 'psy' disciplines in the nine-teenth century, and what can account for the transformation of both practices? I also wish to offer a radical rethinking of the term 'biology' and to begin to think about ways in which we can engage with the biological as one of the processes, alongside the historical and social, which together produce the possibility of experience. This will entail looking at the interplay of biology, psychology and the social within very specific practices, at very specific historical moments, and looking to the wider social, ethical, political, theo-retical and historical conditions which made their specific combinations possible.

This effectively means that the terms 'biology', 'social' and 'psy-chology' are not constants (or separate categories), but rather that their meaning(s) are always situated in relation to individual and discursive practices. This does not mean that the individual merely becomes a discourse-user, picking and choosing from the cultural narratives at their disposal, nor does it mean that the norms of the 'psy' disciplines fix subjects in relation to their explanations with no room for manoeuvre. A main focus of the book will be on the new forms of subjectivity made possible in the gaps, silences and contradictions surrounding 'psy' explanations and understandings. The book does not argue that the problem of the relationship of the biological, psychological or social is over, but that it can offer some new tools for thinking through these relations. These tools come from the later work of the French poststructuralist philosopher, Michel Foucault (developed in Chapters 3 and 7), cultural phenomenology, critical psychology and some of the debates which offer the term 'embodiment' as a revision of the biological (developed in Chapter 8).

The term 'embodiment' is useful as it explores the ways in which we live out our bodies' psychology and biology through the social. Within these formulations the 'body and sociality are inseparable' (Burkitt 1999:116), and attention is shifted to the ways in which we embody, somatically and sentiently, different 'culturally elaborated ways of attending to and with one's body' (Csordas 1994). One question which arises if we follow these revisions, is how and in what ways do both biological and psychological explanations impinge on individual experiences of psychiatric symptoms, such as hearing voices? Such questions will be addressed through a study of the HVN, paying particular attention to the basis and ways in which hearers are able, and manage to, transform their relationships, both affectively and discursively to their voices. This study, developed in Chapter 7, draws out two main conclusions in relation to the biological and the psychological: firstly that biology is generative and productive; it is a potentiality, rather than a static entity which can be offered deterministically as a cause of certain experiences. Secondly, that both the biological and the psychological are amenable to the same sorts of cultural analysis as phenomena that have become the mainstay of cultural studies: identity, subjectivity, and so forth.

In the chapters to follow the phenomenon of 'hearing voices', and its status and significance within the 'psy' disciplines, will be unpacked and interrogated. Within the explanatory frameworks of the social sciences, to hear voices is largely seen as an aberrant phenomenon, a sign that the person has lost certain capacities of social existence. In much popular discourse, to hear voices is to be feared, evidence that the person has lost control and can no longer distinguish between fantasy and reality. And yet, in another realm of popular discourse voices are viewed as prophetic, to be listened to and heeded. Doris Stokes, the popular clairvoyant, made her career from describing the voices she heard, and offering them as messages from the dead, to members of her empathic audience. The notion of an 'inner voice' is offered as the basis of creativity, the listening and acting upon, viewed as the path to self-development and self-actualisation. The concept of the muse embodies some of these views, the voice visiting on certain days and allowing the writer to tap into his or her inner potential. What all these discourses share is a notion that the voice is something to be listened to, rather than an experience to be tamed, controlled and even denied.

However, the notion that the voice is a meaningless epi-phenomenon of disease, is one that in certain contexts has the status and authority to explain the meaning of such experiences. It is this belief, which despite some of the competing discourses in popular explanation, tends to structure the ways in which individuals 'hear voices'. Chapters 1 and 2 will examine how the 'psy' discourses frame the problem of hearing voices. What kinds of explanatory structures, concepts and terms are used to make the voice-hearing experience intelligible, and how are these concepts deployed to distinguish those voices we all may hear, upon waking or falling asleep for example, from those which are directly linked to disease and illness? The chapters will also examine how the social and the biological are combined within these explanations, and specifically by those perspectives which claim to focus more on the social dimensions of the voice-hearing experience, such as more phenomenological, social psychological and ethnomethodological arguments. Transcultural psychiatry will also be examined, as again, this is one area of psychiatry which claims to represent a more socially attentive practice.

Chapter 3 will examine arguments within 'critical psychology' which have begun, with degrees of success, to reconceptualise the subject-matter of the 'psy' disciplines. The 'turn to language' characteristic of the last decade or so of critical psychological practice, will be compared with an approach which favours a more historical focus on the production of experience. Developing the archaeological (Foucault 1972, 1973), and later work of Michel Foucault on ethics and 'techniques of the self', the questions shift to 'how' it has become possible, for certain categories of psychological experience, to become part of the landscape of an interior world, lived out by individuals in their own self-understandings and practices. Rather than simply viewing these self-understandings as produced by the discourses of the 'psy' disciplines, the focus will be on how the biological and the psychological are processes which are made intelligible and embodied by individuals within a matrix of historical and social processes. This way of rethinking the biological and the psychological refuses any notion of stable, constant entities influenced by the social, to a view that the biological and the psychological are generative potentialities, rather than acting as limits to sociality.

This chapter will also review similar kinds of studies, both within and outside 'critical psychology', which have privileged historical investigation to understand how present understandings are made possible. It will focus upon arguments which suggest that the human sciences, alongside the life sciences, are taking on a more and more authoritative status in our everyday conceptions of what makes us human, and how to understand all those so-called deviations from normal thought and conduct. Foucault's study of the rise of clinical medicine (1973), and the ways in which the human and life sciences constantly transform and 'modernise' will be examined. This chapter will argue that it is not enough to simply move to a linguistic and discursive-based analysis, without careful consideration of the role these practices play in the production of human subjectivities.

Chapter 4 begins at a historical moment when the notion that voice-hearing was linked to structural disease and degeneration had not taken place. The chapter will chart shifting and changing definitions of hearing voices (hallucination), from the seventeenth century through to a point in the eighteenth century when hallucination began to be framed as a particular convulsive condition of the brain. The chapter will pay particular attention to those social, theoretical, political and ethical conditions, which helped to produce a shift away from 'moral' explanations, to a notion that hallucination was a specific marker of disease. The chapter will argue that it was only when madness became to be seen solely as a disorder of the brain, that the meaning of hallucination was divided from delusion, and comes to stand as a marker of a discrete disease entity, dementia praecox (viewed as the modern precursor to schizophrenia).

Chapter 5 will develop the historical investigation of modern 'psy' understandings of the voice-hearing experience, by examining how the practice and knowledge base of psychiatry shifted and transformed throughout the nineteenth and early twentieth centuries. It will examine the status of evolutionary theory within 'psy' explanations, and how these understandings were deployed in relation to arguments beyond psychiatry about the relationship between crime and insanity. Despite the unifying of psychiatric understandings within wider social practices, such as the legal system, during this period, moral and psychological explanations from William James (1902) to Hack Tuke (1872) argued that the hearing of voices was an expansive phenomenon, having deep psychological significance. Despite these 'softer' approaches, hallucination became the fulcrum within biological psychiatry, and the legal apparatus of judging individuals' ability to be responsible both to themselves and others.

Chapter 6 will consider transformations in the practice of psychiatry from the mid- to late twentieth century. During the inter-war years, explanations of mental distress radically transformed, allowing for the possibility of symptoms being produced beyond the materiality of the brain. The mind as a clinical object reentered the practice of clinical medicine, through a newly emerging dichotomy between the neuroses and the psychoses. This invention of a new psychological space rested upon a psycho-geographical way of understanding mental health, and its relation to the surrounding environment of the individual concerned. This chapter will specifically focus upon the significance and differentiation of hearing voices within this dichotomy, which began to see the problem of hearing voices, in and of itself, as not necessarily signalling disease. Hallucinations became more finely differentiated according to a number of concepts such as vividness, complexity, and level of recognition, which operated to establish whether the voice-hearer was likely to act upon them as mandatory wishes or demands. The notion of 'heritable constitution' had transformed to an understanding of the 'enfeebled personality'; a concept which understood those who were more likely to act on the voices, as those whose life history was seen to predispose them to lose touch with reality. The chapter will discuss significant events which led to the invention of the neuroses/psychoses, to include the two world wars, the discovery of the unconscious, and the 'LSD' experience. The chapter will explore related arguments, which suggested that it was the psychiatric definition of hallucination which to a large extent produced the psychological and social reaction to the experience.

With this view in mind, Chapter 7 will focus upon the Hearing Voices Network (HVN); a group of voice-hearers attempting to transform their discursive and affective relationships to their voices. The majority of the voice-hearers who join the self-help groups, which run on a national and international basis, have been through the psychiatric system. Many of them have psychiatric diagnoses, and are attempting to transform how they 'hear' voices. In many cases, psychiatry has failed them. Despite cocktails of drugs, the voices still remain. This chapter will examine some of the different practices and techniques the groups engage in, in order to facilitate changed emotional experiences of their voices. The chapter will argue that ironically, 'psy' explanations and understandings, in their gaps, silences, and contradictions, make possible some of the new forms of subjectivity being produced within the network. The chapter, through the use of a methodology developed from Foucault's later work (1985, 1987, 1990), will cogently illustrate how these 'techniques of the hallucinatory self' are not at all continuous with CBT (cognitive behavioural techniques). The chapter will focus upon specific practices to include the telepathic, traumatic and the spiritual as interesting case studies, to illustrate how voices may be embodied and lived in very different ways, engendering different kinds of 'emotional economies'.

Chapter 8 will develop some of the conclusions of this study, by relating the arguments to wider debates across the disciplines of critical psychology, cultural studies and sociology, which have begun to explore the concept of embodiment as a way of revising the biological. These debates have emerged, for example, in relation to practices of health and illness and the emotions. The chapter will illustrate the radical rethinking of the psychological and the biological, made possible by this work, and begin to draw out some of the possibilities for therapeutic practice. The chapter will explore the role of the 'emotional' in processes of change and transformation. Practices of the HVN will be compared with those more aligned with personal development, to illustrate the different psychological landscapes produced through practices, which are often compared with each other. The cultural and psychological significance of these different practices will be discussed.

The final chapter will review arguments within critical psychology, which suggest that the human sciences, and the 'psy' disciplines more specifically, are central to the formation of modern subjectivities.[5] It will argue, that although these disciplines help to construct the ideal behavioural norms, and vocabularies and concepts through which people understand themselves, it is important to examine the processes of translation in situated practices (such as the HVN), which may create new forms of subjectivity. The important point stressed in this concluding chapter is that it is not the 'autonomous self' per se, but how individuals embody, relate to and live this injunction in their everyday lives. This attention to embodiment must also examine the different kinds of strategies that people develop, to defend against and resolve feelings of pain and distress (Lucey and Reay 2000).

The book will conclude with its central argument: that we are indeed embodied and following Denise Riley, that this awareness 'need entail neither a fetishism of the "body", nor a dissolution into the clouds of the social' (1983:41). This new and novel approach is increasingly pertinent as we witness the rise of genetic science and the mapping of the human genome project. With their claims to finally realise the project of the 'psy' disciplines, to discover the truth about human nature, and all its deviations from the normal, a re-engagement by critical psychologists and cultural theorists with these questions is of absolute importance. If we choose to dismiss and leave the life and human sciences to continue on their journey of discovery, then we will only have ourselves to blame when our work has little impact on those who suffer and struggle with the very real realities of these issues.

1
The Psychiatric Architecture

> we should cease posing our analyses of the political function-
> ing of psychiatry in terms of an opposition between a
> reactionary medical model of madness that is supposedly
> blind to social factors in aetiology or amelioration, and a pro-
> gressive social theory whose explanations and remedies
> recognize the social conditions underlying mental distress.
> (Rose 1986:45)

In the introduction we began to consider some of the landscape of
modern psychiatry which is structured through a combination of
biological and psychological explanations and interventions. Some
have termed this a 'psychosocial matrix' (Shepard 1983) which
despite some of the biomedical techniques which tend to dominate
the practice, also situates psychiatry within a broader social matrix
where psychological understandings also have an important role
and function. Psychiatry is not only located within clinical spaces
bounded by biomedical interventions, but also targets psychosocial
factors which play a part in the alleviation and support of mental
distress. This attention to the specific combining of the biological
with the psychological is pertinent for the kinds of critiques we
may wish to make of the practice, and for how we may wish to
analyse the 'psy' disciplines more generally as critical psychologists
and cultural theorists. The following two chapters will begin some
of this work by analysing in more detail the ways in which psychiatry and psychology make the voice-hearing experience intelligible.
We will begin to explore how the meaning of hallucination has
been created through the kinds of concepts and explanatory structures, which are embedded within psychiatric theorising and
experimentation. We will then be equipped with a better starting
point and place to reflect upon the theory and practice of the 'psy'
disciplines. We can then begin to consider how we as cultural theorists wish to create a dialogue with those sciences, which claim to
be based upon an understanding of normal and abnormal biological and psychological functioning.

The building of black boxes

> The investigator is not just interested in any kind of answer
> to specific questions; he or she is only interested in obtaining
> such answers on certain terms that have been set in advance
> ... These formal prescriptions, which dictate in advance what
> form the knowledge product shall take, often become quite
> specific ... the kind of knowledge product desired has a
> decisive influence on the choice of investigative procedures.
> (Danziger 1990:180)

Most critical psychologists and cultural theorists tend to view the
make-up of human subjectivity as being tied to historical, cultural
and social processes, rather than existing within stable, private,
interior psychological landscapes which are pre-social and
inevitably reducible to biology. There is a sense then, that psychological phenomena are socially constructed, and that the
investigator sets out to explore such phenomena on the basis of a
set of prior assumptions, values and beliefs. This is not a new claim,
as even within the natural and life sciences, which the 'psy' disciplines base themselves upon, the unshakable sense that the
scientist is a neutral, objective observer has been questioned again
and again (Howard 1985, Kuhn 1962, Latour 1987). It is taken for
granted (in differing degrees), that any observation of the social or
physical world is imbued with theoretical, epistemological, and
ontological presuppositions. Popper (1969) proposed that even
within the framework of positivist science, the simplest scientific
descriptions are dependent upon a range of theoretical assumptions, what he termed the 'theory dependence of observation'.

For many then, the constructed nature of psychological knowledge is a given, and has been explored and analysed in many
different ways, as we shall see in Chapter 3. Kurt Danziger
(1990:180) has cogently illustrated, through studies of some of the
psychological phenomena any student of the discipline will
encounter, that there is always a relationship between theories,
methods and ways in which the object or subject-matter of psychology is constructed. Citing Ebbinghaus's (1913) approach to
memory, Danziger (1990:144) illustrates how his conceptualisation
of memory as a series of inputs and outputs, based on an analogous
model within the physics of time, led him to look at the energy
invested in strengthening the internal memory image. Memory
had nothing to do with quality, content, or accuracy (Neisser 1976).

Nor with why historical actors constructed their memories in a particular way at a particular time (Middleton and Edwards 1990, Potter and Edwards 1990, Shotter 1990). It was conceptualised as the amounts of quantitative energy (memorising) used to strengthen the image. Scientific and psychological knowledge always therefore 'bears the mark of the social conditions under which it was produced' (Danziger 1990:191).

This does not simply mean that psychological phenomena are brought into being within the immediate investigative context, but that they are made possible by allied systems of explanation. These systems of explanation circulate within wider social practices, and help to create and structure certain areas of life for 'the insertion of a certain kind of psychological knowledge' (ibid.:191). Many commentators on the social sciences and their claims to 'scientificity', have highlighted how the knowledge produced in this context, the human sciences, is never simply produced within the discipline. It is always posed in relation to problems, which occur in the various spaces and sites which 'make up' the social. Osbourne and Rose (1999:390) develop this argument in relation to the 'creation' of the opinion poll within the social sciences: 'inventions or discoveries emerge first in relation to specific practical problems, be they those of intelligence in schools or shell shock in the army ... or those of the morale of the population in total war'. These problems are then addressed through particular kinds of theories, concepts, research technologies and so forth, which attempt to make the problem intelligible and amenable to treatment and cure.

This chapter will begin to explore the kinds of concepts and theories used to create the meaning of hallucination, and to distinguish it from other kinds of experience. It will focus upon what Latour (1987) has termed 'science-in-the-making': the ways in which theories have become incorporated into research tools, and exist as entities which can then be used to explain other entities (for example the ways in which duration is used as a concept to explain schizophrenia). These entities exist as phenomena which can then be 'explained, analysed, refined, purified, categorized, classified and utilized' (Osbourne and Rose 1999:372). They exist as particular kinds of explanation which circulate across a range of theories within the 'psy' disciplines. The strength of association of particular kinds of concepts and explanation contribute to what Latour (1987:103) has termed 'black boxes'; those 'hard facts', 'powerful theories' and 'indisputable evidence' which together

combine to produce what is taken to be the 'truth' of certain phenomena. This helps to explain why some theories have more
credibility, legitimate certain spokespersons and make possible particular actions and interventions on the basis of these explanations.
We will explore in this chapter how some theories and concepts
have a high level of consensus in relation to their truth status, even
if there are marginal levels of dissent and controversy. Let us begin
to think about some of the parameters of explanation within psychiatry, which structure the various modes of inquiry and have
been subjected to a mass of experimental research.

The 'interaction' of the biological with the social

Within psychiatric discourse some of the broadest assumptions are
made about what is natural (i.e. can be located within neurology
for example), and what is social. Psychiatric discourse, despite its
commitment to examining the social as well as the biological, is
preoccupied with causality. This causality is ultimately grounded
within materialist explanations, which seek to locate the exact
neurophysiological mechanisms, which produce the possibility of
the hallucinatory experience. These have shifted and changed over
the last decade. There is less focus upon specific neurochemical
receptors such as dopamine, to a focus at the latter end of the twentieth century on brain lipids (Walker et al. 1999), circuit
malfunctions within the brain (Feinberg and Guazzelli 1999), defi-
ciencies of glutamine (Carlsson et al. 1999) and so forth. Even
when psychiatry operates in its most biophysical mode there is no
unified explanation, and many of the causal mechanisms are contested and are far from gaining validity within the discipline.
However, with the rise of genomic techniques and more sophisticated biotechnologies, there is still a sense that the exact
mechanisms and conditions of risk (calculated in genetic terms)
will eventually be offered up for scientific scrutiny (Kerwin and
Owen 1999, Parker et al. 2000, Buckley and Friedman 2000).

As well as the focus upon neurology and genetics, there are also
research perspectives, which are committed to the more social
dimensions of psychiatric experience. These include studies examining the role of race and ethnicity in the outcome of psychosis
(Goater et al. 1999), and misdiagnosis (Hickling et al. 1999). There
are also concerns with what are termed the 'psychosocial' factors or
influences, which are seen to play a role in the facilitation and

progression of disease (Eisenberg 2000). There is much more of a sense that patients should be listened to and their symptoms understood within the context of their lives (Eisenberg 2000), rather than simply being given medication. There is more of a concern with treatment-resistant symptoms, and how to understand and intervene in this area (Wykes et al. 1999). As we saw in the introduction, psychological techniques and understandings such as Cognitive Behavioural therapy (CBT) are viewed as useful adjuncts in the treatment of non-compliance and medication-resistant symptoms (Haddock and Slade 1996). As we will see the split and intersection of the psychiatric with the psychological is overlaid by differentiations made between negative and positive symptoms, transitory and chronic disease processes, and the neurotic as opposed to the psychotic. It is these sets of differentiations and combining of the psychiatric with the psychological which the next two chapters will examine, in what I will term 'the problem of hallucination'. As we will see there are two problems: the first is how to differentiate the 'pseudo-hallucination' from the hallucination, and the second is the problem of non-compliance and those voices which persist in spite of the administering of psychotropic drugs.

What does it mean to hallucinate?

This section will begin to explore the way the object, hallucination, is specified, classified and differentiated from other kinds of experiences within contemporary psychiatric discourse. It is worth noting that psychiatry starts from the premise that in some contexts, to hear voices is a sign of pathology. This pathology is articulated as both an internal pathology (paying attention to those mechanisms and deficits producing the possibility of such an experience), and a social pathology. The voice-hearer is viewed as having, or potentially losing contact with, the social world, and simultaneously losing certain capacities of social existence, such as the ability to function in work and social relationships. The voices are viewed as a sign that individuals can no longer self-regulate and control their behaviour, and are at the mercy of the voices' demands and wishes. The following quote is taken from the *Diagnostic and Statistical Manual* (*DSM III R*), the bible of most psychiatrists, and is cited again and again as the diagnostic definition of hallucination:

A sensory perception without external stimulation of the relevant sense organ. A hallucination has the immediate sense of reality of a true perception, although in some instances the source of the hallucination may be perceived as within the body. The term hallucination, by itself, is not ordinarily applied to the false perceptions that occur during dreaming, while falling asleep, or when awakening. Hallucinations occurring in the course of an intensely shared religious experience generally have no pathological significance. Transient hallucinatory experiences are common in people without mental disorder. (*DSM III R* 1980:498)

However, 'the problem of hearing voices', for the 'psy' disciplines, is the fact that they traverse a whole range of experiences. These include reactions to traumatic events and potentially life-threatening situations (Comer et al. 1967, Belensky 1979), hostage situations, bereavement (Reese 1971), sleep deprivation, fasting, drugs, organic illness and before falling asleep and waking up. The problem then becomes one of differentiating the 'pseudo-hallucination' (those we all might experience at some point), from the hallucination (seen to indicate underlying mental pathology). This section will explore the concepts which psychiatric discourse deploys to operate these distinctions. What does it mean to say that someone is hallucinating? What does it mean when a psychiatrist pronounces somebody's experience as hallucinatory?

The conceptual armoury

It is not enough then, to say that somebody is hearing voices for their experience to necessarily be pronounced as a sign of illness and disease. Psychiatric discourse has a range of concepts and explanatory structures which it uses to distinguish the 'real' from the 'pseudo', to include source, vividness, duration, location and control. These concepts are embedded in the following quote from Mayer-Gross et al. (1969:45), and indicate the extent to which the 'psy' disciplines operate finer and finer distinctions in order to understand and make intelligible the 'problem of hearing voices'.

The source, vividness, reality, manner of perception, content, and all other circumstances of the experience are important; its content, especially if auditory or visual, must be reported. When do these experiences occur, at night, when falling asleep, when alone? Any peculiar bodily sensations, feeling of deadness? Unreality?

Let us look then, at how these concepts combine in order to make intelligible the supposed distinction between the 'real' and the 'pseudo' hallucination.

The source – where are the voices coming from?

This concept is articulated in relation to the location of the voices and whether the person attributes them to an internal or external source. Are they perceived as coming from inside or outside his/her head? Does the person locate them within the television, for example, or from other external sources such as the wardrobe, or are they viewed as emanating from within the person's own head? Within psychiatric definitions, it is the location of voices within an external location, outside the head for example, which is more likely to yield a pathological status.[1]

However, within the literature it is not so conceptually clear-cut. Despite the inside/outside distinction, there are also seen to be voices which are attributed to the person's own psychological processes, and not located in external sources. The distinction made is that these voices are 'different' from a person's so-called normal thought processes. They operate in an authorial mode of address, running a continual commentary on the person's own behaviour and conduct; insulting, judging, commanding or directly addressing. Most of the literature focuses upon the disembodying feeling generated by this constant retort, where a person is seen to lose the capacity to attend to outside experience. 'Auditory hallucinations may accompany every action of the patient with their comments, even repeating aloud what he is silently reading. In some cases, they consist of whistling only, or of inarticulate voices; or they consist of words, which, in spite of an honest effort the patient is unable to repeat, although they absorb his attention' (Mayer-Gross et al. 1969: 275).

This 'inner-directed' focus, produced by third-person commentary, does not allow the inside/outside distinction to be the only means of differentiating the 'real' from the 'pseudo' experience. This concept is one boundary within a complex constellation of concepts, which are articulated in relation to each other. The next concept within this assemblage of explanatory structures is vividness.

Vividness

This criterion focuses upon the vividness of the experience, and the extent to which the intensity of the voice or image allows the person to distinguish between self-generated images or thoughts, and those objects external to him-/herself. For example, day-dreaming may be vivid, but it is still deemed to be within the realm of the 'normal', because the person can distinguish between the inside and outside. It is not so much the vividness of the voices or imagery therefore, but the extent to which individuals can recognise their self-generated nature. Vividness cannot therefore stand alone as an index of disease, as it is how it combines with other categories within the conceptual armoury.

For example, a person who takes mind-expanding drugs such as mescaline, may well experience extremely vivid images, which they may even consider 'real', but they are not likely to be viewed as signs of schizophrenia. They may under certain circumstances be aligned with an induced Organic Mental Disorder. Here the hallucinations are viewed as transitory experiences, not linked to a pre-morbid disposition. The important, yet fundamental, distinction is that 'real' hallucinations are synonymous with disease; they are signs which relate to underlying neuro-physiological defects. The important discriminating principle therefore, is whether the person has insight into their pathological nature, and can judge and control them (i.e. not act upon them). As with the concept of source, vividness does not stand alone as a means of differentiating the 'real' from the 'pseudo'. It is how it is linked, combined and articulated, with other concepts within this assemblage, which sets the boundaries through which the 'problem of hallucinations' is specified.

Control

Control is a central discursive concept used to make the distinction between the normal ('pseudo'), and the pathological ('real') hallucination. It is an explanatory structure, which organises the dispersal of other concepts, which link together within this assemblage of elements. There may be a whole myriad of vivid imaginings or sensory misperceptions which a person may engage in, such as illusions, vivid imagery, creative thought and so forth, but those signalling pathology relate to the degree of control a person has over those imaginings. Hallucinations (proper), are not random occurrences, related to specific times or situations, such as day-dreaming or sleep, but systematised, all-powerful, all-pervading 'events' which engulf a person's general cognitive capacities. They are viewed as overwhelming individuals' normal psychological propensities, leaving them unable to control themselves.

How then is the concept of control articulated and made intelligible? Control is taken to be a measure of social and work functioning, where the focus is upon specifying how well a person is seen to be functioning within the external milieu. One mode of explanation drawn on within the *DSM III R* (p. 398) to distinguish the normal from the pathological, is that there has to be a reduction in social or work functioning. Control is therefore not measured in relation to vividness, but with a person's relation to the external world. It is a measure of behaviour and conduct, and not a measure of the quality of a person's own internal reverie. Within this division, 'pseudo-hallucinations' are those which do not interfere with the person's daily functioning. In other words, the person appears to maintain an element of control over them. Thus, time of occurrence is used as another distinguishing criterion. Where they occur only upon falling asleep or awakening, hypnagogic and hypnapompic hallucinations, they are viewed as the twilight state between dreaming and consciousness, when we are still living in both worlds; the mundane and the fantastical.

However, although this form of explanation emphasises control, articulated within the context of the imagining, and whether the person can engage with the external world if called upon, there is another criterion which conflates these two modes of explanation. These two distinctions are seen to relate to the duration of the occurrence.

Duration

Duration is combined and articulated with the other concepts already discussed, and reduces the complexity of explanations forming the object, hallucination, into a differentiation, based upon the length of time the hallucination has endured within the person's psyche. Pseudo-hallucinations are transitory, fleeting occurrences, which do not affect a person's general level of social functioning. Hallucinations are viewed as more permanent and impermeable aspects of existence forcing individuals to lose contact with their external surroundings.

In two of the many scales variously used to make diagnoses, the duration of the hallucinations has become a key way of distinguishing between the 'true' and the 'false'. The Manchester Scale (Kraviecka et al. 1989), focuses upon the frequency of hallucinations, within a range from 0–4. Categories 3 and 4 are where 'true' hallucinations fall, 1 infrequent, and the category 4, relating to those hallucinations that have 'occurred frequently in the past week'.

Within the Positive and Negative Syndrome Scale (PANSS), another psychometric tool used to distinguish the pathological from the 'normal' (Kay et al. 1989), there are seven categories to differentiate the normal from the pathological. Thus 1–4 cover those deemed to be minimal, mild and moderate; in the authors' words, those of 'questionable pathology'; they may be at the 'upper extreme of normal limits'. Categories 5–7 encompass those where hallucinations frequently occur, and also have a disrupting influence on thought, behaviour and conduct. For example category 6 is used to describe severe hallucinations, 'present almost continuously, causing major disruption of thinking and behaviour. Patient treats these as real perceptions, and functioning is impeded by frequent emotional and verbal responses to them' (ibid.:65).

The concept 'duration' attempts to tie together the various concepts through which the normal and the pathological are distinguished. The psychometric tests, examples of which have been discussed, attempt to make the concept calculable, measurable and classifiable. They are what Latour (1986) terms 'inscription devices'; ways in which the prior assumptions and presuppositions of this explanatory structure are rendered into a form which produces those very properties as amenable to investigation. The object of study, in this case, duration, forms a perceptual system whereby persons are viewed as embodying the very properties that the prior assumptions embodied by the tests, presuppose. This way of approaching the 'psychology of individuals' is one which assumes that in order to understand human subjectivity, one needs to turn inwards, beyond the envelope of the skin. These processes are then viewed as amenable to investigation through devices, which abstract the individual from their social environment, and attempt to measure some characteristic, which has been privileged by the investigator as a measure of psychological functioning. These 'manipulable, coded, materialised, mathematised, two-dimensional traces' (Rose 1989:129), can then be combined with other traces, to render intelligible the gamut of human subjectivity.

However, we can see within this example, that these devices are always used in conjunction with measures made about social functioning which exist beyond the immediate investigative context. Even when the hallucinations are present almost continuously, the ultimate differential factor is how the person reacts to the voices; i.e. whether the person judges them to be 'real' or not. These judgments, as we have already seen, are made in relation to work and social functioning. In the end, despite the conceptual armoury, which attempts to tie the gaps and contradictions in 'psy' explanations together into a coherent set of explanations, the ultimate measure of hallucinatory experience is made in relation to social norms of conduct and functioning. Even though psychiatry, as we saw in the introduction, is a biological discipline, it is not enough to dismiss it along those lines. It is how a conception of the biological is combined with the social, and the psychological, in order to create the meaning and consequent treatment of experiences possible.

In the next section I will consider a relatively recent transformation within the concept of schizophrenia, which is changing the internal relations between the categories used to 'think' pathology, and the structure of the theoretical framework. I will argue that this theoretical framework is attempting to incorporate into its schema the differing concepts referred to in the above analysis. I will argue that it is here we can clearly see psychiatry attempting to produce a coherent framework of explanation from all the inconsistencies, gaps and contradictions in the concepts it deploys. The main problem which the concepts address themselves to, as you will remember, is that the hearing of voices is seen to traverse a range of conditions including space flight, traumatic events, hostage situations, bereavement, sleep deprivation and so forth. How then can the psychiatrist be sure to distinguish the pseudo-hallucination from the hallucination?

The type 2 syndrome

The type 2 syndrome has been offered as an explanation of all the contradictions and dispersals within the literature. This syndrome is contested (Taylor and Liberzon 1999), but is a good example of the ways in which psychiatry, despite its heterogeneity, is attempting to provide coherent causal explanations of psychotic experience. Thus the complex constellation of behaviours and thought processes, which are problematised within the discursive practice, could be viewed as originating from two distinct disease categories. Within this set of theories, hallucinations have become markers of a 'type 1' syndrome which is viewed as an acute phase, responsive to neuroleptic drugs and occurs as a result of increased dopamine receptors. This is delineated from a second phase, a 'type 2' syndrome which is more chronic, marked by flattened affect and poverty of speech, having a poor response to neuroleptic drugs and possibly being irreversible and permanent. It is viewed as a consequence of structural changes in the brain (cf. Crow 1989:16). This delineation is used to describe why some persons do not respond to the chemotherapy, and why some symptoms disappear at the expense of more enduring debilitating 'symptoms': the notion of positive and negative symptoms.

Within this particular conceptual framework hallucinations appear as temporary markers of pathology which are amenable to 'cure', thus offering a trajectory which is used to explain why 'hearing voices' appears across the range of disease classes as a 'symptom'. This offers a grid, which imposes an order on 'hearing voices' which was encountered within practice, but not in theory. In other words, the contradictions and dispersals between the concepts used to make the distinction between the real and the pseudo-hallucination are being recombined within a different theory of disease, incorporating a concern with neuro-physiology and the context of the experience. The key categories used to think this distinction are duration, severity and chronicity. These recent transformations could be linked to the relatively recent emergence in the *DSM III R* of a group of non-organic psychoses (Brief Reactive Psychoses) also known as 'borderline' transitory conditions. The forms of argument here use the concepts discussed previously (duration, control, insight and severity) to 'think' the normal/pathological distinction. This may be one explanation of the renewed interest in 'hearing voices' not as first-rank symptoms of schizophrenia (Schneider 1959), but as signs which operate within and across these transitory conditions. If this is the case then psychiatry needs systems of explanation which more finely differentiate and discriminate the complexities of hallucinatory experience. The problem of hallucinations can no longer be thought of purely in terms of control, vividness, duration and so forth, but the patho-physiology of the individual must be raised as a causal factor. This creates a space within this set of theories for genetic and heritable conditions of risk, and the underlying (dysfunctional) brain mechanisms, which are seen to cause the type 2 syndrome, to be offered as explanations.

Within this framework of explanation, hearing voices is viewed as a possible sign of temporary psychosis, which traverses many species and is not viewed as the sole marker of schizophrenia. The contemporary grid of perception appears to be mutating in response to its own internal criticism and anomalies. The gaps and contradictions created within the technical apparatus, such as the flow-charts, tables and diagnostic tools are transforming the theoretical framework. A new conceptual grid is offered as a way out of the differences encountered within clinical practice. This also transforms the space circumscribed by the individual, where the endurance and chronicity of the disease process are seen to be a function of genetic and hereditary factors. Although the subject within psychiatric practice has displaced to a certain extent and been replaced with 'risk factors' (social and epidemiological), the notion of an 'at risk' personality plays a paramount role in the so-called more enduring, degenerative 'type 2' processes. Let us now examine how conceptions of the social, biological and psychological, in relation to the psychiatric subject, combine to frame the 'problem of hearing voices' in a particular way.

When is a hallucination not a hallucination?

As we are beginning to see, despite psychiatry's object being the 'timeless mind', and all its potential deviations from the normal, the conceptual basis of the discipline incorporates particular ways of thinking about social functioning and norms of conduct and behaviour. Traditional histories of both the disciplines of psychiatry and psychology (Alexander and Selesnick 1966, Zilboorg 1941), argue that they have been organised around fundamental timeless questions concerning the nature of the human mind and psyche. Historians such as Nikolas Rose have cogently shown how these disciplines have always focused on problems articulated in relation to aspects of existence considered socially abnormal or pathological (Rose 1985). Although, as we shall see throughout this chapter, the 'psy' disciplines tend to turn to statistics and the experimental method to warrant their 'truth-claims', arguing that their explanations are based on statistical norms of mental functioning. We shall see that these norms are derived from very historically specific and situated ways of thinking about the nature of human subjectivity, rather than the psyche (as a timeless object) itself.

If we turn to the *DSM III R* (p. 398) we can begin to see how a combining of a particular way of thinking about the social and the biological is incorporated into its judgements concerning the diagnosis of hallucinatory experiences. There are four different modes of explanation which are deployed, and to some extent, one could argue that the experience is considered a hallucination if there appears no other plausible explanation for it. To qualify for pathological status the experience must occur in the absence of any organic factors such as alcohol, drugs or sensory deprivation, not occur in the course of an intensely shared religious experience, and for there also to be a reduction in social or work functioning.

The important and fundamental point to make is that the symptoms do not 'speak for themselves'. Despite the conceptual grid used to divide the normal from the pathological within psychiatric discourse, the psychiatric gaze concerns itself with what is 'absent' to the immediate gaze of the psychiatrist. The 'absent' may be conceptualised in a number of ways, but in short is the gaze which takes into account the context of the hallucination. For example the use of psychoactive substances such as drugs or alcohol which may have induced the hallucination are known as organic hallucinosis (see *DSM III R*, p. 110). Other organic factors include fever or Delirium (ibid.:101). Both these kinds of experiences are viewed as transitory and linked to an identifiable organic stressor.

Other 'absent' explanations include psychosocial stressors, which may have caused the hallucinatory experience, such as bereavement, divorce and so forth. If the symptoms are brief, have a sudden onset and last for no more than one month, with a return to pre-morbid functioning, then they are considered signs of a brief reactive psychosis (*DSM III R*). This is deemed a severe reaction to stressful events within the realms of the 'normal'. In other words, these are severe experiences, causing severe psychological stress, likely to cause a particular reaction in most people. It is the 'event' which is outside the bounds of the normal and not the person. This point is highlighted in the following quote taken from the Glossary to the *DSM III* describing reactive psychoses or non-organic psychoses: 'this category should be restricted to the small group of psychotic conditions that are largely or entirely attributable to a recent life experience'. These 'reactions' as Stroemgren (1989:49) suggests, are given names such as Panic Disorder, Schizophreniform Disorder, Post-traumatic Stress Disorder, Schizoaffective Disorder and so forth. Gordon Turnball, writing in a broadsheet newspaper, suggests these psychological reactions are 'a natural reaction to a calamitous event'. As stated it is the 'event' which is disastrous, producing in most people what are deemed psychological symptoms, such as flashbacks and hallucinations, cardio-vascular problems and so forth.[2]

Psychiatric discourse has then produced a taxonomy of natural diseases, of which certain symptoms, such as hearing voices, are viewed as first rank signs. The 'pure' psychotic states are those where psychotic symptoms are viewed as signs of disease and illness, such as schizophrenia. These are often viewed as degenerative and linked either to structural changes in the brain, or biochemical or neurological deficit or imbalance (the type 2 syndromes). An inscription device which purports to tell this story can be viewed in *DSM IIIR* (p. 285). It is a visual display outlining the relationships and associations between various degrees of psychosis and their borderline states. Therefore, depending upon the combination of symptoms, and how well one is coping with them, one might receive a diagnosis of brief reactive psychosis as opposed to Schizophreniform Disorder. One, as we have already seen, is viewed as a transient condition in response to a stressful life event, the other a more enduring condition, a close partner of schizophrenia which has less than a six-month duration. The contradictions and theoretical incoherence of the discursive framework as a whole are inscribed in the form of a flow chart, an easy, unproblematic step-by-step guide to diagnosis. As the name describing the flow chart implies it is a 'Decision Tree for Differential Diagnosis of Psychotic Symptoms'.

The third aspect to the psychiatric gaze is one whereupon the 'psychology' of the individual is subjected to a series of probing questions, incorporating particular ways of thinking about normal and abnormal psychological functioning. These questions and ways of problematising aspects of existence are ways of thinking about human subjectivity, which I will suggest are based on the concept of the 'enfeebled personality'.[3] This is based upon a notion that there are certain persons deemed constitutionally lacking in the so-called normal propensities to equip them to deal with the stresses and strains of life. I will investigate how this concept is instrumentalised and routinised through the course of a psychiatric examination.

The psychiatric interview

Within an examination of a potential psychiatric patient there are two distinct phases; the first is a description of the present mental state and involves a 'provisional' diagnosis. The second phase of history-taking is undertaken to pinpoint any 'patho-features' of the person's biography, which may have made them more vulnerable, or in psychiatric terms, 'at risk' to a disease process. These 'patho-features' resemble reconstructed readings from a present vantage-point, to try and detect signs which could have been read as earlier warnings of the developing disease.

The examination focuses on those elements of life deemed to be most important in 'thinking' the distinction between the 'normal' and the 'pathological'. Mayer-Gross et al. (1969) describe these elements, conceptualised as a longitudinal description of those peculiarities, which could have been retrospective indications of 'risk'. A family history is always taken to establish any links such as other family members, especially parents (mother) who may also be 'lacking' the normal mental constitution. The first five years of life are investigated as sites of potential 'risk' development, as are other important 'life-stages' such as puberty and adolescence. Were there any outward signs, such as 'asocial' or 'anti-social' inclinations which may be signs of 'risk'? What is the person's relationship history to work, military service and social functioning, now, and before the person's presentation to the psychiatric gaze? What is their marital history; are they single? Can or could they maintain long-term relationships? Are there any other signs which might reveal their 'enfeebled personality'? Some of the social factors used to make intelligible the 'enfeebled personality' are social conformity (Sarbin and Juhasz 1967, Shean 1973, Whitman 1961), social competence, social maturity (Phillips et al. 1956) and 'lack of interest in the social environment' (Stein 1968). These variables have then been broken down further into smaller component features, i.e. social competence is defined in terms of level of education, steady employment and marital status and has then been used to explain the excess of 'schizophrenia' in the so-called lower classes (Blackman 1996, Hollingshead and Redlich 1958).

This 'social history' is then used as part of the grid of perception for making sense of the person's experience. The discursive space opened up to make the distinction between what is deemed normal and what pathological is disparate and heterogeneous. It is a complex assemblage of concepts, which attempt to make it conceptually possible to 'think' in terms of disease and pathology. These include the status of the 'personality' of the individual, and the context of the experience, which is rendered in relation to the key concepts of source, vividness, control and duration. However, the most general specification, which underpins the dispersal of concepts within psychiatric discourse, is the notion of the 'enfeebled personality'; one who is viewed as unable to maintain particular kinds of relations with themselves and 'others'. This personality is one whose 'psychology' is directly linked to biological inferiority or inadequacy. In the next section I want to begin to unravel the ways of thinking about the 'enfeebled personality' which underpin the psychiatric gaze.

The enfeebled personality

What conceptualisation of the body and its social environment is brought into being through this discursive framework? As we have seen the disease is seen to follow a more severe, disabling and enduring course if one is viewed as constitutionally lacking in certain biological propensities. If one has a 'normal' level of pre-morbid functioning, the disease may take a transitory, less disabling course. The body is viewed as the distorting feature, the object that must be scrutinised through sets of questions premised upon a particular way of thinking about the biological and the social. These include questions, as we have seen, designed to elicit signs of risk (associated with possible genetic inheritance), such as past history, alongside questions designed to assess social functioning (behaviour). The outcome of the interaction between the body and its social milieu is viewed as producing the ultimate site and course of the illness.

There is then a split or dualism within psychiatric discourse between the natural and the social. The natural (body) is made intelligible through particular ways of thinking about the body and biology, derived in part from evolutionary theory. Biology is viewed as a static, invariant set of characteristics which predispose persons to particular forms of thought, behaviour and conduct. Biology then sets limits on how a person is able to interact with the social, and also the levels to which the social can impact or impinge upon the individual. The broadest assumptions about what makes up the 'natural' and the social are then overlaid by other dualisms, such as inherited/environmental, somatic/psychological, psychotic/neurotic and even the pseudo-hallucination/hallucination. These dualisms underpin the following quote, which encapsulates the aim of the psychiatric gaze at this point in time. 'To illuminate the nature of the relationship between genetic and environmental factors in the aetiology of schizophrenia: it implied that a causal continuum exists, with genetic factors at one pole and environmental at the other' (Tarrier et al. 1989:629).

Does the 'use of "interaction between biological and social factors" work as a way of resolving the problem of the intersection between the biological and the social'? (Riley 1983:28). In the intro-duction I argued that it is not enough as cultural theorists to dismiss psychiatry as biologically reductive. Psychiatry is not a homogeneous discipline, and combines 'hard' (biologically oriented studies) with 'softer' psychologically oriented studies. What needs attention is the ways in which the 'interaction' between the 'biological' and the 'social', make possible particular ways of thinking about and acting upon phenomena, such as 'hearing voices'. Psychiatry targets both the biological and the social, but does this in ways in which biology is conceived of as an originary point. Biology is opposed to the social, and the social becomes a measure of the individual's competence in social inter-actions. Social and psychological life ultimately is explained with reference to biological[4] causes. The complex heritage of these divi-sions and ways of thinking about the biological and the social will be explored in Chapter 6. We have already seen how some of these assumptions make possible the conceptual armoury, which psychi-atry uses to distinguish the 'pseudo-hallucination' from the hallucination.

Let us now look at how these concepts and explanatory struc-tures have become part of the 'black boxes' of contemporary 'psy' discourse. It is important to raise here that there is one concept underpinning the various concepts and explanatory structures which we have examined, which seems to have already taken on a 'truth-status': the concept of schizophrenia. It is assumed for the most part that schizophrenia is a discrete unproblematic classifica-tory system (cf. Boyle 1990), which is further broken down into 'type 1' and 'type 2' syndromes and which other concepts are used to explain the existence of. It has therefore become an entity, which other concepts attempt to describe, categorise, classify and so forth. It has the status of 'science-already-made' (Osbourne and Rose 1999), and many of the research perspectives encountered in the literature, would not be possible without the notion of schizo-phrenia. There may be dissent over the mechanisms which produce the psychotic symptoms seen as markers of this disease process, and the different theories deployed to account for its existence, but schizophrenia has what Osbourne and Rose (1999:372) term a 'reality effect'. In Chapters 4, 5 and 6 we will begin to look at the genealogy of this concept in relation to the phenomenon of hearing voices. We will begin to explore what historical conditions made it possible to think according to this concept, and how research has developed in particular directions in relation to this entity. There is no simple or single lineage to explain the existence of this phenomenon, and as we will see it is made possible by a con-tingent set of theoretical, social, political and historical conditions of possibility.

In the next section we will look at how other concepts are deployed in experiments and research designs, to account for the existence of this entity. We will begin to see how this concept is inscribed within the research techniques which claim to represent it, and more finely differentiate it, and forms the unproblematic backdrop against which theories are assessed and subjected to forms of scientific validation.

The experiment

The various end-points of this discursive framework, the inscription devices such as graphs, nosological tables, charts and so forth, are said to merely reflect the accumulation of knowledge built up through scientific experimentation. Experiments are said to be the sites where these 'truths' are tested and subjected to scientific scrutiny and judgement. The concepts that we have already examined are those which have become part of the theories which psychiatry deploys in its diagnostic measures. They become the 'black boxes' (cf. Latour 1986), the objects to which the psychiatric gaze addresses itself in an attempt to discern finer and finer dis-criminations. Psychiatric theories are based upon the production of truth, conceived of in statistical terms. It is not the case that anything uttered by various spokespersons can 'claim truth', as only certain evidence counts. These are the points where the 'truth' is battled out and continually judges itself and is judged by others. The range of devices such as journals, experiments, conferences and so forth, are where the claims are made and alliances built.

The experiment is the primary site of 'truth production' where the concepts used to think the difference between the 'normal' and the 'pathological' are continually judged. These are the concepts which are deployed to further differentiate the phenomenon of hearing voices and its relationship to schizophrenia and its close counterparts. If we take a few examples from the literature, we will see the ways in which dissent and controversy are subjected to scrutiny, and used to investigate and analyse the existence of schizophrenia. Each experiment takes a part of the conceptual assemblage and subjects it to the 'test of truth'. A large part of the experiments cited are addressed to the 'enfeebled personality', which again largely already has the status of truth. The questions centre around a 'will-to-know' what it is that makes certain persons 'risky personalities'. The following titles capture this 'will-to-know':

- Schizophrenia and the Perception of Emotions. How Accurately do Schizophrenics Judge the Emotional States of Others?
- Season of Birth and Childhood Psychoses
- Pre-morbid Psychopathology in Schizophrenia
- Pre-morbid Psychopathology in Schizophrenia Spectrum

Each study makes links to previous studies where alliances are built and more 'black boxes' used, to construct one's claims as indisputable and 'highly significant' evidence. Parnas and Jorgensen (1989:623) cite Gunderson et al. (1983) and Torgensen (1985), as well as the founding fathers, Bleuler and Kraepelin, to assert their claims that; 'several dimensions of pre-morbid behaviour, centred around the axis of "peculiarity", predicted subsequent schizophrenia or schizotypy'. Such 'peculiarity' was said to include nouns such as 'fatuous', 'awkward', 'clownish', 'giddy', 'queer' and 'eccentric', 'dreamy', 'cautious', 'shy', 'inhibited', 'introvert', 'shut-in', 'cool', 'reserved', 'detached', 'silent' and 'withdrawn'. The assumption that these studies are predicated upon are that people who experience psychotic symptoms are genetically predisposed, therefore there must have been signs prior to their emergence. These signs are measured using various psychometric tests, which purport to 'tell the truth' about the extent a person differs from a mean (norm) of behaviour. Thus differences are viewed as both distinct and quantifiable. These tools have also become embedded in theories which start from the assertion that people differ statistically across the population according to a standard distribution curve. Those who become diagnosed as schizophrenic must statistically fall in the outer extreme ends. They are 'peculiar' and as Parnas and Jorgensen (1989) claim; 'only peculiarity was a significant predictor' (ibid.:625).

The biological and social are viewed as separate categories, and in this example, the classification of one's biological status is further broken down into a psychological measure, 'peculiarity', articulated through particular characteristics. One then seesaws between genetic and environmental interpretations. Are they 'peculiar' because they are schizophrenic and is this rooted in their genes, biochemistry, neurology and so forth? Are there environmental factors to account for their conduct, and did this lead to schizophrenia? Or, the favoured way of uniting the two: what combination of environmental and inherited factors have led 'peculiarity' to be a significant measure of pre-morbid risk? And where does this interaction happen? One account in the literature is that these factors interact in relation to the season in which the person was born. These studies are not viewed as certain and given, but the intensification of research in these areas is constructing stronger and stronger links.

Fombonne (1989), makes links with Boyd et al. (1986), who found that 10 per cent of people deemed to be schizophrenic were born in the winter months.[5] This concept has also been used to determine cross-cultural comparisons across the latitude of the equator (Parker et al. 2000). What do these experiments tell us? The psychiatric gaze offers these as possible 'risk factors' justifying a proliferation of research. Other explanations posited include vitamin deficiency, malnutrition during pregnancy, obstetric and perinatal complications, viral infection and a 'seasonal pattern of conception amongst parents of schizophrenics' (Bradbury and Miller 1985). One could also view these claims as an attempt to make more and more links with other elements, in relation to a will-to-prove that the 'enfeebled personality' is ultimately the site and cause of schizophrenia. All these 'risk factors' and 'sites of interaction' are continually being judged according to norms of statistical truth. Although they are viewed as speculative, their plausibility within the framework motors this push to prove that biological and neurological referents are the ultimate anchors and basis of human conduct.

Thus what else can psychiatric practice 'discover' about the 'enfeebled personality'? Cramer et al. (1989) found that those deemed schizophrenic failed to judge the emotional states of others, and were seen to make 'deviant' sets of responses to photo-graphs. Although the authors state that 'however there is little agreement' (p. 225), and 'contradictory results' (p. 225), they also cite other studies, e.g. Tarrier et al. (1988) and so on and so forth to add weight to their findings. Although 'judgement of emotional states' deployed within this particular context is far from a 'black box', it is building allies and alliances along the way. The antecedent or 'a priori' of these kinds of studies is of course that notion that risk is located in the body and can be measured along different axes. The 'enfeebled personality' is the given, taken-for-granted object underpinning this process of verification which is taken to be a measure of schizophrenia.

The questions are viewed as technical matters, discerning more subtle distinctions and differentiations. The truth will gradually be revealed through a process of scientific discovery and innovation. These experimental 'effects' are written down, compiled into graphs and tables, combined and compared and may eventually become embodied in theories and concepts themselves. Each element is given a position within this complex assemblage and becomes part of the 'thought space' used to distinguish pathology from all those deviations from the normal. It is through this process of verification and 'judging' that possible explanations become statements organised in particular ways. For statements to be 'in the true' they must be validated using the experimental method. While these concepts remain plausible, within the terms set by the discursive formation itself, they will form the parameters through which experimentation is structured within the discourse. There are suggestions that the enfeebled personality has displaced within psychiatry, to a consideration of 'risk factors', a concern with those 'events' or factors, which are likely to produce so-called psychotic reactions. Psychiatry is concerned with social and epidemiological 'risk' factors, which we will examine in the next chapter (as we have seen it is concerned with both the biological and the social), but in light of advances in genetic science, these are only consid-ered alongside calibrations of genetic risk.

Consider the following statement from an article in the *British Journal of Psychiatry*:

The completion of the human genome project will result in a quantum jump on our ability to identify the hereditary compo-nents of mental diseases. (Eisenburg 2000:3)

Although concerned with what are seen as 'psychological and social influences' (ibid.:7), the majority of studies carried out within the psychiatric literature are concerned with measuring and classifying genetic risk factors including, gene mutation (Blackwood et al. 1999), gene–diet interaction (Walker et al. 1999), the ability of drugs to target genes (Kerwin et al. 1999, Paul 1999) and so on. In order to understand why psychosis and the 'problem of hallucination' are framed in this particular way, we need to understand the historical conditions of possibility which have enabled certain divisions between the body and mind, veridical and illusory, rational and irrational, and the natural and the social to be made and articulated. Before we begin a genealogy of the modern voice-hearing experience, in the next chapter we will begin to examine how the social is configured and conceptualised in relation to these particular ways of thinking about the role of neurology and genes in the production of psychotic experience. We will specifically look at the role of psychological explanations, which are increasingly seen as useful in relation to the problem of non-compliance and treatment-resistant symptoms.

2
The Social and the Psychological

We saw how in the introduction, one of the most compelling problems in relation to hallucination is the problem of compliance and treatment-resistant symptoms. The problem is not simply that some people hear voices, but that some people, despite being prescribed medication, either do not take it or experience little relief from the voices. In this context the problem is one of the authoritative status of some voices to instruct a person to commit acts, such as murder in the case of Christopher Clunis, beyond their apparent will. It is the framing of this problem, as we will see throughout this chapter, which is creating the possibility of a new status for psychological techniques within the discipline and practice of psychiatry.

Conditions of risk

Castel (1991) argues that psychiatric practice has gone beyond the concrete relationship between the doctor and the patient and now involves an 'epidemiological clinic'. He terms this a system of multifarious practices, which have superseded the doctor–patient relationship, to include psychiatric social workers, community nurses, psychologists, skills management experts and so forth. He suggests that the 'site of diagnostic synthesis is no longer that of the concrete relationship with a sick person, but a relationship constituted among the different expert assessments which make up the patient's dossier' (Burchell et al. 1991: 282). He suggests that this reconfiguration of the agencies targeting the patient are transforming the notion of a 'dangerous' or 'at risk' personality, to the conditions liable to produce 'risk'. Although this conceptualisation within British psychiatric practice accounts for the role of the 'social', and those extreme events likely to cause psychological stress to most people, the 'at risk' personality, as we have seen, still plays a fundamental role within psychiatric understanding and intervention. The transformation of those agencies now concerned with mental health has opened up a discursive space to consider psychological and social 'influences' in the treatment and management of mental distress. As Griggers (1998) argues in relation to

'Post-traumatic Stress Syndrome', the standard protocol for psychiatric diagnosis is the definition of a patient as either psychotic or non-psychotic and amenable to either medication or psychosocial interventions. This kind of split or differentiation is being challenged by those symptoms, which seem to cross or disturb diagnostic boundaries, such as hallucination. As she argues (ibid.:136), 'for traumatised individuals, many of the usual assumptions about symptoms do not apply. For example, the presence of hallucinations may not indicate psychosis.' Alongside the disturbance of diagnostic boundaries, are concerns with non-compliance and treatment-resistant symptoms and a fear of those who may run the risk of dangerous, violent or threatening behaviour. In a newspaper article, 'Fear on the Streets' a psychiatrist, Dr Victor Schwartz, has argued for a 'scale of dangerousness' against which to gauge potential risks according to 'agreed criteria'.[1] This controversy surrounded the case of a psychiatric patient, Stephen Findley, who upon being released into the community went on to murder a pensioner, acting upon the wishes of the voices he heard.

> Findley was diagnosed as 'extremely dangerous' and confined by a Sunderland hospital under Section 2 of the Mental Health Act. A week later he was transferred to Garlands Hospital, Cumbria, and placed on anti-psychotic drugs. The psychiatrist made an unusually early appraisal, which caused some surprise among fellow psychiatrists at a subsequent inquiry when he concluded that Findley was not a risk to others.
>
> At home he received a 45-minute visit by a community nurse, who came away suspecting that Findley might be dangerous but took no further action, intending to see him again after Christmas. By then it was too late. On the morning of December 23, Findley took a bus to Carlisle. The streets were bulging with people with that present-hunting look in their eyes. Findley also appeared frantic, but his hunt was of a different nature. Voices were telling him to kill someone – anyone. As it happened he selected a 67-year-old pensioner, walked up to him and stabbed him 32 times.

This case again highlights the perceived failure of psychiatry to provide techniques of cure, which will allow the person to return safely to the community. The psychiatrist who released Findley had his expertise questioned and had to undergo a period of 're-training'.

Because of the ways in which psychiatric expertise is now spread across a range of practices and locales, as was highlighted in the introduction, it is easy for a person to slip through the net. Castel (1991) suggests in view of this that there are now far more potential irruptions of risk or danger within the social milieu and corresponding new objects of intervention. Rather than the psychiatrists' expertise diminishing, it has actually penetrated further, forming a new administrative mode of surveillance intervening in a wide range of social problems. However, with so many objects and people involved, the mismanagement of beaurocracy and administration of risk becomes more uncertain and unpredictable. Because of the new objects of risk, other agencies are deployed to act and intervene on the basis of a medico-psychiatric diagnosis. This involves other agencies' records and gazes, which co-exist alongside the psychiatric gaze, and create the potential for more slippage to occur.

Activities of daily living

Prior (1991:412) writing about an ethnographic study carried out on a modern psychiatric ward in Dublin, highlights one of the most striking features of patients' case notes. He claims that 'responsibility for mental illness was widely dispersed'. Each patient had two sets of records – a set of medical records and a set of social services records. The social services' notes provide information about family relationships, employment history, social networks and the pre-morbid (enfeebled) personality. The medical notes contained a set of psychiatric case notes – symptoms and a diagnostic category, and a list of attempted treatments. However, the nursing care notes were focused on what Prior (1991) refers to as Activities of Daily Living (ADL). Nursing practice was aimed at normalising the patients' behaviour and moving beyond the effects of institutionalisation. As Prior (1991:145) highlights,

> It was patient behaviour. Indeed it was 'behaviour' more than anything else which dominated the routine activities of the ward. It was the behaviour (rather than disease or illness) which determined the amounts and kinds of medication, which a patient might receive.

Prior proposes that; 'what is important to note from our point of view is that the focus on behaviour (and/or social networks and social relationships), is not conducive to treatment in a hospital milieu. Indeed the normalisation of behaviour and the creation of supportive social relationships inevitably direct the therapeutic effort beyond the walls of the hospital and into the community itself.' Prior argues that this has been a key condition for the extension of psychiatry beyond the immediate hospital setting. This relates to a new administrative mode of surveillance where, as Castel (1991) argues, the practice of psychiatry is extended and enmeshed within a range of experts all attempting to realign the person with certain objectives: self-discipline, self-management and the monitoring and inspection of one's symptoms through a medico-psychiatric gaze.

This mutation within the discursive complex is also opening up a new space where psychological techniques and understandings are viewed as useful in dealing with negative symptoms and treatment-resistant symptoms. Slade and Bentall, cognitive psychologists writing in a book called *Sensory Deception* (1988:133) propose five approaches to the treatment of negative symptoms which all focus on the use of psychological techniques to transform behaviour. Briefly, these are the use of token economies; a form of behaviour modification which is used to 'motivate patients to behave appropriately and constructively by giving them tokens whenever they behave in an acceptable manner'. Social skills training is seen as a useful approach to improve negative 'symptoms' which result in a lack of social skills. Combined with this is a form of 'life-skills' training, which focuses on interpersonal skills training, nutrition and meal planning, health and hygiene, managing money and the use of community resources and social networks. They also advocate a form of Self Instructional Training (SIC) where patients are taught to plan and control their own behaviour. Finally a problem-solving approach is posited as a solution to solving long-term interpersonal problems. To reiterate, the focus is primarily on the self-regulation and management of behaviour.

This split and intersection of the psychiatric with the psychological is overlaid by differentiations made between negative and positive symptoms, transitory and chronic disease processes, and the neurotic and psychotic. It is these sets of differentiations and combining of the psychiatric with the psychological, which have created a space for psychological techniques and understandings to take on a new status within psychiatric practice. In a recent edition of the *British Journal of Psychiatry*,[2] the issue focuses on the use of psychological techniques in the treatment of mental illness. It is important to state that, again, these techniques, including CBT are viewed as a useful adjunct to manage acute positive symptoms, such as hearing voices, and drug-resistant positive symptoms (Drury et al. 2000). The notion is one of psychological techniques complementing the administering and self-administering of neuroleptics. One of the key issues surrounding compliance and obstacles to care and cure, is that of the patient feeling that he or she can exert some kind of control over the illness. One solution by pharmaceutical companies has been to experiment with different kinds of drugs (such as those which are soluble) to try and get round the problem of the person who refuses to take medication.

However, pharmaceutical companies and psychiatrists realise that in order for psychiatry to be perceived as helping those living in the community to manage their own symptoms through self-administered medication and prophylactics, the person also needs to believe in the efficacy of the drugs. One role for psychological techniques and CBT in particular has been to help patients believe that they can feel in control of their illness. This focus on 'belief' is a key target of CBT, 'where the individual develops a curious approach to their illness and views it as something they can exert control over' (Drury et al. 2000:13). These techniques have also been found to be useful for those who experience 'treatment-resistant' voices, and are seen to facilitate 'coping skills' and to help rationalise the phenomenon, so that they experience them as 'coming from within rather than outside their own minds' (Turkington et al. 2000:101). As well as particular kinds of techniques to facilitate these kinds of engagements with the voices, such as not paying attention, distraction and focusing techniques, and 'rational responding' (ibid.:101), patients are presented with evidence so that they may consider the voices' status as self-generated.

CBT is a technique and set of practices which has developed from cognitive psychology which focuses upon the internal mechanisms which allow people to represent the world to themselves (Sampson 1981). Various hypothetical models of the mind are presented to explain how this internal representation and ordering of the world is made possible. These include 'schemas' (Neisser 1976), reality-discriminating skills (Bentall 1990) and so on and so forth. The mind is viewed as a 'system' which processes, stores and codes information or 'input', reified as a repository which has a hardware, metaphors which originate within the 'technological revolution' in computers which accompanied its rise in the psychological sciences. Although perception is viewed as an interaction between one's cognitive structures and the environment, the environment is conceived as a set of influences or variables, which influence or facilitate cognition. In relation to the 'problem of hallucination' four variables have been proposed to influence or facilitate the onset of hallucinatory experience: predisposing factors, environmental stimulation, reinforcement and psychological stress (Bentall 1990). Taking one concept from the psychiatric armoury, the distinction between the inside and outside, these factors are said to influence whether a person is likely to misattribute their thoughts and not view them as self-generated phenomena (ibid.:90). The misattribution is located within a person's 'reality-discriminating skills', allowing much of the psychological literature on hallucinations to be integrated as variables which affect discriminating awareness. These include stress-induced arousal (Eysenck 1976, Schwartz 1975), sensory deprivation, white noise (Margo et al. 1981), effects of suggestion (Barber and Calverley 1964), the hallucinations of 'normal' people (Bentall and Slade 1985, McKellar 1968, Posey and Losch 1983, Sidgewick et al. 1894, West 1948), and subvocal speech (Inouye and Shimizu 1970). The interventions based on these theories are treatments which train hallucinators to re-attribute thoughts to themselves (Bentall 1990). This as we have seen then opens up a space for psychological theories to be useful in helping to transform people's relationships to their own voices and beliefs about their illness.

This intersection of the psychiatric with the psychological is overlaid by distinctions drawn between the brain and mind and negative and positive symptoms, and is part of what is constituted as the bio–psychological–social jigsaw. If we turn to psychological theorising in more detail, we will see that these kinds of techniques have emerged from a complex range of theories and concepts attempting to explain the phenomenon of 'hearing voices'.

Changing our minds

Psychology, like psychiatry, is not a unified discipline, and is made up of a range of disparate theories, concepts, explanatory structures and techniques and understandings. Many different theories within psychology have been deployed in order to understand the problem of hallucination. Many of them have similarities with psychiatric understandings, attempting to locate the exact psychological, rather than strictly neurological mechanisms, which are seen to underpin the hallucinatory experience. Again, like psychiatry, only some concepts have the status of science-already-made (Osbourne and Rose 1999), and there is much dissent and controversy surrounding many of the theories offered to explain the nature of hallucination. Slade and Bentall (1988:114) offer a useful introduction to many of the theories, which have been offered, judged, evaluated and subjected to scientific scrutiny. Many of these theories are, again, attempting to provide coherent explanations for all the gaps, silences and contradictions encountered in psychiatric and psychological practice. However, as we will see they all differ in the mechanisms they suggest, and the ways in which the hallucinatory experience is seen to be produced.

Hallucinations as a disorder of consciousness

Within this conceptual framework hallucinations are viewed as a disorder of consciousness. As Slade and Bentall (1988:114) highlight, seepage theories are 'those theories which despite their differences, explain hallucinations in terms of some kind of "seepage" into consciousness of mental activity that would normally remain preconscious'. Therefore, the problem of hallucination is construed within the terms of consciousness and its preconscious workings. The notion of consciousness in psychological terms relies on Freud's (1922) concept of the mind as a psychic apparatus, made up of an unconscious, preconscious and conscious level. For example, West's (1962, 1975) theory proposes that,

1. life experiences affect the brain in such a way that they leave permanent neural traces or 'engrams' that subserve the neural physiology of memory, thought, imagination and fantasy.
2. that the current mental and neurophysiological state of the individual is a product of the interplay of psychobiological forces that originate both outside and within the individual. (Slade and Bentall 1988:114)

This explanation posits some kind of interaction between a biological mechanism (the ascending reticular activating system in the brain stem is offered as a likely candidate (West 1962, 1975)) and a psychological mechanism which monitors the sensory field and filters the information to be processed (Frith 1979, Shallice 1972).[3] The failure of this psychological mechanism to monitor the conscious and preconscious aspects of perception is located within this underlying neurological mechanism. The concept of the internal/external, which we explored in the last chapter, is then used to explain why the person may misattribute these internal pseudosensory products and experience them as coming from outside his or her head. Within this framework hallucinations are experiences related to dreams, originating in the preconscious imaginary realm of the mind. When the rational mind is relaxed then these subterranean forces are brought into play. Freud viewed dreams as the 'royal road to the unconscious activities of the mind' (Wright 1984:11). During the condition of sleep the force of repression is relaxed and the release of engrams into consciousness occurs.

The difference between hallucinations and dreams within this framework is that the state of consciousness, which occurs during the dreamstate, is considered a normal function of sleep. Many researchers during the late nineteenth century suggested the apparent similarity between dreams and hallucinations. The notion that 'dreams are hallucinations during sleep' or 'hallucinations are dreams during awakening' has been linked with neurophysiological evidence. Consider Hughlings Jackson's (1880) proposition that hallucinations are release phenomena related to 'dissolution of cerebral function' (Itill 1969:86). However, the neuro-physiological mechanism underpinning hallucinations is considered deficient, whereas during sleep the mechanism is merely relaxed.

Other evidence amassed to give this theory more 'truth-status' comes from studies of sensory deprivation. It is argued that during sensory deprivation, stimulation is decreased, but arousal levels are maintained, permitting the flow of engrams from preconscious to consciousness, thus resulting in hallucinations. We have already seen how hallucinations are common, for example in hostage situations, where sensory deprivation is a common experience. But of course, these are considered pseudo-hallucinations, rather than hallucinations linked to psychosis. In order to differentiate the experiences, West (1962, 1975) draws on theories of schizophrenia, which focus on the role of arousal. These theories suggest that schizophrenia is akin to a state of hyper-arousal, which deleteriously affects cognitive information-processing capacities. The state of hyper-arousal is used to explain attentional deficits, which lead the 'schizophrenic' to inadequately screen and process input from the external environment (Gjerde 1983). It is this state which leads to the focus on the internal as opposed to the external, where a person misattributes and confuses the location of stimuli. Although there is a focus upon neurology and biology, there is also a sense that the main problem is with misattribution of internally generated phenomena. Thus, psychological techniques may be useful in facilitating the re-attribution of phenomena to the internal, helping to transform the experience of these neurological symptoms (as we saw in the last section). Here again, we can see a space opening up for the intersection of psychiatric and psychological understandings in the treatment and conceptualisation of hallucinations.

Hallucination as an example of 'inner speech'

Within this conceptual framework, the classical conditioning model of behaviour has been utilised to explain the nature and origin of hallucinations. Based on the Pavlovian model of learning (1927), hallucinations are viewed as conditioned responses to internal or external stimuli. Behaviourism has been criticised for its objectivist reductions where the individual is viewed as a passive recipient to outside forces. This notion of the passive individual moulded by social forces is reified, where individual behaviour is contingent upon reinforcement and punishment schedules. Within the Pavlovian model involuntary responses are conditioned, whereas in operant conditioning voluntary behaviour is shaped. Therefore, the main assumptions drawn on are that hallucination is an involuntary response to certain external or internal stimuli, which have been learnt through continued association.

Hefferline et al. (1972) defined a hallucination as a covert thumb twitch to a conditioned stimulus. A thumb twitch was covertly conditioned to a tone; when the tone was omitted a covert key press was still elicited. Because the subjects claimed they heard a tone, which was not really there, they were said to have hallucinated it. Other studies used as evidence have shown that visual after-images can be conditioned to a tone (Davies 1974, 1976, Davies et al. 1982). These studies take one of the concepts embedded within psychiatric discourse – the ability to judge between the real and the imaginary, and attempt to provide evidence to support this explanatory structure. This experimental effect has a long history and was first created in an experimental study in 1895 by Seashore. However, as Sarbin and Juhasz (1978) suggest, this is just one concept used within psychiatric discourse to differentiate the pseudo-hallucination, from the hallucination. As highlighted in Chapter 1, even within the *DSM III R*, a hallucinatory experience is deemed psychotic, if there is no other intelligible explanation for the behaviour and conduct (cf. Coulter 1973, 1979, 1989). Sarbin and Juhasz (1978:124) give numerous examples of contexts where people 'hear voices and see visions', but are not necessarily given a psychiatric diagnosis.

A subject in a psychophysical experiment says, I see it, when no stimulus is presented.

A commuter imagines that he is in a Turkish Harem while he is on a commuter train, goes through many physiological changes associated with sexual activity and says, Ah, How Wonderful, as the train pulls into Penn station.

A Siberian Shaman on a spirit journey converses with spirits.

A person under the influence of LSD tells his friends that they are energy packets from outer space.

An artist says that he is painting from a picture in his mind.

A split-brain subject says that he cannot see an object to which he is responding appropriately through visual cues.

Other concepts such as vividness, control, duration, severity and the 'enfeebled personality' are not assembled within this framework. It is a basic division between the internal/external, which sets the parameters through which the 'problem of hallucination' is framed. Therefore using one mode of explanation reified within psychiatric discourse, and deploying it as an explanation for conditioned responses within a learning paradigm, merely highlights the way statements are used from other discursive frameworks and links are made with other discourses, to make one's own system of explanation both 'intelligible' and possible. There is also much dissent surrounding behaviourist explanations within contemporary psychological discourse. Rather than being viewed as 'blank slates', humans are seen to have 'higher cognitive functions'.

Evolutionary arguments are then often deployed to differentiate these more 'simple' kinds of learning from the rationality seen to characterise humans. Consider how these differentiations between simple and complex and the animal and civilised structure the following set of claims regarding the problem of hallucination.

> These considerations do not rule out the possibility that classical conditioning may play a role in hallucination. A classical conditioning account would have the virtue of allowing hallucinations in animals, for example. However, until firm evidence of the conditioning of hallucinations is collected, it seems that more complex processes will be required to account for the available clinical and experimental data. (Slade and Bentall 1988:114)

Therefore, despite the push to prove that hallucinations are a result of associative learning there is no basic agreement on the 'truth status' of this set of theories. It does not offer a clear trajectory through the gaps, silences and contradictions encountered in psychiatric practice. It plays a part in the web of explanations produced through psychological representation, but does not offer the link which psychology is striving for to provide a coherent explanation of the nature of hallucinatory experience.

Hallucination as a continuum of 'normal' mental imagery

'Normal' mental imagery has been defined as a non-veridical experience involving the sensory or perceptual organs. There are two concepts which structure the dispersal of explanations within this model. The first is the concept of vividness where hallucinations are viewed as an example of extremely vivid mental imagery (Richardson 1969). Within this explanatory framework, 'hallucinations' are viewed as being in some respects similar to other 'normal' forms of mental imagery, such as daydreaming, hypnosis, dreams and so forth, but paradoxically also to be qualitatively different. The notion invoked is one where imagery falls along a continuum with hallucinations appearing at one extreme. This extreme is described either as one of 'vividness' or 'exaggeration' (Seitz and Molholm 1947). In other words, although hallucinations are viewed as proximate to other forms of imagery they are also, by definition, the negation of 'normal' mental imagery.

Questions posed within this framework typically focus on determining individual differences in imagery, thought to underlie the hallucinatory experience. However, the 'problem of hallucination' is delimited further by incorporating and redeploying one of the main modes of psychiatric explanation, 'a belief in the reality of the experience'. The empirical problem is individualised, and the two concepts conflated through attempting to classify and measure 'reality testing' (the ability to judge between real and imaginary events) and the 'quality of mental imagery'. Thus the 'problem of hallucination' is seen as an interaction between the quality of mental imagery, i.e., through mental rotation tasks (Shepard and Metzler 1971), and the person's 'reality testing' skills (cf. Mintz and Alpert 1972). Other areas of research within this framework utilise standardised questionnaire measures of mental imagery. Early studies used questionnaires asking individuals to imagine scenes, for example, a car standing in front of a gate, and were then asked how easy it was for them to change the image, for example by changing the car's colour and turning the car on its roof. The ratings were forced into a standardised scale and then compared inter-individually.

These concepts and their accompanying research technologies have then been used to compare and contrast 'quality of mental imagery' between those deemed schizophrenic and control groups. Mintz and Alpert (1972) utilised a design first used by Barber and Calverly (1964) where subjects are asked to imagine 'a cat sitting on their lap'. Three groups of subjects were used, 'hallucinating schizophrenics', 'non-hallucinating schizophrenics' and 'controls' – those deemed to be normal. When asked to imagine 'White Christmas' being played, 75 per cent of 'hallucinators' reported hearing it, and 10 per cent believed it had actually been played. Similar designs, involving suggestion, have been used to compare 'hallucinators' and 'non-hallucinators'. It was found that 'hallucinating patients' were more likely to report hearing complex stimuli than non-hallucinators (Alpert 1985).

These designs use one concept, schizophrenia, which has the status of 'science-already-made' (Osbourne and Rose 1999), to divide people into predetermined groups to compare, classify and measure levels of mental imagery. Other concepts such as hostility, neuroticism, physical anhedonia and aggression are then used as further measures of predisposition to a hallucinatory onset. These procedures of measurement thus define something to be measured, which is then used as an indication of something else. In relation to this point, Rose suggests that 'they (psychologists) domesticate and discipline subjectivity, transforming the intangible, change-able, apparently free-willed conduct of people into manipulable, coded, materialised, mathematized, two-dimensional traces which may be utilized in any procedure of calculation'.

The paradox is that nowhere in the literature are the norms of 'normal' mental functioning defined. Mental imagery is presumed to be a mental picture of the world as produced internally, thus not dependent upon actual representations of external events. However, the laws governing normal mental imagery functioning are not explained. The 'norm' of mental imagery is a lack of hallu-cination. Thus 'abnormal' mental imagery is a negation of 'normal' mental imagery, which in turn defines and classifies the limits of 'normal' mental imagery. In relation to this point, if one considers Hilgard's 1965 definition of altered states of consciousness,

> the subject loses initiative and the willingness to act independ-ently, his attention is re-distributed, his perception becomes selective and he develops a heightened ability for fantasy pro-duction and for distortion of reality (Wagstaff 1983:210),

there are continuities with this definition, the definition of mental imagery, and the psychiatric definition of hallucinations. All focus upon the involvement of imagery or fantasy production whilst 'awake', or at least in a certain state of consciousness. However, hal-lucinations are differentiated from 'normal' mental imagery by invoking the notion of 'self-conscious' awareness. However, this criterion or mode of explanation does not suffice to delimit the definition of altered states of consciousness from the psychiatric definition of hallucination. In both definitions, the subject loses volition, the willingness to act independently and attention becomes redistributed or refocused. Therefore, what is the concep-tual difference between hallucinations and an altered state of consciousness such as hypnosis?

Wagstaff (1983:86) suggests in relation to this question that hypnosis involves the capacity to produce vivid images, as 'whilst some of us may be able to produce a vivid mental picture of a relative or loved one, sufficient to invoke intense emotional feelings, this is not quite the same as projecting the image so that the person actually appears to be physically present in front of us'.

Again this definition still does not rule out the inclusion of hallu-cinations as an altered state of consciousness akin to hypnosis. Compare this statement: 'if a subject genuinely "hallucinates" an object, then the object to some extent is as vivid as objects actually present' (ibid.: 84). The fundamental difference or division is that hallucinations are viewed as inherently pathological and hypnosis is not. Hypnosis is viewed as a transitory state or role (Sarbin and Coe 1972), whereas hallucinations are a symptom or index of pathology, and become an integral part of the identity of the person. Thus in order to understand why hallucinations are consti-tuted within this framework as a continuum of 'normal' mental imagery, one needs to understand the antecedent for this statement to exist. Neisser (1967) has highlighted that there is no a priori reason for believing that imagery vividness is an underlying condi-tion for a hallucinatory experience to occur – the paradox being that 'normal' mental imagery is defined by what is abnormal, i.e., hallucinations. Thus although psychology aims to extend its knowledge of normal mental functioning to deal with what is con-stituted as individual and social pathology, the questions are posed in terms of deviation from certain norms. As Rose (1985:123) suggests, in relation to this argument,

> individual psychology would seem to diagnose social pathology in terms of deviation from statistical norms. Its conception of normal and abnormal mental functioning would be constructed from the point of view of a theory of populations, averages and correlations, not from a conception of the psyche itself.

As we have seen in this section, there are a plethora of theories and concepts which make up the available professional psychological commentary on the subject. Many of these are directly aligned and linked to those concepts which are embedded within psychiatric discourse. They focus less on the brain and more on those cognitive capacities which are viewed as existing within the mind. They are attempts to locate the psychological, as opposed to the psychiatric mechanisms, which underpin the hallucinatory experience. They claim to be based upon general theories of mental functioning, which are then extended to understand these so-called deviations from normal functioning. However, as we are beginning to see, it is actually the ways in which deviations, understood as pathology, are articulated, which make possible what we understand normal mental functioning to be. Foucault (1987b:73) makes the following set of observations in relation to psychological discourse:

> It must not be forgotten that 'objective' or 'positive' or 'scientific' psychology founds its historical origin and its basis in pathological experience. It was an analysis of duplications that made possible a psychology of the personality; an analysis of compulsions and of the unconscious that provided the basis for a psychology of consciousness; an analysis of deficits that led to a psychology of intelligence.

In the next section we will turn to arguments within other sub-disciplines of psychology and psychiatry, which examine the more 'social' dimensions of the hallucinatory experience. These argue that the experience of 'hearing voices' can never be reduced to an expression of a biological or psychological state. There is more concern with the context of the experience, and the kinds of interpretations, which are used to make sense of the phenomenon.

The social psychology of hallucinations

This section will focus upon other alternative explanations within the 'psy' discourses, which all attempt to contextualise the 'problem' of hallucination, within the social, cultural or historical context which has given rise to such explanations. They all start with the contemporary definition of hallucination, and attempt to locate these explanations within their immediate socio-historical milieu, where interpretations of phenomena are linked to the time and place of their enunciation. They are all relativising modes of investigation, where the social context, history and culture are used to highlight the ways in which different kinds of social and cultural interpretations exist to make sense of the phenomena. Where, in the previous section, the 'problem of hallucination' was viewed as the expression of a psychological process, traditionally viewed as a prediscursive capacity or attribute of the psychological subject, in contrast these are viewed as historically and culturally relative interpretations. These interpretations are viewed as dependent upon particular, often Western, ways of conceptualising the mind and its capacities. These explanations are not considered empirical fact(s), but are akin to folk-models of the culture which provide the implicit foundations of psychological and psychiatric knowledge.

Transcultural psychiatry

Transcultural psychiatry contests many of the concepts and modes of explanation, which structure psychiatric discourse. Transcultural psychiatry attempts to 'rehumanise' the patient's discourse, going beyond the objectification seen to characterise bio-medical psychiatry, i.e. that the hallucination is merely a release product referring to deficient pseudo-sensory activity. Transcultural psychiatry differs markedly by treating the meaning of hallucination as having deep personal and psychological significance. Littlewood (1980) and Littlewood and Lipsedge (1989) incorporate these ideas into their theories where hallucinations are considered functional phenomena. They are viewed as expressions of the active ways people cope and make sense of a confusing and changing world. By directing attention to the social context of the hallucinatory experience, they argue that apparently bizarre and meaningless behaviour can be meaningful and function as a way of making sense of a complex world.

The theoretical approach advocated within this framework is based on a phenomenological perspective, which treats the patient as the arbiter of experience. The meaning of the patients' utterances must be understood by examining their life situation and lived experience. Littlewood and Lipsedge (1989:14) argue that 'the expression of mental illness, while it may not always be valid communication to others, is still a meaningful reaction on the part of the individual to his/her situation'. The role of the practitioner or psychiatrist within this framework is to attempt to understand the lived experience of the patients, and to make their worlds intelligible. There is no absolute 'reality' against which a persons experience can be judged. Rather, there is a pluralism of 'realities' alongside the dominant 'reality', which is embedded within the particular cultural milieu. Littlewood suggests that in heterogeneous, industrial societies like ours, language is over-determined with a wealth of delicate and subtle meanings. Certain groups within society are dominant and control access to and the use of social symbols. Therefore members of cultural minority groups in a society, according to Littlewood (women, children and the 'mentally ill'), have to use the majority culture to articulate their concerns (Ardener 1971).

The notion here is that a person's experience is structured according to 'public symbols' which reflect the way society is organised. These 'public symbols' are constructed as having two poles – a public pole, which reflects the experiences of the commu-

nity group as a whole, and a private pole which represents an idiosyncratic use of a symbol by an individual, which is derived from
one's own experience. In relation to those designated 'mentally ill',
they are either employing their own highly idiosyncratic symbolic
communication system, or if they are not familiar with the
dominant meaning systems (e.g. ethnic minorities), then their use
of these dominant meaning systems to express their concerns may
be 'rickety and cumbersome' and not 'readily assessable to others'
(ibid.:219).

Therefore, according to Littlewood (1980), the reason there is a
disproportionate number of black and ethnic minorities defined as
schizophrenic within the mental health system, is because of miscommunication and misdiagnosis between the doctor and patient.
What is subjectively meaningful and functional for one, i.e. the
patient, may be misinterpreted as signs of mental illness, rather
than a particular way of structuring the world at odds with the so-
called dominant culture. In the following example, a woman's
dramatic delusions and hallucinations, characterised as signs of
psychosis, highlighted instead a breakdown of the symbolic communications systems she was using to make sense of her world.

Littlewood (1980) describes the ways in which she quite literally
constructed the world in terms of black and white. She was the
daughter of a black Jamaican Baptist minister, and moved to
England when she was 18. She had got married and had a baby, and
then her husband had died. At this time her family had also
disowned her. Over the next ten years she became lonely and
depressed, but she did not blame the British, whom she in fact
admired and envied. 'White' to her, according to Littlewood, sym-
bolically represented religion, purity and renunciation. Whereas,
'black' represented West Indians in general, but also sin, sexual
indulgence and dirt. According to Littlewood, her classification
system of black/white first became disrupted when she quarrelled
with her West Indian neighbour in her 'white' front room reserved
for guests. She dealt with this by emphasising internal colour;
whites can be spiritually black, and some blacks can be spiritually
'white'; this helped her to explain why not all people conformed to
her expectations. However, the complexity of her system failed to
cope with 'external reality', when her son came home from the
Notting Hill carnival, and announced that all blacks, by virtue of
their skin colour, are treated unfairly. She identified herself, both
ethnically and morally as white. This is the point, according to

Littlewood when she becomes 'insane', as her symbolic system begins to break down and collapse.

Although attempting to provide an understanding and possible solution to institutional racism within the mental health system, the understanding of ethnicity underpinning this analysis is individualised and located within miscommunication. Although this highlights the important issue of how different groups of people may be differentially treated within psychiatric practice, it does not engage with arguments which bring the issue of power and the productive role of discourse into the debate. Mercer (1986) for example, suggests that the medical stereotyping of black people, for example, as loud, volatile and aggressive, sets limits on the ways in which particular experiences are understood and acted upon within the mental health system. He advocates the adoption and utilisation of post-colonial theory, particularly the work of Franz Fanon (1967) and Homi Bhabha (1994) as a way of intervening in these debates.[4] This is very different from the combination of phenomenology and structuralism which underpins Littlewood's formulations.

The first is that meaning is a product of the 'fixing' of a concept, the signified, to a symbol, the signifier. This 'fixing' of meaning is seen to occur at the level of the social group, who then share these meanings and use them to construct their group identities. Therefore the analytic unit for examining meaning is the social group. Dominant meaning systems are assumed to be those that are 'fixed' by the more powerful groups. 'Madness' is therefore seen to be a form of 'sign conflict', a confusion of different 'realities'. However, it is the place concepts occupy within a number of connected terms or meanings, or within the allied discursive field, which gives signifiers their meaning, rather than that of a concept tied firmly to the tail of a particular signifier. If we take an example pertinent to the last chapter, the meaning of hallucination is articulated through a number of connected concepts which create the possibility of particular ways of articulating and differentiating the experience. The meanings of signifiers are always situated in relation to particular discursive practices, which then create particular 'subject positions' or ways of articulating one's own and another's experience. The question then becomes one of examining the ways in which individual voice-hearers embody and experience their voices. This is a rather different set of concerns, and will be developed in Chapters 3 and 7.

One of the key problems with much of this theorising is that despite the focus on the social dimensions of psychiatric experience it becomes unclear exactly how the social intersects with individual experience. Culture is viewed as a separate monolithic entity which creates 'shared meanings', which are then internalised by the individual and structure their experience. These 'shared meanings' may then be at odds with those employed in idiosyncratic ways by other groups in society, thus causing a breakdown in communication. The kind of experiences which biomedical psychiatry understands as being caused by neurological and biochemical referents are instead seen to be overlaid by cultural and social values, beliefs and symbols. The focus is less on the form of the experience, i.e. the neuro-physiological mechanisms which may underpin the experience, and more on the content of the experiences, which are seen to reflect the ways in which individuals structure their experiences. Thus a distinction is drawn between form and content, which relativises the experience and shifts the focus to the function different experiences play in a person's life.

This dichotomy between form and content is central to the way in which transcultural psychiatry understands particular kinds of somatic experience (cf. Leff 1981). The form, or the symptom, i.e. the hallucination, is viewed as a universal biological or neurological experience. The content of the hallucination is derived from the patient's cultural milieu and thus can vary across time and space (the thesis of universalism).[5] Culture and the social act in a peripheral way filling in the content of the hallucinatory experience. The expression of the experience differs because of the influence of differential norms, attitudes, beliefs and values. This is highlighted in much of the anthropological literature, where the influence of the culture is also viewed as changing the threshold of the experience itself. In a survey of anthropological literature on 488 societies, Bourguignon (1970) noted that in 62 per cent of the societies, hallucinations play a major role in ritual practice. For this reason, hallucinations are often actively sought out, often by resorting to extreme and perhaps dangerous measures, i.e. ingestion of toxic substances, or by pushing the body to extreme exhaustion (Rabkin 1970).

Although these approaches move away from neurological and biological reductionism, they see biology and the cultural as being two separate categories which overlay each other. Questions of causality then oscillate between the two perspectives, where both remain as separate entities, which influence each other in a peripheral way. Rather than adopting a phenomenological perspective this book will explore the radical transformation in understanding brought about by taking up a 'phenomenological methodological standpoint' (Csordas 1994). This perspective does not view biology as a static entity, a substrate merely overlaid by experience, but a condition of possibility of certain kinds of experience, which becomes embodied and transformed through the strategies and practices people use to engage with somatic, bodily experiences. These methodological points will be developed in the next chapter and Chapter 8. In the next section some of the problems with phenomenology as a theory of 'experience' will be introduced.

The phenomenology of perception

> I am the absolute source, my existence does not stem from my antecedents, from my physical and social environment; instead it moves out towards them and sustains them, for I alone bring into being for myself, the tradition which I elect to carry on. When the victim of hallucinations declares that he sees and hears, we must not believe him, since he also declares the opposite; what we must do is understand him. (Merleau-Ponty 1962:336)

The quote above illustrates the orientation to a person's experience which is central to phenomenological inquiry. Merleau-Ponty (1962) was particularly interested, in his book *The Phenomenology of Perception*, in those kinds of experiences such as hallucination which in Western societies tend to signify as abnormal and pathological. One does not judge and evaluate a person's experience within this form of inquiry, but attempts to understand their 'being in the world'. In the context of perception, it is an attempt to grasp how objects in the social world impinge or impact on our bodily senses. One of the methods of phenomenology is hermeneutics, a method that originates from studies of the Bible, attempting to understand and extract the 'true' meaning of the verses. It is a method that has also been used within market research, where through a cyclical process of reflecting back your understanding of the research subject's understanding, you eventually come to some kind of 'true' representation of their experience.[6]

It is a human inquiry into the meaning of hallucination, which is based firmly in the description and experience of the person it (the method) purports to understand. The interpreter must somehow bracket their own experience, understandings, social and historical conditions of existence, language etc., and attempt to harness the existential meaning of the hallucinator's experience. It is offered as an 'objectively, subjective' way of understanding experience. It is a communion of the researched with the researcher. Merleau-Ponty also relies upon the notion of a 'pre-objective body' in much of this work, focusing less on the understandings a person may bring to bear on the experience, and more with the ways in which particular kinds of experience are felt and lived in one's bodily, somatic awareness. It is very much a language of touch and sensation, a concern with the sentient body, and with those kinds of experience which we may have prior to language. This takes us into wider philosophical debates about what comes first, language or experience, a kind of chicken or egg problem. The main criticism of phenomenology is aimed at this notion of whether experience is possible without language, and obviously depends upon how one is defining the concept of experience in the first place. Compare the following two quotes:

> A woman patient declares that someone looked at her at the market, and that she felt the gaze upon her like a blow, but could not say whence it came. She cannot bring herself to say, that in common property space there stood a flesh and blood person who turned his eyes towards her – and it is because of this refusal that the arguments that we can bring against her leave her completely unmoved. For her it is not a matter of what happens in the objective world, but of what she encounters, what touches or strikes her. (Merleau-Ponty 1962:342)

> To claim that I am having a wholly private experience is meaningless. I would not be able to have an experience in the first place unless it took place in the terms of some language within which I could identify it. (Eagleton 1983:60)

This is a debate that has underpinned many of the approaches within critical psychology and cultural studies, which privilege language, discourse, text and representation in the constitution of experience. As Hwa Yol Yung (1996) argues, phenomenology is concerned primarily with what she argues is a traditionally feminine way of understanding bodily experience – hugging, embracing and caressing. Rather than being concerned with what she terms the 'mind's eye', with reason and language, its focus is with the 'body's touch', how the body is touched, glanced at, subjected to blows and so forth. In the next chapter we will explore the ways in which constructionist perspectives (central to much of critical psychology and cultural studies) argue that experience is always the end product of social, historical and cultural processes. We will also examine the move away and negation of biology and somatic experience in the production of experience. The transcultural approach advocated by Littlewood and Lipsedge (1989) is more influenced by Heideggerian phenomenology, which focuses more on language and understanding, but is less concerned with what Foucault (1987b) termed the 'historicity of experience'. Foucault was concerned not so much with 'being in the world', but with how it is possible to have particular kinds of experiences in the world. In relation to 'mental illness', less an examination of either the social or organic basis of mental pathology, than an exploration of the very idea of mental pathology; how historically is has become possible in Western societies to posit certain experiences, such as hallucination, as signs of underlying mental pathology. All these arguments will be explored in the next chapter. In the next section a range of social psychological theories will be examined, which again shift to a focus upon the social dimensions of the experience. These social psychological approaches deploy different ways of understanding the social dimensions of experience in order to understand the 'problem of hallucination'.

Role-strain

the conduct of an individual cannot be understood without taking into account the texture of the social environment. To understand 'hallucination' requires an examination of the social roles enacted by a particular person and the reciprocal roles enacted by others in efforts to solve their interlocking problems. Thus, within the field of social psychology itself, our approach is a role theoretical one. (Sarbin and Juhasz 1978:117)

This approach attempts to understand the 'problem of hallucination' by grouping together imaginings, daydreams and hallucination and viewing all these experiences as a-linguistic and asocial actions which a performer will intentionally shift into when 'the going gets tough'. This move into what is conceived as the world of 'abstract things' is regarded as a strategic, action-oriented, pragmatic accomplishment. The world is seen to exist at a variety of fictive levels which people as actors move in and out of (Singer 1966). The problem of hallucination is only a problem when a person wishes to communicate about these abstract worlds; a process of translation between an a-linguistic mode and a linguistic and social mode. This problem of translation creates the potential for miscommunication, where hallucination is considered a pejorative term to dismiss someone's imaginings and place a negative valuation on them. This approach encounters some of the problems with phenomenology discussed in the previous section. There is a split or dichotomy between those experiences, which are viewed as prior to language, and then how a person uses the symbols at their disposal to translate these worlds. Imagining is viewed as preceding or predating this communication system. As Sarbin (1967:136) suggests, 'instantiation or perception precedes language use by a good two years'. He draws on further experimental evidence to support this statement citing Piaget and Inhelder (1971) and Paivio (1971). However, this statement reifies the 'myth of the innocent eye' that we somehow observe, perceive and classify without using the theoretical and conceptual resources we have available to us to 'make sense' of objects. This is a key debate across many disciplines underpinned by splits between perception and signification, essentialism and constructionism, the body and culture, which we will deal with in some depth in the next chapter.

This approach also presumes a particular relationship between power and subjectivity, such that power is seen to repress and control the self, and the world of imaginings is seen to be less susceptible to power relationships. This is a particular way of thinking about power and the ways in which it acts upon the human subject. Foucault (1985:94) in *The History of Sexuality* offers a different way of thinking about the ways in which power functions. It does not repress a core or essential self, but rather acts upon and through individuals' actions, such that they come to want or desire certain things and ways of acting for themselves. It works, according to Foucault, in a productive mode, such that discourse and knowledge provide the parameters through which people come to think about, understand and act upon themselves in particular ways. The concept of social control or social constraint, drawn on within the role perspective, views power as prohibiting and repressive, rather than productive and positive. The imagination is then conceived as an experience which falls outside of discourse and power, and can be adopted as a strategy when a person is suffering from stress. 'At this point, we want to stress that the imaginer is far less under social control than is the thinker' (ibid.:135).

The problem of hallucination then becomes a problem when the person experiences 'role-strain'. This is viewed as a practical incongruence between certain social role expectations and a participation in the realm of imaginings.[7] Role-strain is used to refer to the cognitive strain someone may experience, which may be a precursor for shifting perspectives to the world of fantasy and imagination, and also for why problems may then occur in relation to the kinds of role-expectations they are also having to deal with. This may then account for why their experiences may be pejoratively dismissed as hallucination.

> As we have said before, it is not the overt, autochthonous features of the behaviour that determine whether the reported imagining is diagnosed as hallucinatory or creative imagining. It is rather the social variables, which single out the individual as a proper candidate for degradation to the status of mentally ill. (ibid.:138)

The implications of this perspective, much like phenomenology, are that we must try and understand people's experiences, and not judge them according to divisions made between the normal and the abnormal. The authors cite a variety of culturally sanctioned 'shifting perspectives' which allow a person to enter the world of imagination and fantasy: ritual, drama and the spirit quest. The implication is that the psychiatrist or psychologist should act much like a shaman or spirit guide, allowing the person to explore these new perspectives, and to share them with the psychiatrist/psychologist. It is postulated that within traditional psychiatric thought the therapist actually freezes the person in the role of mental patient and discounts their imaginings. This approach is also very influenced by some of the more 'anti-psychiatric' perspectives which view psychiatry as an institution, which makes moral judgements about behaviour and conduct, masked under the mantles of science and objectivity (Sarbin 1967:7).

This approach tends to reverse some of the distinctions, which although shifting and changing in the twenty-first century, were very much embedded within psychiatry at the time of much of this writing. Where the person was seen to be objectified within the medical model, the role theoretical model focuses on intentionality (a strategic shift to the world of imagination). Where the medical model infers hallucination as being a referent of underlying pathology, the role theoretical model concludes that there is no identifiable referent, i.e. the person is not mentally ill. Hallucination is a pragmatic moral judgement on another person's ability to meet the expectations of their social roles. The act of 'shifting perspectives' is viewed as an offence against the 'public order' and therefore as a form of moral deviancy.

> Far from being culture-free, such 'symptoms' are themselves offences against implicit understandings of particular cultures. Every society provides its members with a set of explicit norms – understandings which govern conduct with regard to such central institutions as the state, the family, and private property. (ibid.:7)

Within this perspective, the person labelled as mentally ill is also romanticised as a potential revolutionary. Their behaviour is not only considered an idiosyncratic 'voyage of discovery', but a public challenge.

> Perhaps the time has come to consider that the reality that the so-called schizophrenics are out of touch with is so appalling that their view of the world may be more supportive to life than conventional reality. (ibid:19)

We will see in Chapter 6 how some of these ways of specifying particular kinds of experiences, such as hallucination, although operating as points of resistance in relation to orthodox psychiatry, helped to shape the restructuring and reconfiguration of psychiatry following the Second World War. They also borrowed from some of the notions which psychiatry was beginning to deploy to differentiate and make intelligible the realm of mental distress. Within this shift a space opened up for psychological understandings and tech-

niques to be deployed in relation to those forms of mental disturbance which were considered mild (neurotic) and not completely
disabling the person. The notion that there were different types of
reaction emerged, where the schizophrenic reaction (although not
considered insurrectionary) was a more severe and incapacitating
reaction linked to a prior vulnerability or inherited disposition.
Although the role-theoretical framework positions itself as a more
general critique of the function and role of psychiatry, it neverthe-
less also translates some of the concepts central to psychiatry at a
particular point in time to make its own theory intelligible. In the
next section we will consider a development of this theory to look
at the ways in which judgements about what is normal and
abnormal behaviour are also viewed as culture-bound.

Beyond roles to attitudes

This theory combines concepts from labelling theory (Sarbin and
Juhasz 1967, 1978) with social anthropological theories to unsettle
the reliability and validity of some of the concepts and modes of
explanation drawn on within the medical model (Al-Issa 1977,
1978). It argues that the criteria drawn upon to distinguish
between the pseudo-hallucination and the hallucination are not
self-evident means of classifying and differentiating the experience. Evidence cited by authors such as Bugelski (1971), McKellar
(1968), McLemore (1972), Richardson (1969), and Stoyva (1973)
are linked together to show that the criteria of 'individual control'
cannot be used as a means of classification because hallucinations
have been shown to be related to internal and external cues
(within a classical conditioning model), and that the 'imagery of
normal subjects is by no means voluntary or subject to personal
control' (Al-Issa 1977:571).

Another criterion central to psychiatric discourse, 'a belief in the
reality of the hallucination' (ibid.:571) is also attacked by citing
counter-experimental evidence. The author suggests that it is the
'conviction', which a person expresses which may make all the difference, such as using the phrase 'as if' (Sarbin 1967). The following
quote indicates how this approach also attempts to understand
some of the cultural differences encountered within the
doctor–patient relationship which, as we have seen, are used to
explain why there are a disproportionate number of black people
within the mental health system in Britain.

A special problem exists for the diagnostician when the suspect lacks language sophistication and cannot indicate his ellipses with appropriate qualifiers. This is especially true of children, adults with limited language skills, persons with meagre vocabularies such as recent immigrants, etc. Expressing the concept 'as if' requires a fair degree of linguistic skill. Thus when a 4-year-old child insists on talking to an imaginary playmate, the as if is supplied by the mother and the child is not likely to be referred to a therapist for help in stamping out hallucinations. When reading the productions of great poets, the readers supply the suppressed as if. In order to interpret any sentence properly, the listener must consider the total context, i.e. he must be ready to supply missing qualifiers. (Al-Issa 1977: 574, quoted from Sarbin 1967)

Added support is amassed by linking experimental studies showing that 'normal subjects under some conditions are liable to the confusion between vivid imagery and externally generated signals', commonly referred to as the Perky effect (Perky 1910, as cited in Al-Issa 1977:571). This somewhat contradictory evidence is then used to support the assertion that psychiatric diagnoses are founded upon criteria, which are unreliable and invalid. We can clearly see within this perspective the ways in which some of the concepts central to the psychiatric architecture are deployed and disputed. The perspective then draws upon other statements in order to make its own framework of explanation intelligible (cf. Henriques et al. 1984:104). Ultimately the theories are made possible by the very discursive concepts they seek to dismantle, such as individual control and vividness (cf. Chapter 1).

However, as stated at the beginning of this section, this perspective is one which claims to examine the social dimensions of the 'problem of hallucination'. This is set up in a particular way where it is framed in relation to how 'the social' affects the individual and where does it register its effects? This question is trapped within the individual/society dualism where the individual and the social are constituted as two separate entities (much like the individual/cultural dualism we have already examined). The social is welded on as an outside restraining or sometimes facilitating force. Seen as an entity, it is easy to divide the social domain up in terms of variants or factors, which influence or affect the individual and his or her psychological capacities. This dualism characteristic of psychology remains continuous in one form or another right across the various 'sub-disciplines' of psychology (Blackman and Walkerdine 2001, cf. Chapter 3).

Al-Issa (1977) has drawn upon one of the most popular and widely used psychological concepts, the attitude, to account for where the social registers its effects. It is the social beliefs of the culture which are internalised and become part of the individual's make-up. Attitudes are viewed as relatively stable and enduring traits, which can be measured using psychometric tests (Potter and Wetherell 1987:33). It is also proposed that people act on the basis of these sets of fixed attitudes or beliefs. Attitudes are also seen to vary across time and space and are therefore seen as culturally relative. The cultural beliefs concerning the origin of hallucinations have been offered as an explanation of differing means of controlling the occurrence and the cultural differences in content (Al-Issa 1977).

Much of the work in critical psychology which we will examine in the next chapter has moved away from a notion that there are stable psychological entities, such as attitudes, which can be measured, described and compared across individuals and groups. This is an offshoot of the assumption that the individual and the 'social' or 'culture' exist independently from each other and yet interact. Within social psychology, the language that people use to describe themselves and others, is viewed as a tool which reveals these inner psychological thoughts and beliefs. Potter and Wetherell (1987) have shown that people are inconsistent across time and space, and use language to 'do' things. In other words, language is pragmatic, action-orientated and rhetorical. This orientation to language directs attention away from the notion that people possess stable, enduring attitudes, to examining the context in which utterances are embedded, and the 'linguistic repertoires' that people may use to make sense of phenomena. The concept of 'linguistic repertoires' is problematic, as we will examine in the next chapter, but does direct attention to the various ways hallucination may be conceptualised, and therefore, the variation in accounts of hallucinations. However it is also important to examine how it is possible for the 'linguistic repertoires' surrounding hallucinations to exist as possible systems of explanation and how they co-exist within a whole web of discursive practices.

If one conceptualises the intersection of the psychological with the social through the concept of attitudes, then there are particular modes of intervention made possible by this account. Al-Issa (1977) argues that people's 'attitudes' must be changed to alleviate the anxiety felt by people who 'hear voices', because of the negative attitudes people and the voice-hearer may have towards them. This is one of the central propositions and aims of a psychiatric-user group, the 'Hearing Voices Network' which is currently contesting the assumptions embedded within psychiatric discourse and society at large. Al-Issa advocates a range of therapeutic methods along these lines. The first goal is to reduce anxiety by using various behavioural approaches such as systematic desensitisation (Wolpe 1958), or to eliminate the hallucinations completely by using methods such as aversion therapy (Bucher and Fabricatore 1970) or operant conditioning (Lindsley 1959) by varying stimuli such as social reinforcement. The assumption underpinning these methods is that hallucinations are under the control of certain internal and external cues, which can be regulated (Schaefer and Martin 1969).

The other therapeutic intervention advocated within this system of explanation draws on psychoanalytic concepts. Hallucinations are viewed as being akin to dreams, which within Freudian psychoanalysis are viewed as the acting-out of 'motive fulfilment' producing cathartic effects. This directs attention to the function of hallucinations within a person's life (Juhasz 1972, Sarbin and Juhasz 1970, Singer 1970). However, because of the negative attitudes towards hallucinations they are proposed to become more functionally autonomous and less relevant to the immediate social stimuli, and therefore the person may have less control over their occurrence. Thus the concepts of location and control which make up the tapestry of psychiatric discourse are not viewed as natural divisions within which to distinguish hallucinations, but differentiations which are a product of the influence of the actual social and cultural setting within which these experiences take place.

The different cultural responses are seen as a product of the negative attitudes of Western cultures, which are then contrasted with the positive attitudes of non-Western cultures. The apparent differences in the conceptualisation of the experience known as hallucinations are reduced to a single explanatory concept, rationality.

> The rationality of the culture and its distinction between reality and fantasy may well result in different attitudes toward hallucinations, and these in turn could affect both the detection and report of hallucinatory experiences. (Al-Issa 1977:576)

'Rationality' is constituted as an outcome of the extent to which a culture distinguishes between 'fantasy' and 'reality'. Anthropological evidence is cited to make intelligible these apparent differences between 'Western' and 'non-Western' cultures. For example, Wallace (1959) found in a comparative study that a group of Indians reported socially meaningful visions, reacting to them in an aura of calmness and satisfaction. The notion is that in less 'rational' cultures the distinction between reality and fantasy is more flexible and individuals are encouraged to observe their hallucinations and imagery. These events in turn are positively valued and are frequently communicated to others. The experience is not anxiety-arousing or disturbing to the individual. The experience is even actively sought out by a variety of methods: lack of sleep, fasting, prolonged physical exercise, social isolation, drugs and so on and so forth (Bourguignon 1970). Therefore, the notion of attitude is conceptualised as a register of the culture's distinction between reality and fantasy.

All of the above evidence illustrates how some of the concepts used to make the distinction between the pseudo-hallucination and the hallucination (seen to indicate underlying mental pathology) within psychiatric discourse are tied to a very specific historical and cultural context. It also shows how within the field of psychological theory, there are a number of conflicting and different perspectives which attempt to make the voice-hearing experience intelligible. Several of these, including behaviourism, studies of the mental imagery of normal people, and psychoanalysis are conflated within this account. The evidence drawn from anthropological literature within this account adds further weight to the main 'problem of hallucination' within psychiatric discourse, that under certain circumstances it is possible for most people to experience hallucinations. In the next chapter we will begin to think about different ways in which we can understand the intersection of the biological with the social. Although one tactic could be, as with this perspective, to provide counter-evidence for some of the assumptions embedded within psychiatric discourse. One of the aims of the book will be to examine the different kinds of voice-hearing experience made possible through the ways in which actual voice-hearers understand and act upon their own voices.

What this chapter has illustrated is the intersection of psychology with psychiatry in the rendering of the 'problem of hallucination'. This space shows how psychiatry is not homogenised by biological, neurological or pharmacological responses to the voice-hearing phenomenon, and mental distress more generally. There is a space for psychological techniques and theories, particularly as we have seen, in relation to the problem of non-compliance and treatment-resistant symptoms. What we will see in Chapters 4, 5 and 6 is that since the beginning of this century, and particularly following the First World War psychological theories and techniques (in the terms which we now understand the psychological) have been part of the landscape of psychiatric discourse. Rose (1986:77) has argued quite cogently that there have always been spaces within orthodox psychiatry for those 'who are in one way or another resistant to its techniques of normalisation'. We will examine some of these in future chapters. What this does point to however is the urgent need to rethink how as critical psychologists and cultural theorists we wish to think about the role and function of the 'psy' discourses in our everyday lives. In the next chapter we will take on this challenge by exploring how we might analyse the relationships between the biological, social and psychological along different lines. This difficult task is one which must be attentive to the ways in which psychiatry neither functions along the lines of a reactionary medical model, nor can only be explained by moving to social explanations which deny and negate biological processes altogether. The next chapter will examine what tools are available within critical psychological inquiry and allied disciplines, to reframe what we might understand by the 'problem of hallucination'.

3
Critical Psychology

So far we have explored the tapestry of explanations across the disciplines of psychology and psychiatry which attempt to provide coherent theories, concepts and research technologies to understand and make intelligible the 'problem of hallucination'. We have seen the ways in which particular concepts and specific kinds of explanation circulate across a range of theories within both disciplines. We have also seen the ways in which the 'social', 'psychological' and 'biological' become combined in particular ways in order to frame and understand the voice-hearing experience. The last two chapters were important to elucidate exactly what kinds of explanation have a 'truth-status' within these knowledges in order to consider how we might wish to enter into a dialogue with the human sciences. Much critique has been generated in relation to both knowledges' claims to be 'sciences of the individual'; to be discovering the psychological and neurological mechanisms which define normal mental health and all the so-called deviations from normality. This chapter will engage with some of these critiques and begin to develop some conceptual tools that will be useful to examine the 'problem of hallucination' from a radically different perspective. Let us start with one of the key dualisms which structures much of this critique: essentialism versus constructionism.

Beyond the skin

This dualism frames debates which argue that what we understand to be 'the psychological', rather than located within or inside the person, are actually interpretations embedded within the very languages one uses to describe oneself and others. Thus all those psychological entities and mechanisms which are taken to define and describe individual subjectivity are actually part of a discursive landscape which maps and constructs subjectivity in particular ways. It is important to chart the trajectory of these arguments and to explore some of the problems with moving from essentialism to constructionism. We will start with exploring how these arguments developed within a sub-discipline of psychology – social psychology – and have produced a range of critical and discursive psychologies.

The vagaries of social constructionism

Many writers commenting on the role and function of psychology over the past decade have problematised the claims to scientificity which characterise the discipline. There are certain concepts – truth, objectivity and progress – which psychology uses to warrant its privileged position in making claims about the nature of subjectivity. Both psychology and psychiatry (despite not being unified disciplines as we saw in the last two chapters), assume that there are stable, enduring psychological capacities and mechanisms which are amenable to classification, description and calibration through the application and utilisation of the scientific method as a key research technology. We saw in Chapter 1 the way in which even if there is dissent and controversy surrounding some of the concepts and explanatory structures central to both disciplines, the experimental method is used as a means of validating and strengthening associations with other concepts, which have already gained the status of 'science-already-made (Osbourne and Rose 1999). The concepts which make up the discursive landscape in relation to particular phenomena such as voice-hearing, claim to be descriptions and means of classifying and differentiating entities which exist within the psychological, neurological or biological structures of the individual. This perspective on what makes us human is often described as 'essentialist', seeing human subjectivity as produced by underlying and pre-existing psychological and biological capacities. One good example for our purposes is psychology's reliance on the concept of *human nature*, which broadly encompasses, depending upon the perspective, all those essences taken to define the human subject. These essences are taken to be pre-social and pre-discursive, easily reducing to biological, neurological and even genetic dispositions.

Fuss (1989:2) aptly sums up essentialism in the following quote:

> Essentialism is classically defined as a belief in true essence – that which is most irreducible, unchanging, and therefore constitutive of a given person or thing.

The 'psy' disciplines operate upon the notion that there are basic building blocks of human nature, which can be uncovered through 'psy' inquiry. This set of presumptions has been critiqued in many different ways, starting within the discipline itself by social psychologists in the 1970s who felt the experimental method could not capture the complexities of human behaviour (Armistead 1974). This method, when applied to human subjectivity, was considered mechanistic and dehumanising, reducing human beings to mere automatons. In other words, how could the meanings human beings develop about themselves and the social world in which they exist be reduced to statistics and laws of probability?

Some argue that this led to the first crisis within the discipline where it was argued that to understand human subjectivity one needed to study how subjects make sense of and understand the world in which they live (Parker 1989). Psychological study should focus upon language and sense-making rather than the calibration of internal psychological mechanisms. The argument hinged upon the insight that humans could only come to know their worlds through social action and negotiation. There was nothing innate or predetermined about human sense-making activity. This was a move away from essentialism, which was viewed as reductionist and deterministic, to the study of language as a human and cultural invention. This reinterpretation of the nature of psychological inquiry involved the development of research methods enabling the study of human sense-making. These methods were interpretive rather than statistical, qualitative rather than quantitative. These more ethogenic approaches (Harré and Secord 1972) prided themselves on their basis in an image of human life which revered and reflected the diversity, subtlety and complexity of human behaviour (Fox 1985). The research process no longer relied upon the illusion of the objective, detached, neutral observer. Rather the relationship between the researched and the researcher was viewed as dialectic; a process of mutual construction, between the subjects' or co-researchers' own understanding and meaning(s) of their own and others experience. This research became known as new paradigm research, encompassing a range of interpretive methods such as hermeneutics, participant observation, dialectical methods and feminist methodologies to name a few, where research was done *with* and not *on* people (cf. Reason and Rowan 1981).

This shift in perspective allied social psychologists less with their own discipline, and more with perspectives originating within sociology, anthropology, philosophy and so on and so forth. Key new paradigm researchers drew from a range of theories from neighbouring disciplines including micro-sociology and the philosophy of social action (Shotter 1974) and hermeneutics and structuralism (Harré 1974). The aim of new paradigm research was to make psychology more social, and therefore other disciplines within the human sciences that were committed more to social explanations of the world were drawn from. Although new paradigm research was a move away from essentialism it has been critiqued and considered problematic by many critical psychologists in the Eighties who were also unhappy with the general mores of psychological inquiry (cf. Henriques et al. 1984). Although grounded within an individual's understanding of the world, it was also considered important to examine the conditions of possibility of certain understandings to exist within the social world (cf. Blackman and Walkerdine 2001). The *individual* is the central analytic unit to which new paradigm research retreats to explain the existence of the social world, rather than examining how individuals are constituted through the social domain (cf. Henriques et al. 1984).

Although a move away from biological essentialism, new paradigm research was seen to replace one set of essentialisms with others which credited humans with what were seen as more sophisticated psychological capacities. Rather than replace one set of essential characteristics with others, leaving psychology bound within an individual/social dualism, it became viewed as more important to explore how individuals come to relate to themselves as if they were *selves* of a particular type (Henriques et al. 1984). The psychology or subjectivity underpinning new paradigm research was based upon an image of life characterised by agency, intentionality and responsibility. New paradigm research relied upon a pre-given subject or psychology without explaining the process(es) through which subjects were formed and form themselves in relation to particular images and regulatory ideals. The social world existed as a function of the way(s) individuals represented or made sense of it. The approach therefore assumed an implicit voluntarism focusing upon the fluidity and flexibility of sense-making activity, rather than the processes through which subjects come to see themselves *as if* they are *selves* of a particular kind. Because this research was formed in opposition to *realist* or *positivist* psychology it was considered as having failed to adequately or radically rethink the relationship of the human subject to the discursive field in which he/she exists (ibid. 1984).

Morss (1990) has termed new paradigm research one of the first waves of criticism of orthodox psychology. More recent critiques have evolved from these debates, and have come to be known as discursive or postmodern psychologies (Burman 1990, 1992, Curt 1994, Gergen, 1973, 1989 1991, 1992, Harré 1981, 1983, 1985, 1989, 1992, Kitzinger 1990, Parker 1990a, 1992, Parker and Shotter 1990, Potter et al. 1990, Sampson 1989, 1990, Shotter 1984, 1986, 1987, 1989, 1990, 1993, Stenner and Eccleson 1994, Wetherell and Potter 1992). Despite their differences, they all share a commitment to the central role of language in constructing human understanding. As the preface to *Texts of Identity*, a key text in these critiques highlights, *central to the emerging dialogue is a recognition of the critical role played by linguistic constructions in social life* (Shotter and Gergen 1989:x). Within these critiques language is seen as having subjectifying force – it creates and forms individual understanding. Culture is made up of a series of texts or narratives, which are available as resources through which the individual makes sense of the social world. These cultural narratives are studied or accessed through individual *talk,* which is viewed as symptomatic of these wider texts. These forms of discursive psychologies are thoroughly committed to constructionism, which Fuss (1989:2) defines as

> ... articulated in opposition to essentialism and concerned with its philosophical refutation (and) insists that essence is itself a historical construction. Constructionists take the refusal of essence as the inaugural moment of their own projects and proceed to demonstrate the way previously assumed self-evident kinds are in fact the effect of complicated discursive practices ... What is at stake for a constructionist are systems of representations, social and material practices, laws of discourses and ideological effects.

A constructionist perspective would concede that there is nothing natural or inevitable about human and psychological life, and that to understand subjectivity one needs to look outwards to history, culture, language and systems of representation. Constructionist perspectives within discursive psychology have tended to negate, silence and ignore biology as an explanation of human subjectivity and view these very processes as effects of historical, cultural and discursive processes. These perspectives tend to be at odds with many approaches within the human and life sciences which through nanotechnology, the human genome project and the mapping of DNA are attempting to provide a genomic blueprint for what it means to be human. Biological and genetic approaches are viewed with suspicion within discursive psychology, primarily because of the ways in which particular versions of biology have been used within eugenic strategies for categorising the population, and in intelligence testing promulgating the idea of genetic determinism (cf. Blackman and Walkerdine 2001). Essentialism, as within many disciplines, is viewed as part of our historical legacy from the enlightenment, which we need to move beyond and reject. Before we move on and look at some of the problems with this rejection of biology in the constitution of human subjectivity, let us look at precisely how the 'psychological' is reconfigured within these accounts.

Discourse and the psychological

One of the main assumptions underpinning discursive psychology is that those once solid measures of subjectivity, previously located within the internal psychological realm of the individual, such as the psyche, mind or self, are actually viewed as existing within the very languages one uses to describe oneself. The implications of this argument are that there can be no access to internal mental states, as these are constructed through language (Wittgenstein 1963, Ryle 1949). What was previously located within the inside has been folded outside into the realm of linguistic and social practices. The intra/psychic is located within language. Thus what people say is not treated in any way as a window on the world or into their minds. Rather, people's accounts are studied for the ways they *vary* across conversational contexts according to the different *functions* talk is performing within and across differing contexts. This view is one which views meaning as a social accomplishment, tied to particular ends, mediated by culturally available narratives or interpretive repertoires.

Within these discursive approaches talk can be studied as a rhetorical resource, exploring the ways in which it can be used to different ends: to blame, excuse, persuade or accomplish other forms of social action (Edwards and Potter 1992). Some writers adopting these ideas have argued that the concepts of truth and objectivity which traditional psychology uses to warrant its claims, are merely rhetorical devices which it uses to maintain its privileged status, i.e. to produce its accounts or versions of the world as factual (Kitzinger 1987).Thus, truth is seen to function as a form of legitimation masking claims which are arbitrary and value-laden. Psychological knowledge is not *objective*, but partial, maintaining and reproducing particular ways of seeing the world, which are perspectival, contingent and culturally specific. It maintains its privileged or illusionary position, according to these accounts, through the very terms and strategies it uses to warrant its claims.

Therefore, to study psychology is to study the very texts and cultural narratives through which our notions of ourselves and our relations with others are constituted. This perspective on the nature of language and its relationship to social reality shares many commonalities with those approaches to emerge from the crisis, despite their commitment to broader interdisciplinary moves such as poststructuralism, semiotics and the postmodern (Potter and Wetherell 1987).

Another version of discourse analysis, rather than analyse talk as functionally oriented, also uses talk as a resource to uncover some of the culturally mediated discourses available for self-articulation. Potter and Wetherell (1987) discuss the range of self-discourses embedded within psychology which one can use to make sense of oneself and others. Thus, psychological discourse becomes a set of textual resources or linguistic repertoires, which provide a range of possibilities for self-expression. Self-expression is no longer considered the expression of one's internal psychological essence, but a form of accounting located within the strategic and functional use of language (Michael in Kvale 1992). The self is a form of narration – dialogic – constructed through a range of possible models or ways of accounting for subjectivity. As Potter and Wetherell (1987:102) argue, these language-based approaches call for a move from the *self-as-entity and focus (it) on the methods of constructing the self.* They give as examples some of the popular theories about the self embedded within psychological discourse which all claim to be describing the true nature and form of subjectivity i.e. trait theory, role theory and more humanist conceptions of the self. As they claim (ibid.:102),

It is suggested that methods of making sense are the key to any kind of explanation of the self, as people's sense of themselves is in fact a conglomerate of these methods, produced through talk and theorising. There is not one self waiting to be discovered or uncovered but a multitude of selves found in the different kinds of linguistic practices articulated now, in the past, historically and cross-culturally.

We can see from the above quote that this particular discursive approach to psychological knowledge relativises these theories of the self, seeing them as possible linguistic practices. One consequence of this analysis is that if the ways people talk about phenomena, including their own relation to self, can be changed, then new forms of social relation and ways of being can be created (cf. McNamee and Gergen 1992, Shotter 1993). Potter and Wetherell (1987:104) argue that cultural analysis which approaches subjectivity in this way has important ethical and political consequences – i.e. that each method of constructing the self positions the self and others in specific ways producing subjectivities which may be negative, destructive, oppressive as well as liberating. This is a rather idealist position rooted in the prioritisation of language as the primary site of subjectification. We will consider later in this chapter some of the problems with reifying talk in this way.

A key uniting principle of these approaches is the argument that those concepts and explanatory structures which are taken to define and articulate what makes us human within the 'psy' disciplines, do not map or describe human subjectivity in any way. Indeed, as we have seen, the very idea that there are stable, enduring characteristics, which can be mapped, has been thrown into radical doubt. Within this work one of the key ways in which human subjectivity has been defined, within the 'psy' disciplines, is through the concept of the autonomous self – a self that is primarily independent, in control, responsible and able to rationalise and make choices about its life (cf. Rose 1990). The concepts which are taken to constitute this form of selfhood are those which structure and define how psychological normality and health are articulated and made intelligible. Different writers within this tradition have engaged with this construction of selfhood in different ways.

Some have sought to expose the autonomous self as false and to show how this concept was actually seen to function as a way of reproducing particular social arrangements as natural and inevitable. It is viewed as culturally-specific (Gergen 1985), and bound up with the maintenance of capitalism and protestantism (Sampson 1977). Despite its emergence within certain historical events it has become part and parcel of what Shotter (1990) terms liberal humanist thought and is constructed, sustained and managed through commonsense conversational practice (Shotter 1993). Harré similarly argues that we have inherited this way of speaking about ourselves from Judeo-Christian civilisation, which has become reified through its rootedness in the language-games we use to account for ourselves and others. All these writers share a commitment to language as a textual resource, which the human subject uses to position him-/herself and others in specific ways. Much of this work has its ancestry in the theories to emerge from the crisis, and also from the seminal ideas of Potter and Wetherell (1987) and their particular strand of discourse analysis.

Stenner (1993) has developed some of these constructionist arguments in relation to jealousy. Commonsense practice tells us that jealousy is a property of the individual; there are jealous types who cannot control their feelings in relation to another. Stenner troubles this view where jealousy is regarded as a property of mind, and instead approaches it as a subject position produced through the deploying of particular cultural stories about jealousy. These stories are examined for their consequences in the relations between a couple, Jim and May. For example, jealousy can be used to position somebody as unaware and unenlightened or as being emotionally weak and insecure. Both of these strategic uses of jealousy have particular implications for the person positioning and being positioned according to these narratives or stories. Thus, Jim positions himself as enlightened and progressive and May as fragile, unstable and weak. Because of this relational positioning he sees himself as having to walk on eggshells, therefore crediting himself with the power to hurt or protect May according to his actions. Stenner argues that this account cannot be viewed as being about the relationship, *reflective* of emotions or *expressive* of May's or Jim's personality – as if a reality existed independently beneath the discourse – but rather as *constructive* of the relationship, *productive* of contradictory and non-essential identities and *generative* of emotional experience. Stenner views it as a jealousy story available as one of the cultural narratives through which people can account for their own and others' experience.

One problem with these kinds of discursive accounts is the refusal to engage with the psychological other than through its locatedness within language. The human subject becomes a discourse-user creating meanings of the social formation in their local, specific accounting practices. Let us pause here for a minute and think about how these kinds of arguments would reframe the 'problem of hallucination'? If we were to follow these moves then one implication would be that we would no longer be interested in mapping underlying internal psychological or neurological mechanisms, and would instead concentrate on the different ways in which the voice-hearing experience is mediated through culturally available narratives. Thus, through examining talk, and the ways in which hallucinations are made intelligible through talk, we could explore the variations in accounts of hallucination, and the ways in which particular accounts are used to position someone who hears voices as deficient, lacking and pathological. This would be a useful strategy, and would indeed bring to light the different narratives or texts, which construct the meaning of hallucinations in markedly different ways. But let us begin to also think about some of the problems with moving to this linguistic constructionist position, in relation to the 'problem of hallucination'.

The old tired theme of social constructionism

As we saw in the last section, the rise of discursive psychologies over the past two decades, characterised by their focus on the subjectifying force of language, has led to a reluctance to engage with the psychological, other than through its narrativisation. The once 'interior' realm of the psychological has been enfolded and located in the very languages we use to speak about selfhood. This move from essentialism to constructionism, Riley (1983) argues, leaves us with two unhappy alternatives. On one side we have essentialist views where social and psychological life are easily reduced to biological and neurological referents. We saw this clearly in the last two chapters where although there is a focus upon 'psychosocial' factors, mainly in relation to treatment-resistant symptoms and non-compliance, the main focus of psychiatric and psychological research is on locating the neurological or psychological mechanisms which are seen to cause the hallucinatory experience. These mechanisms are easily reducible to biological processes (the brain, biochemistry, the gene etc.) and are offered to explain the existence of hallucinations. These 'biological' approaches attract large amounts of funding from pharmaceutical companies and the biotechnology industry.

On the other side we have perspectives, such as those in discursive psychology, which appeal to the social, where most human behaviour, thought and action is viewed as a social construction produced by the workings of language, discourse, ideology and so forth. Within these views, as we have seen, biological explanations are rejected, but no radical rethinking of this area is offered. Essentialism and 'biologism'[1] are therefore dismissive terms that it could be argued move from one form of determinism to a more sophisticated form (linguistic and discursive) (cf. Fuss 1989 for a similar argument). What this does is to effectively leave the biological/social dualism intact, and to simply move from one side of the dichotomy to the other (Riley 1983). Is it then enough for social and cultural theorists to drop the biological altogether?

> Psychiatry will probably become progressively more 'biological' over the next 25 years. (Kendall 2000:7)

One strategy as cultural theorists and critical psychologists could be to 'drop the biological' and focus instead on talk and discourse as the primary site of subjectification. If we wish to enter into a dialogue with the human and life sciences however, this may be a little premature and not take into account the ways in which, as we have seen, the biological, psychological and social are combined and articulated within these disciplines in particular ways. On the one hand we have claims such as the one above which argue that with the rise of biotechnologies and genomic techniques, psychiatry will develop a more sophisticated understanding of the psychopharmacology of some of the new anti-psychotic drugs (i.e. become more biological). Alongside this argument we also have psychological and 'psychosocial' interventions being championed as important in the management of hallucinatory experience. It is therefore easy for the 'psy' disciplines to counter constructionist arguments through an appeal to the 'interaction' of the biological with the social central to the articulation of experience within these practices.

I am not suggesting that appeals to an 'interaction' between the psychological and the social, or the biological and the social are the way out of this problem. As Riley (1983:30) poses in relation to this problem, 'where does this interaction happen?' The appeal to an interaction effect presumes that the biological and the social are two separate categories, which somehow interact. This version or view of biology Riley (ibid.) argues is based upon a myth of origins, or what Pile and Thrift (1995) term a 'metaphor of depth' where the bare essentials of the body can be mapped internally. This presents biology as that which is most pure, untainted and instinctual about human nature – a language of animality. As Riley (1983) cogently argues, this myth is incorporated into traditional socialisation accounts within psychology (cf. Henriques et al. 1984 for further discussion), connected to the idea that you get more and more social as you age and then return to biology in old age. What we need to do, Riley and many others argue, is to offer a revision and radical rethinking of how the biological intersects with the social, such that it is never lived out in a pure and unmediated form. This will entail neither a complete rejection of biology nor a move to a form of linguistic or discourse determinism. In a later section of this chapter, we will develop some of these arguments in relation to the concept of embodiment, which is being offered by cultural theorists, as a possible solution to the intersection of the biological with the social. Hoy (1999:4) puts it this way:

> While the term embodiment certainly suggests that there is a biological dimension to comportment, it is not a term that refers directly to the biological phenomenon independently of related concepts and of cultural context.

In relation to the 'problem of hallucination' this will entail a consideration of those cultural and discursive strategies and practices that voice-hearers develop to engage with particular kinds of somatic and neurological experience. Before we move on to develop the concept of embodiment in relation to the 'problem of hallucination' I want to turn to some related problems with linguistic determinism.

The historicity of experience

> The only conclusion that can be drawn from discursive psychology is that the objects of traditional psychology must be reconceptualised as no more than the ephemeral and epiphenomenal consequences of the rhetorical devices or linguistic strategies employed within particular interactive sequences of discourse. (Nightingale 1999:420)

One must be careful of paying attention to the differences between different strands of discursive psychology (cf. Blackman and

Walkerdine 2001). However in the move from essentialism to constructionism, which we explored in the last section, there is a sense that psychological capacities are not inherent properties of individual minds or brains. Rather they are possible ways of accounting for selfhood located within cultural narratives which mediate psychological experience. As we have seen, many forms of discursive psychology situate individual experience within their immediate social context (often conversational or interactive), and then read off either the functional nature of a person's conversational reality, or attempt to uncover the cultural narratives which mediate their experience. In this section I want to consider some of Michel Foucault's moves towards what he termed the 'historicity of experience' (Foucault 1987b, Rabinow 2000) and consider how his concept of discourse is rather different from those which privilege talk and language as being the main sites through which 'the psychological' is constituted.

Technologies of truth

There have been many studies of the role of particular forms of knowledge and discourse in the government and management of the population (Adlam et al. 1977, Dean 1994, Miller 1998). Many of these studies are indebted to the work of Michel Foucault, and tend to explore how particular kinds of knowledge and discourse structure individuals' own self-understanding and practice such that their own desires, aspirations and will become connected up with wider governmental objectives and aims (Burchell 1993). A key focus of much of this work is on the governmental role of the 'psy' discourses, which are seen as central to the modern management of the self (Rose 1990, 1996a). Rimke (2000) explores how, for example, the concept of 'self-help' and the kinds of concepts which articulate 'self-help', have become central to how we problematise and understand the mundane problems of everyday life. Concepts of psychological adjustment, self-fulfilment, self-actualisation, personal growth and so on and so forth, become part of a technology through which problems are made intelligible, and particular practices on the basis of these understandings are made possible. Thus, Rimke (ibid.) discusses the kinds of practices and techniques, such as self-inspection, self-monitoring, decipherment, writing activities, questionnaires, checklists etc., which enable people to transform their thought, behaviour and action in particular kinds of ways. This is a way of defining discourse, which moves simply beyond a focus upon talk and conversation, to explore the practices and interventions made possible by particular kinds of understanding. In other words the ways not only in which particular kinds of knowledge and discourse mediate our self-understanding, but with the kinds of strategies, practices and ways of acting upon selfhood which emerge from particular discourses.

One of Rimke's (2000) key arguments in relation to psychological discourse is that the language of choice, personal freedom, personal responsibility and self-autonomy which articulate the psychological healthy individual within these knowledges, facilitates, through our own actions, the development of forms of selfhood, which modern neo-liberal governments rely upon for their functioning. This is an argument very derivative of the seminal work of Nikolas Rose (1990, 1996a) who has cogently explored how the 'fiction of autonomous self-hood' promulgated by 'psy' experts, rendering individuals entirely responsible for their own successes and failures, produces 'citizens who are psychologically "healthy" inasmuch as they are governable, predictable, calculable, classifiable, self-conscious, responsible, self-regulating and self-determining (Rimke 2000:63, Rose 1990).

This work links practices of government with practices of the self, and views psychological discourse and knowledge as being a key link point between the ways in which authorities seek to govern individuals and how individuals understand and act upon themselves (Rose 1990). Psychological discourse is not simply one discourse among many, which renders our everyday successes and failures meaningful in particular ways, but according to many writers sharing Foucault's commitment to discourse, has a privileged 'truth-effect' or 'reality-effect' (cf. Blackman and Walkerdine 2001, Henriques et al. 1984, Miller 1998, Rose 1990, 1996a, Walkerdine 1990). Foucault argued that the human sciences have been key sites through which particular kinds of 'truth' have been established about what makes us human. These are not 'truths' in an essential way (i.e. reflections of our essential human nature), but particular kinds of concepts and explanatory structures which make certain kinds of experiences intelligible and divide experiences up according to divisions made between the true and the false, the normal and the abnormal. We saw in the first chapter the ways in which particular kinds of concepts are used to differentiate and make intelligible the apparent divisions made between the hallucination and the pseudo-hallucination. The question, 'what does it mean to hallucinate?' is answered through particular kinds of explanatory structures which divide up and constitute the experience in specific ways. Concepts make it possible to think about phenomena according to a specific perceptual grid – the internal 'rules of sense' (cf. Blackman 1994 for further discussion). Concepts do not simply describe experiences but become means of classifying, calibrating, differentiating and constituting experiences in particular kinds of ways. They make possible particular kinds of self-understanding, practice and intervention. These concepts, although not simply describing the truth of experiences, take on a certain status in establishing what is taken to be the truth of experience. Thus, in the context of psychiatry, certain concepts gain the status of 'science-already-made' (Osbourne and Rose 1999) and are used to make judgements about what counts as a hallucination and a pseudo-hallucination.

Rather than evaluating these concepts or statements (Foucault 1972) according to their truth status,[2] Foucault (ibid.) asks us to consider 'how' it has become possible for certain statements to exist as ordered, regulated bodies of knowledge consituting experiences such as hallucination, in particular kinds of way. This kind of 'how' question directs our analytic attention to the 'historicity of experience' – to the ways in which concepts have combined and recombined historically, as well as the conditions which have made it possible for particular truths to be established about experience. These 'truths' are not simply what is said about phenomena such as hallucination, but what kinds of practices, techniques and institutions are formed on the basis of particular ways of problematising experience.

Foucault argues then that truth is *historical* and *regulative*. Every society/epoch has its own regime of truth – those discourses which function-in-truth – and has the status to divide up the social world in particular ways, i.e. to pronounce the good from the bad, the normal from the abnormal, the rational from the irrational. As Foucault (1980:131) highlights:

Truth is a thing of this world: it is produced only by virtue of multiple forms of constraint. And it induces regulatory effects of power. Each society has its own regime of truth, its general politics of truth: that is the types of discourse which it accepts and makes function as true, the mechanisms and instances which enable one to distinguish true and false statements, the means by which each is sanctioned; the techniques and procedures accorded value in the acquisitions of truth; the status of those who are charged with saying what counts as true.

Foucault's historical approach to the production of truth is often referred to as an archaeological method (Foucault 1972), or a 'history of the present' (cf. Blackman 1994 for fuller elucidation). By asking 'how' questions rather than 'why', this directs our attention to the different ways in which conceptual apparatuses have established truths about experience, as well as to the conditions of possibility for these truths to be established and circulated. Foucault (1972) argued then that it is imperative that one go beyond simply analysing talk and conversation, to exploring the a priori, the concepts, objects, strategies and subject positions which organise statements prior to individual reception (cf. Blackman 1994). Language is part of the assemblage but is what Foucault (1972) termed the endpoint of discourse or what is given to the speaking subject. In order to understand the subjectifying force of language we need to go beyond the text or individual account, and explore how particular terms and concepts are linked within specific material and discursive practices. As Foucault (1972:23) highlights:

> The frontiers of a book are never clear-cut: beyond the first line and the last full-stop, beyond its internal configuration and its autonomous form, it is caught up in a system of references to other books, other texts, it is a node within a network.

We have already seen how an analysis of concepts allows us to examine the ways in which experience is differentiated, made intelligible and constituted within a specific discursive formation, such as psychiatry. 'Objects' directs our attention to the spaces and places through which particular experiences, such as hallucinations, are problematised prior to their rendering within specific discursive formations. Foucault (1972) argued that 'surfaces of emergence' are those spaces, sites, institutions and general divisions through which particular experiences are problematised and marked out for attention as troublesome in some way or another.

The notion of 'problematisation' is important for Foucault's analyses, and stresses the concern of the human sciences with aspects of being which are considered troublesome, abnormal, lacking, deficient or deviant in some way. As Rose (1996a:26) argues in relation to this point and the function of psychological discourse more generally:

> our vocabularies and techniques of the person, by and large, have not emerged in a field of reflection on the normal individual, the normal character, the normal personality, the normal intelligence, but rather, the very notion of normality has emerged out of a concern with types of conduct, thought, expression deemed troublesome or dangerous.

To what extent then, does the rendering and problematising of experience depend upon knowledge which claims to be producing truth about experience? Although there may be many different ways of making experiences such as hallucination intelligible, the focus of an archaeological approach is those knowledges and discourses which claim a particular status for the ways in which they differentiate and act upon experiences – those who produce scientific stories about the consitution of our humanness and normality, which play a key role in establishing the limits and boundaries of what is considered normal experience. This approach has been found particularly useful by critical sociologists and psychologists such as Nikolas Rose (1984, 1985, 1986a, 1986b, 1988, 1989a, 1990, 1992, 1996a) and Valerie Walkerdine (1990, 1997), to explore the place of the social and life sciences in apparatuses of social regulation. 'Strategies' refers to the ways in which particular ways of understanding 'what makes us human' can become intertwined with broader, more general strategies of regulation. This is a way of exploring how particular forms of sociality may become presupposed within particular strategies for governing and managing populations.

We have already encountered this argument in relation to the 'psy' discourses in the work of Nikolas Rose (1990, 1996a) and Rimke (2000), who has developed these ideas in relation to the burgeoning literature on 'self-help'. These studies develop Foucault's concept of 'governmentality' (cf. Burchell et al. 1991 for further development of the term), as a way of exploring how particular discourses become central to the ways in which subjects are managed and manage themselves within the current political rationality. Gordon defines governmentality as 'a form of activity aiming to shape, guide or affect the conduct of some person or persons' (1991, cited in Burchell et al. 1991:2). This is a conceptualisation of power as bio-power (Foucault 1980), a power which acts on and through a person's actions. This directs attention to the ways in which subjects inculcate particular relationships to themselves, such that their needs, desires and aspirations are aligned with wider governmental objectives and aims. This is not a form of power, which is simply constraining or repressive, but rather a form of power which works through knowledge, such that a person will come to want or desire certain norms or ways of behaving in relation to themselves. Power is not an entity but embedded in routine practices, techniques and understandings through which we act upon ourselves as subjects. As an example, Nettleton (1992) has developed this concept of bio-power in relation to the modern dental institution and its fabrication of the modern dental subject. Adopting a historical form of analysis also indebted to the genealogical and archaeological work of Foucault (1972, 1973), she asks us to think of the words 'mouth' and 'teeth' in a nominal fashion. In other words, to assume that these words or terms do not have a continuous meaning throughout history. She explores how the mouth and teeth have been constructed and constituted at different historical moments, and even how the terms 'pain', 'fear' and 'sugar', which are central to the lexicon of modern dentistry, do not mean the same thing if we look historically. Rather than look for the origins of some of the categories we use in the present to construct the mouth and teeth, she looks for shifts, ruptures, discontinuities and different ways of 'seeing' and 'doing' in relation to these objects. This way of 'doing history' (Blackman 1994) also allows one to explore how particular kinds of knowledge, such as the behavioural sciences, have become central to the articulation of the dental subject in the twentieth century and beyond. Moving back to the concept of 'strategies' and 'governmentality' she explores how we are now produced as subjects responsible for our own dental health, particularly through the discourses of psychology and sociology, such that we are incited and required to act as guardians of our own mouths. The targeting of psychological blocks and barriers to good dental health is, according to this argument, a strategy whereby we become caught up in those mechanisms of power which constitute us.

Similar arguments have been made in relation to the concept of 'healthism' within the sub-discipline of the sociology of health and illness. This concept is seen to articulate a set of shifts which are seen to have occurred in the last two decades or so, within and outside health-care disciplines, where the customer or client (as opposed to the patient) is increasingly addressed as a subject, who should be willing and able to take on more personal responsibility for the maintenance of their own health (Turner 1997). There is seen to be a governmental concern with 'cultures of risk' (those environments where health risks to the individual become uncertain and unpredictable),[3] creating the need for a more intensive micro-surveillance and discipline of the population based on more subtle and systematic forms of management and regulation. Within these arguments, 'healthism' as a moral injunction and personal responsibility, is evaluated as a normalising strategy which produces the very kinds of enterprising, healthy, self-determining and responsible citizens that neo-liberal societies rely upon for their functioning (Kinsman 1996, Lupton 1997, Ross 1992). There are some problems with the generic ways in which the concept of strategies is used to evaluate practices of the self, as we shall see later in the chapter when we explore the concept of embodiment. However, some of the examples covered show the possible interdependence between practices of the self and practices of government, and vice versa.

The fourth aspect of Foucault's analysis of discourse is the notion of 'subject-positions'. This directs attention to the kinds of relationship constructed between those such as psychiatrists who claim the capacity to pronounce the 'truth' of hallucinatory experience, and those such as voice-hearers who may become subject to these truths. As we saw in the last section, there is a concern that with many practices of the self, subjects may become the object of particular kinds of truths and authoriative relationships, both with themselves and others, which depend upon positive knowledges (those which claim a scientific status). These knowledges, and the concepts which articulate them, may have particular consequences for the ways in which individuals judge, understand, experience and act upon aspects of their own selfhood. The concept of subject-positions then begins to look at the kinds of relationships constructed between, for example, the psychiatrist and the voice-hearer, and will be examined in more detail in the case study of the Hearing Voices Network in Chapter 7. Before we move on to consider some of the problems with approaching discourse and the relationship to self-formation using Foucault's archaeological approach, let us sum up the different aspects of discursive activity that he saw as central in understanding the constitution of experience.

The analytic tools

As we have seen then, Foucault's (1972) archaeological approach identifies four different domains which one must examine to understand 'how' it has become possible to frame and understand experience, such as hallucination, in particular kinds of ways in the present. The first are the 'concepts', which, as we have seen, direct our attention to those discourses in the present which have a particular kind of status in constituting and differentiating what it means to hallucinate. The first two chapters of the book so far have explored the kinds of concepts and explanatory structures which constitute what it means to hallucinate within the discursive formations of psychiatry and psychology. 'Objects' directs our attention to the ways in which aspects of being are problematised prior to their specific rendering within particular discursive formations. The 'problem of hallucination' for the most part appears as a problem within the social, for those who are unable to control and manage their voices and may become subject to the voices' wishes, demands and requests. Thus voices tend to appear as a disturbing aspect of existence in relation to those who may harm themselves or others and become subject to media and legal scrutiny. Also voices which affect family and other social relationships, including work and personal relationships, become problematised in particular kinds of ways, and as we will see later in the book are those which tend to become subject to medical and 'psy' forms of expertise and authority. 'Strategies' explores how particular forms of sociality and individuality are presupposed by particular ways of rendering experience, and are bound up with wider strategies for governing populations. The fourth aspect of this relational matrix are the subject-positions created between those who take up particular authoriative positions, and those who become subject to their knowledges. The most important aspect of this relational dynamic is that these relations and the ways in which they are constituted are never static, but shift, change, transform and combine in different ways as we look historically. This is the crux of a 'history of the present' which uses these analytic concepts to explore how present configurations of truth and meaning are made possible. In the three chapters to follow this chapter (4, 5 and 6), shifts or discontinuites in the ways in which the 'problem of hallucination' has been made intelligible and constituted from the eighteenth century to the present will be examined. The focus of this historical investigation will be on the general explanatory structures and conditions – social, theoretical, philosophical, moral etc. – which constitute and have constituted hallucination, in all its varied forms. We will particularly focus upon 'how' it has become possible for a particular configuration of truth and meaning to establish what it means to hallucinate (within certain contexts), at this particular historical moment. This focus upon the 'historicity of experience' is important, not to simply state that experience is 'socially constructed', but to show that things once were and in some areas of life are still otherwise (Foucault 1987b). It is a way of countering the inevitability of certain understandings and practices, which although they may claim scientificity, as we will see throughout the book, are producing the possibility, through the gaps, silences and contradictions in their explanations and practices, of new forms of subjectivity and sociality. These new forms of subjectivity and sociality, in relation to the 'voice-hearing' experience are the subject of this book.

Embodiment

One of the problems with the kind of discursive analysis I have just outlined, although moving beyond conversation and talk to examine the constitution of psychological phenomena, firmly leaves out the issue of how actual people engage with particular kinds of understandings and practices in the relationships they form with aspects of their own selfhood. An example will suffice. We have already explored some arguments which link particular practices of the self with practices of government (Kinsman 1996, Rimke 2000, Ross 1992). These studies tend to explore the kinds of concepts which for example articulate 'self-help' (Rimke 2000), health behaviour in relation to HIV and AIDS (Kinsman 1996) and 'new-age' practices (Ross 1992), and then draw homologies between the kinds of sociality and individuality presupposed within these practices, and those which neo-liberal societies rely upon for their functioning. Ross (1992) for example, makes the claim that 'new-age' practices, those which he defines as being articulated through a philosophy of individual responsibility and a language of growth and potential, align people's own desires and self-forming activity with those of liberal ideology. Firstly there are problems with these kinds of studies, which through textual analyses of the concepts which articulate these practices, tend to read off and draw conclusions about the role and effectivity of these practices in people's lives. Lati

Mani (1992) in a discussion of Ross's (1992) article, argues that this kind of claim is disembodied, paying little or no attention to the ways in which these interventions and practices often come from marginalised groups within society. This is an interesting critique and asks us to be much more attentive to the ways in which different people in society live, survive and cope with the different and often contradictory ways in which they are addressed as subjects (Blackman and Walkerdine 2001).[4] There are many examples of those advocating self-help practices, where 'self-help' is articulated through different kinds of discourses, not public health and medical advice, but discourses of survival in a world structured by inequalities and oppressions (Lorde 1996). There is a danger then, if one remains at the level of textual analyses, of making generalised and generic claims about the role and function of practices of the self in people's lives. This raises the issue of embodiment which directs our attention to the ways in which people actually engage, understand and act upon aspects of their own experience, in relation to the exigencies of their lives.

I argue with Valerie Walkerdine (2001) in a book called *Mass Hysteria: Critical Psychology and Media Studies*, that even though the production of a rational, autonomous subject has been central to practices of government within liberal democracies, we must be wary of seeing these discourses as all-determining. We need to explore how actual people embody and struggle with the fiction of autonomous selfhood in their everyday lives (Lucey and Reay 2000). For example, it is clear that we are increasingly required to understand self-transformation as a key issue in relation to how we manage the circumstances of our lives. We are continually addressed as subjects who are capable of understanding, judging and amending our own psychologies as solutions or resolutions to problems in relationships, the world of work, within the school, social work offices and law courts (Blackman and Walkerdine 2001, Blackman 1999a, 1999b).

The necessity of being able to transform oneself is more than a simple human accomplishment. It is a struggle to live in the context of job insecurity, the uncertainties meeting young people with little or no job qualifications, saturation marketing techniques that attempt to create demand for marginal goods and services, loss of certainty and the new 'cultures of risk'. This painful necessity of self-invention, we argued, also creates in its gaps, silences and contradictions new forms of subjectivity, new practices of sociality, and new ways of coping which offer testimony to the ways in which ordinary people struggle with the necessity of self-invention in a rapidly transforming world. Walkerdine (1999) argues, for example, that the extended mourning practices following the death of Diana in Britain in September 1997 by ordinary people, included extended spiritual rituals garnered from new age practices and the discourses of self-help. These discourses had given many (including Princess Diana), the psychological resources to cope with the pain, loss and love that Diana embodied. Although one can see the ways in which particular 'psy' discourses made possible some of these practices, it is also interesting that many were not socially sanctioned by the media (cf. Blackman 1999a), showing us clearly where the 'official boundaries' of self-transformation lie.

> The people who sat around the trees of Kensington Palace Gardens lighting their candles were not waiting to be led – they were leading. They were daring to express those maligned characteristics of emotionality and spirituality, and they were making new practices of sociality, fashioning them out of the cast off detritus of rational government. The regulation of them as subjects was of course formed from the discourses and practices through which their psychological and social reinvention was socially sanctioned to appear, but they made something out of what they had. It is they who showed what can be done without the benefit of any intellectual leadership to show them the way. (Blackman and Walkerdine 2001:195)

Although discursive analysis is important to understand the ways in which particular kinds of discourses frame and constitute experience, if one wants to understand the effectivity of these discourses and practices, one needs to also examine how actual people engage with them in their everyday lives. We must be wary of the determinism and reductionism of talking about experience at the level of the discursive. The discursive, as a matrix of relationships, must consist not only of all those practices, knowledges, theories, problems and concepts which Foucault (1972, 1973) cogently described and analysed in his archaeologies of the human sciences. It must also include analyses of the emotional and psychological economies – themselves discursively produced – as well as the biological potentialities, which make certain experiences possible. Let us consider the first point.

As I have already argued in this chapter, discursive psychology tends to locate psychological phenomena within the very language one uses to describe and talk about experience. This is a very relativising claim, and although highlighting the field of cultural options available to a person, does not adequately theorise why people may have a subjective commitment to certain discourses and practices in relation to aspects of their own selfhood. I have explored this argument particularly in relation to discourses of self-help which circulate within women's magazines (1999b). The concepts which articulate self-help within these magazines present the psychological experiences of the difficulties of living, particularly failure in the world of work, relationships, health, beauty and friendships, as potential transformative experiences. The way that conflicts signify within these discourses promotes and maintains the 'autonomous self' (one who is self-contained, integrated, independent and able to exercise choice over all aspects of one's life), as normal and natural. The very difficulties of living this practice of individuality and sociality are contained within self-help discourses as potential stimuli for change and improvement. We must begin to recognise how an economy of pain, fear, anxiety and distress may be part of the apparatus through which this fictional identity is produced, lived and kept in place. In other words, the difficulties of living the fiction of autonomous selfhood ironically form the very basis of the individual's incitement to change. They are potent and seductive points of identification within these practices.

This example I hope shows how it is also important to engage with psychological and emotional economies – guilt, shame, fear, anxiety, frustration – which although discursively produced, are embodied and experienced by individuals as bodily, affective symptoms. We must find ways of re-engaging with bodily and psychological experiences where we neither view them as essentialist, nor as experiences which can be explained away with recourse to a social constructionism. We must then re-engage and radically revise how we theorise the body, biology, psychology and the emotions. As I stated earlier in this chapter, one of the aims of the book is to develop the notion of embodiment through exploring some of the strategies and practices a group of voice-hearers (the HVN) have developed, to engage with particular kinds of somatic experience. The tools for this analysis will come from some of the later work of Michel Foucault (1985, 1987, 1989, 1990) on ethics and practices of the self (cf. Rabinow 2000), theories and debates surrounding embodiment, and theories of cultural phenomenology, originating within a sub-discipline of anthropology, which focuses upon practices of health and illness (Csordas 1994). This work will be developed in Chapters 7 and 8. I hope that this work will extend the project of critical psychology, so that those both within and outside the disciplines of psychology, who wish to enter into a dialogue with the human sciences, are able to do so without being trapped within an essentialist/constructionist dualism. There is much work to be done, so let us start in the next three chapters by exploring 'how' it has become possible for a particular configuration of truth and meaning to frame the 'problem of hallucination'.

4

Contesting the Voice of Reason

In the preface to *Madness and Civilisation*, Foucault (1971:xi) outlined one of the premises of an archaeological investigation in relation to a historiography of madness. 'What is constitutive is the action that divides madness, and not the science elaborated once this division is made and calm restored.' This quote emphasises the historicity of those phenomena, such as hallucination, which have become the object of the human sciences, and specifically psychiatry and psychology (cf. Still and Velody 1992). As we have seen, these discourses establish and circulate particular kinds of truth about the nature and function of hallucinatory experience. This chapter will begin a historical investigation exploring 'how' it has become possible for the 'psy' disciplines to frame the 'problem of hallucination', as one of differentiating the pseudo-hallucination from the hallucination through a particular set of explanatory structures and concepts. We have already explored the tapestry of these explanations in Chapters 1 and 2. Now it is time to start exploring 'how' it has become possible in this particular set of historical circumstances, for certain statements to exist as ordered, regulated bodies of knowledge constituting experiences such as hallucination, in particular kinds of way.

As a starting point, let us consider how a psychiatrist or psychologist might be inclined to write the history of their discipline (cf. Buxton 1985, Flugel and West 1964, Kantor 1963, Peters 1953, Richards 1987, Thomson 1968). Starting from a perspective of 'scientificity' there may be an attempt to justify present explanations as a progression and development beyond past explanations. These might now, with hindsight, be exposed as irrational, prejudiced and tied to particular attitudes and beliefs. Thus, within this viewpoint, we can now reinterpret the errors of the past and view them as misguided and false. As an example, Zilboorg (1941:391) argues that by projecting back from the present we can see that Socrates' inspiration was actually a manifestation of auditory hallucinations and his trances a form of stupor. These experiences have been captured by the medical gaze and reinterpreted as disturbances of an underlying mental pathology. The present has triumphed over the irrationality of the past. Certain figures are credited with the leaps and bounds, which have led to present conceptualisations. Esquirol, a psychiatrist practicing in the first quarter of the nineteenth century, according to Zilboorg (ibid.:391), was one of the first modern figures to introduce the medical understanding that is central to the constitution of hallucinatory experience in the present.

> He introduced the term hallucinations, giving it the clear-cut definition of today, that is, limiting it only to hearing or seeing things which are not there and understanding that these are not false perceptions (illusions) but actual pseudo-sensory products of the mental disturbance itself.

These arguments also reveal the racist and ethnocentric pretensions which underpin the founding of psychiatry as a modern truth-telling practice. Whitwell (1936:1) compares modern psychiatry with cross-cultural explanations and is led to the following conclusions:

> it is only necessary to move through a few degrees of longitude or latitude in order to find some community, small or large, at a different stage of evolution, which holds today the same views concerning mental disorder as those current in this country only a few centuries ago'. In a similar direction, demonical possession and the Mongolian possession by 'Damchan' show 'merely the various stages in evolution through which all civilisations have to pass in the slow and laborious climb from magic, and its congeners, to science'. (ibid.:2)

Psychiatry is a modern scientific practice, which represents, according to this position, the pinnacle of civilised thinking. It still battles against 'backwaters of resistance' (Whitwell 1936:3), such as 'unusual cults, freak forms of religion, spiritualism, astrology and the palmistry of today', which for him, float or drift, 'like coral reefs in the full tide of civilisation'. They are viewed as remnants of the archaic and the past which still remain despite psychiatry's march towards truth. These kinds of explanations are represented in a schematic form throughout histories of the emergence of psychiatry, represented as a linear movement from the magical to the organic, through to the psychological; or from the priestly, religious, priest – physician through to the purely medical. Thus

Alexander and Selesnick (1966:3) divide their account from the 'Ancients, Classical, Medical and Renaissance, through to the Era of Reason laying the foundations for the Enlightenment and the Modern Era'. They argue that 'The evolution of psychiatry has been a central part of the evolution of civilisation itself.' Certain figures, such as Hippocrates, are represented as forefathers or forebears to modern understanding, embodying the essence and key to the future of the human condition, those 'of an entirely different type of mind, sceptical, analytical, logical and scientific' (Whitwell 1936:142).

These are very seductive arguments, which pioneer psychiatry and clinical medicine as progressive and humane. As we saw in Chapter 2, many critiques of psychiatry (anti-psychiatry), instead view psychiatry as an institution which makes moral judgements about behaviour and conduct, masked under the mantles of science and objectivity (Sarbin 1967). Madness is a form of moral deviancy pathologised as disease and illness. The history which this book develops is not 'anti-psychiatry' in this sense, and does recognise that most professionals, and the aims of psychiatry, are to alleviate suffering and distress. However, we will see that the evolutionary account which allows psychiatry to trace its lineage through concepts of progress and scientific discovery, do not stand up to historical scrutiny. It is easy and reassuring to read back from present understandings, and find their lineage in the thought and practice of particular individuals. These individuals can then become the lynchpins from which modern psychiatric practice was seen to emerge.

These arguments are probably familiar and are often conflated when talking about what is taken to be the most common and intractable form of mental distress, schizophrenia. Kraepelin (1919) is viewed as discovering this disease in its then disguised form, dementia praecox. Despite its elusiveness, this 'modern disease' will be captured and forced to lay bare its secret(s) to the clinical psychiatric gaze. As Alexander and Selesnick (1966:296) optimistically pronounce, 'the Gordian knot of schizophrenia will not be slashed suddenly by a sword in the hands of one man, but will slowly be untied by the collaboration of groups of scientists'. Schizophrenia, although a contested category, as we saw in Chapter 1, has taken on the status of 'science-already-made'. It has what Osbourne and Rose (1999:372) term a 'reality-effect'. It has become an entity, which other concepts attempt to describe, categorise, classify and so forth.

Certain experiences, such as hearing voices, are viewed as one of the first-rank symptoms of such a disorder. Even though there is dissent over the mechanisms which produce the psychotic symptoms seen as markers of this disease, and the different theories deployed to account for its existence, it is largely taken for granted within the literature. This chapter will begin to show that there is no simple, linear ancestry to explain the existence of this phenomenon, and that it is made possible by a contingent set of theoretical, social, political and historical conditions of possibility.

As outlined in Chapter 3, an Archaeology focuses on the internal 'rules of sense' of a discursive practice and its conditions of emergence, by utilising four analytic concepts; objects, concepts: subject positions and strategies. These recognise the fundamental interweaving of power and knowledge in the strategic governance of the population. As Foucault highlighted (1991a:169), 'it is a question of problems that are clearly situated historically in a determinate period'. From their inception, discursive practices such as psychology and psychiatry emerged in relation to particular problematisations of social existence, providing the explanatory frameworks through which they were to be understood and acted upon. Rose (1985:5) cogently develops this argument whilst considering the conditions of emergence of psychological expertise.

> Practices whose object was the identification and administration of abnormality were more than merely external conditions for the development of the psychology of the individual. This psychology sought to establish itself by claiming its authority to deal with the problems posed for social apparatuses by dysfunctional conduct.

If one views the object, hallucination, as historically constituted within an adjacent field of discourse, historical investigation should be oriented towards describing this field of discourse, and its conditions of possibility, rather than the description of the gradual development of medical understanding and progress. This frees the writing to become something 'other'. It is not one of knowing the answers and using history to chart the progress of that certainty, but to disrupt the certainty of present understandings, in order to think about the voice-hearing experience differently. As Foucault (1989:121) suggested, 'we must produce something that doesn't yet exist and about which we cannot know how and what it will be'.

In this manner the following history will be an attempt to suspend our beliefs and certainties about the voice-hearing experience, and to open up a space to think differently about this phenomenon. Foucault (1989:71) remarked that an experience is something you come out of changed. In this sense the historical investigation undertaken in the following three chapters, it is hoped, will be experienced as a critical and transformative experience, in order to think about the 'problem of hallucination' in a markedly different way. As stated in Chapter 3, this is not merely to re-echo the old tired theme, that hallucinations are a 'socially-constructed' phenomenon, but to explore how it has become possible to understand, experience and act upon voices 'as if' they are signs of disease and illness.

There are key terms or categories which will appear throughout the following three chapters – particularly the terms 'moral', 'physical', 'psychic' and 'biological'. These terms are not continuous, and one of the focuses of these chapters is to show that they shift and change in meaning, in relation to the wider concepts and explanatory concepts, which map their terrain. We will also see that there have always been interrelationships between 'hard' and 'soft' approaches, but that the concepts, which map and differentiate them, are quite different at particular determinate historical periods. There are no biological and psychological spaces waiting to be discovered, but what we take the biological and psychological to be (to take two examples), create very different kinds of self-understanding and practice at any particular time. The historical chapters to follow will not consider this question of embodiment specifically, but will pay some attention to some of the practices made possible by different discursive territories. We will also look at some of the different places in which the 'problem of hallucination' was constituted, and the different kinds of relations mapped between the voice-hearer and different authoritative figures, such as the Doctor.

Aberrations of mind

Hallucinations have played a definitive role in the divisions made between 'moral insanity' and biological models of mental illness. It also crosses the divide between current biological and 'psychosocial' explanations of mental illness. It will be argued that as the space constituting hallucinations divided between the mind and the brain, hallucinations have come to signify as one of the primary symptoms of psychosis. It will be argued that it is only when madness becomes solely to be seen as a disorder of the brain that hallucinations are differentiated from delusions and it becomes possible to talk about them as first-rank symptoms of schizophrenia. This historical narrative will start at a point when hallucination was a fairly undifferentiated experience, discussed co-terminously with illusions, delusions and other allied states of consciousness such as dreaming and somnambulism. It will attempt to reconstruct 'how' it has become possible for hallucination to shift and transform into a highly differentiated object, constituted in relation to a number of key explanatory concepts, as discussed in Chapter 1.

Hermeneutics of voices

During the seventeenth century, as many authors have argued (MacDonald 1981, Sarbin and Juhasz 1967), there was a range of possible explanations of hearing voices which co-existed. These included religious, scientific and magical discourses, none of which had any specific diagnostic pertinence. They were all possible ways of making sense and acting upon the phenomenon. This narrative will not consider this historical configuration in any detail. It will start at the point when, I will argue, 'hearing voices' were becoming secularised at the beginning of the nineteenth century. I will consider a text which was written as a point of resistance against this secularisation, coming from a viewpoint which problematised the hearing of voices and seeing of visions along a religious dimension.

Within this framework of explanation the particular act of hearing voices or seeing visions was not in and of itself abnormal, although discussions often centred on whether the hallucinated state of consciousness was abnormal. Hence Carpenter (1805:66) arguing in the early nineteenth century against the 'secularisation of voice hearing', talked about whether the state of consciousness offering the most fertile soil for voice-hearing was most related to a weak and fragile mind.

> And these errors of judgement, which appeared a temporary interruption to harmony, caused the attentive observer more to esteem him as an instrument, inasmuch as they were proofs, that, although weak, he was not deceptive; for even his failings were on virtue's side.

The existential state of mind allowing the possibility of hallucinatory experience was often viewed as erring on the less rational, reminiscent of notions of 'the mad fool' as being one who is closer to the deity. However, the person was viewed as merely an ear or an instrument of communication utilised by the higher powers – the paradox being that this state of consciousness was seen as being closer to nature in both a primitive and 'fallen' sense – less human and closer to God. In other words the person could not be erring as he or she was not capable of wilful deception (i.e. had lost the power to reason), and yet the weak mind had allowed access to experiences beyond the corporeal senses, which were not simply the product of an error in reasoning.

The voices or visions were therefore made intelligible and problematised along a religious and ethical dimension. They were 'taken out of the body' and subjected to a hermeneutical inquiry where the source of the voices and their particular message was judged and evaluated.

> In these observations, I am not giving an opinion from what source the thing came, but thus much I owed to truth and numbers, as well as myself, know that the man possessed not the talents to put them together, ... they came not from the man, but were in language dictated to him: whether from a good, or from an evil source, the reader will determine for himself. (Carpenter 1805:35)

The body of the voice-hearer is seen as a container for the ethereal soul, the metaphysical entity which is considered the divine source of humanity. The body can then be dismissed as it merely acts as the foundation from which all that is spiritual emits and travels through. Much like a lightning rod, the body conducts and is conducted by all that lies beyond the corporeal senses. In many of the discussions of voice-hearers reference is made to this third eye – the spiritual sense through which divine communication takes place. As with the iconography of the 'mad fool' or 'wise fool' as being unwitting channels, there are also those who wittingly focus on the development of this ethereal sense.

Carpenter (1805:20) discusses the notion of the 'spiritual eye' in the following quote:

> But thus it really was with the man who will be the subject of the following pages. He conceived himself to be spiritually

informed; that is, at times he could hear spiritual voices articulately, and clearly see spiritual objects. This, without serious reflection, may to us, who have only the faculty of seeing what is material, appear very mysterious; but, firmly believing Scripture, I find in the 2d of Kings, Ch.vi.17, that, at the prayer of Elisha, his servant's spiritual eye was opened; which makes me believe that we are constantly surrounded by spiritual objects, but that, blind in consequence of sin, we cannot see them.

The voices or visions are then subjected to a hermeneutical inquiry, from the most fundamental differentiation, 'it either came from God or the devil' (ibid.:40), to an epistemological quest to settle their final 'truth status' or revelatory potential. As Carpenter professes,

> what he has said of Joanna is, that she professes to have revelations of what will befall both church and state. Would he but take pains to search out truth, he would find that many revelations, which she has had, have been literally fulfilled. (ibid.:10)

At the time of this writing there were many ambiguities and arguments as to how the phenomenon of hearing voices should be understood. The fuel for the iconoclastic writings of Carpenter and others, was in its very nature a point of resistance to those scientists opposing God, who by asserting what Carpenter could only view as a depraved argument, view voices and visions as delusions; as errors in reasoning. These arguments located the hearing of voices as a form of 'moral insanity'.

It is important to highlight at this point, that although most accounts chart the path of hearing voices from the religious to the moral, as one of a linear directionality, these arguments existed alongside one another. There was not a path of linearity from one discursive space to another, but a space where it was possible to problematise voices along a number of dimensions. A significant shift in the way 'hearing voices' was conceptualised in the early nineteenth century occurred within a space of new problematisations focusing upon the nature of 'man', the mind, and his external relations with the world.

During the eighteenth century, a physical view of madness saw it as an internal disequilibrium of bodily fluids. Mayo (1838) discusses this view of madness as hinging upon the notion of sympathy; certain fluids such as bile were seen to circulate in varying proportions, upsetting the overall balance of fluids and resulting in particular disordered temperaments, such as the bilious, nervous, sanguine and serious. These elements, the notion of sympathy, circulation, and the body, remained a fiercely debated division within which to view the so-called ravings and despondencies of the mad. In parallel to religious constructions of certain phenomena, their physical counterparts waged for acceptance against their metaphysical allies. Certain authors have termed this as a period marked by a challenge between faith and reason.

The 'age of reason' was according to Alexander and Selesnick (1966) marked by superstition, magic and religious constructions. It was a 'dark and deadening time(s)' (Whitwell 1936:142) which would eventually be rescued and reinterpreted from ignorance by modern clinical medicine. As we saw earlier, a view which would revisit what were seen as spiritual phenomena and reinterpret them as signs of underlying mental pathology. This challenge between faith and reason was to shift and change in relation to discussions of the mind and the nature of man through an emerging notion of the 'moral'. This notion of a moral space is however very different from notions of the moral which may circulate within current understandings. We need to think of the term 'moral' in a nominal fashion and begin to look at the concepts and explanatory structures which articulated this discursive space. Let us begin to explore how notions of a 'moral' space were differentiated from notions of 'the physical', particularly in relation to what were taken to be signs and symptoms of madness. It was in relation to the concept of a moral space that conceptions of madness, the body and so-called mental phenomena, such as 'hearing voices', radically shifted in their meanings and that to which they were supposed to refer. As Rose (1985:23) highlights when discussing the notion of the 'moral',

> it appears to refer to the mental as opposed to the physical, to the emotions and the will rather than the body, its organs and fluids. Hence it is used to designate causes of insanity other than physical ones, and treatment of the mentally deranged through kindness, appeal to conscience and to the will of the insane person.

The 'moral' created a space through which earlier physical conceptions of madness were problematised. Rose (1985:24) discusses these eighteenth-century conceptions of madness in relation to the specific techniques of cure practised on the basis of these under-standings. The goal of these practices was to 'adjust(ing) the movements of the bodily fluids, partly in an attempt to restore the links between the deranged internal time of the body and the real external time of the world'. He has argued along with others such as Foucault (1971), that one of the conditions of possibility for the emergence of the 'moral', was the 'very intractability of madness to these physical cures, and the conclusions that were drawn from this that madness was beyond cure' (ibid.:24).The 'moral' as a space of problematisation particularly in relation to the question of 'what makes us human', allowed for a consideration of mental faculties, not directly ascribable to the body and its fluids, such as hallucina-tions, dreaming and somnambulism.

Is 'man' a moral being? The age of sensibility

One of the aspects of this particular configuration was a preoccu-pation with the characteristics of humanness. Rose (1985) discusses the 'Wild Boy of Aveyron' as playing a key role within Enlightenment philosophising at this time, as to the nature of man in a state of nature. This problem was posed in relation to the question of 'what makes us human'. Victor, the Wild Boy, who had lived outside 'human' terrain and therefore what were taken to be civilising influences, presented a hinge upon which these debates could take a practical and material foundation. Rose argues that Victor stands as a marker of the shift into modernity; a shift away from religious conceptions to more 'moral' ways of specifying humanness. These debates were concerned with what is 'natural' and therefore unchanging and fixed about 'man'; what is it that defines the essences of 'what it means to be human'. Within this newly emerging discursive space new objects and concepts were established and circulated in relation to the question of 'what makes us human'.

The parameters of this discursive space radically transformed how madness was to be understood and acted upon. Earlier eigh-teenth-century conceptions of madness as an internal disequilibrium of bodily fluids transformed into a concern with the mind and its relation with the external world. The philosophers Locke (1689) (within the British context) and Condilliac (1930) (within the French context) were important figures within these

transformations. Locke's philosophy of mind was a secular philosophy in contrast to what he saw as religious dogmatism,
authoritarianism and dictatorship. His chief epistemological stance
was agnostic, and this was clearly reflected in his statements concerning the nature of the anima or source of humanity.

For Locke, the mind and not the soul was the living force of
humanity. He argued that the mind was a tabula rasa, a blank slate
with no innate ideas. To have ideas involved perception, as ideas
came to the individual through sensation grounded in experience.
These elements – ideas, sensation and experience – were key
concepts constituting the structure of the mind. The ability to
internally represent ideas to oneself was the capacity which Locke
viewed as distinctly human and characteristic of reason. The mind
therefore represented the citadel of reasoning characterised by the
processes of reflection, association and combining of ideas. As
Locke (1689, ed. 1929:104) describes when discussing the mind:

> Whence has it all the materials of Reason and knowledge? To
> this I answer, in one word, From Experience: In that, all our
> knowledge is founded, and from that it ultimately derives it self.
> Our Observation employ'd either about external, sensible
> objects; or about the internal operations of our minds, perceived
> and reflected on by our senses, is that, which supplies our under-
> standings with the materials of thinking. These two are the
> Fountains of Knowledge, from whence all the ideas we have, or
> can naturally have, do spring.

Locke also introduced certain concepts which I will argue provided
some of the key explanatory structures within which the 'problem
of hallucination' took shape, and became differentiated in the
nineteenth century. There were three concepts which were important to this restructuring and reconfiguration – the concept of
development and the notion of simple and complex ideas. Simple
ideas were those grounded within sensation and received through
one or more of the five corporeal senses. Locke argued that the
mind was passive in relation to these simple, concrete, un-
compounded ideas, what he termed 'simple and unmixed' (p. 119).
This was one stage in a sequence of developments towards the
acquisition of reason. It is in relation to complex ideas that the
mind becomes an active agent. Complex ideas were those where
the mind was viewed as operating in a mode of thought which

actively processed ideas, using abstraction, combination, turning itself inwards and contemplating its own actions.

These different modes of thinking centred around a division made between the voluntary and involuntary, where ideas may simply float around as in dreaming and states of reverie, or where attention is focused upon ideas away from the senses and their relations with the external world. The power of the mind is, however, in its will, its freedom to choose or determine its own thought. The will therefore stands as the censor, which can be disturbed by Desire, or judgement (error), where Reason is dazzled or bewildered by the errors of the mind. According to Locke (ibid.:681) therefore, reason has a maturational sequence whereupon children are capable of simple ideas, up to the highest faculty of abstract thought represented by adult 'man'. This developmental split between children and adults also allowed for differentiations to be made between the so-called primitive and civilised. This contrast of the lower with the higher mapped a hierarchy of thinking from the savage (ideot) to the pinnacle of civilised thought, man, but also highlighted the precariousness of the mind's ability to reason:

> reason, Though it penetrates into the Depths of the Sea and Earth, elevates our Thoughts as high as the Stars, and leads us through the vast Spaces, and large Rooms of this mighty Fulbrick, yet it comes far short of the real Extent of even corporeal Being; and, there are many Instances wherein it fails us.

These kinds of 'moral' arguments about the nature of 'man' and the mind's ability to reason, and therefore to make errors, co-existed as I have already said, alongside more religious and physical frameworks of explanation in the eighteenth century. However, in relation to particular problems of social existence in the nineteenth century the notion of madness as 'error', or 'moral insanity' began to be accorded particular diagnostic pertinence. In order to understand these shifts and changes in understandings and interventions in relation to madness, it is important to examine how particular forms of sociality and individuality were presupposed within newly emerging practices of government and regulation. Madness as error derived from the notion that reason was precarious, in that it could often fail or err. Within this conception there was a division made between those who were viewed as incapable of reason, i.e. ideots,

and those whose reasoning was perverted or in error. As Porter
(1987:86) suggests:

> Within the traditional hierarchical metaphors of psychic health,
> the elite had been seen as sane and the masses raged; in the new
> world, by contrast, bumpkins wallowing in the idiocy of rural
> life remained 'naturals' lacking the wit or sensibility to share the
> English malady.

Moral insanity, in line with some of Locke's philosophical ideas,
was viewed as a (mis)association of ideas, accidental connections
and unnatural associations. The mind was delirious, 'going off the
track' (Donnelly 1983:111) and in error, deluding judgement. As
Porter (1987:86) comments whilst discussing the profound influence of Locke's theories:

> Madmen, he wrote, do not appear to have lost the faculty of rea-
> soning but having joined together some ideas very wrongly, they
> mistake them for truths, and they err as men do that argue right
> from wrong principles.

Within this reconfiguration of the mind as a reasoning apparatus,
came a restructuring of those elements of mind, or mental faculties
seen to play a part in this active process. The new discursive space
made possible a fascination with those twilight states, such as
reverie, illusions, somnambulism, hypnoticism and sleep and
dreaming, which were all viewed as part of the mind's processes of
active reflection and combination. There was also a focus upon
those experiences, such as hallucination and delusion, which were
viewed as reasoning errors, deceiving judgement. Also within this
space, and operating as a central division, was a reverence for the
imagination as opposed to the intellect, and the relation of this
creative process with both madness and genius.

Deception as a mental state

Despite writing in the latter half of the nineteenth century and
associated more with biological theories of mental distress,
Maudsley (1879) typifies the new space of the imagination created
through the space of the moral at the beginning of the nineteenth
century. Although shifts were beginning to occur, especially in

relation to the 'problem of degeneracy' emerging at this time, some of the following quotes highlight the primary place of the imagination within this discursive configuration. There was a focus upon the twilight states of so-called mental deception, where imagination was seen to have a free rein.

> In dreaming as in insanity there are the most strange, and grotesque deviations from the accustomed sober paths of associations of ideas; It is impossible there can be full use of reflection when most of the habitual trains of thought are suspended in sleep; an idea that is accompanied with desire is without the means of becoming a reasoned volition in the ordinary way; it must remain a particular desire, and when it is active, instead of the natural results in following the beaten paths of association, it will rouse some strange, apparently unrelated idea, which being seen as a vision will present itself as a sort of abrupt transformation scene. (Maudsley 1879:9)

The 'power of the imagination' forged links between sleep and dreaming, but also madness and genius. Imagination created a fantastical space of 'vacant reverie' (ibid.:15) where new and novel associations could be made. Porter (1987:99) refers to madness within this conception of the imagination, as the 'condition of poetic fire', making the link between poetics, the action of creative associations or inner reasoning, and genius. This was opposed to the 'ideots' who were seen to congenitally lack imagination. These distinctions between 'ideots' and 'errors of reasoning' were reflected in the nosographic tables seen to represent the various types of madness, which existed at the end of the eighteenth and early nineteenth centuries.

Donnelly (1983) discusses such a nomenclature where moral insanity exists alongside more congenital conditions, such as dementia, paralysis of the insane and congenital idiocy, where intellectual powers have either decayed, weakened, or been entirely obliterated, as with idiocy. However, these naming systems prior to the early part of the nineteenth century did not accord congenital disorders (the biological) a central role in the division of madness and reason. They merely marked the contours or set the limits of rationality.

It was the shift to the primacy of biological/genetic modes of explanation which was to be so decisive in the problematisation of particular kinds of experience, once considered signs of moral insanity, within the latter half of the nineteenth century. However, in the early part of the nineteenth century moral insanity was of central importance. Esquirol (1845:23), writing in the mid-nineteenth century, exemplified the hesitation between the moral and the physical at this time.

> Among the insane, sensibility is exalted or perverted; and the sensations are no longer in relation with external or internal impressions. They seem to be the sport of the errors of their senses, and of their illusions.

The primary focus was on the association of ideas, which the insane person cannot differentiate, deluding judgement by their stream of absurd connections. Esquirol (1845:24) cites an example of reasoning from false principles, or error. 'The city of die is overlooked by a neighbouring rock which is called the u. A young man suggested to himself the propriety of adding the word u to the word die, making it into the word dieu (God). Hence all the inhabitants of die became Gods in his opinion.' Locke's philosophies of mind were particularly important in this conceptualisation of madness as 'error'. 'The insane, are, as Locke remarks, like those who lay down false principles, from which they reason very justly, although their consequences are erroneous' (ibid.:25). Despite the fact that as a historical figure, Esquirol is upheld as enlightening modern psychiatry with the true definition and medical understanding of hallucinations, in histories of psychiatry written by Zilboorg (1941), for example, hallucinations are discussed synonymously with illusions and delusions as being deceptive states, or fallacious perceptions.

Within this discursive space hallucinations were connected with the erroneous imagination, a form of deception resulting in an error of judgement. Hallucinations were conceptually part of the mind's capacity to trick itself and make errors of judgement. This configuration was however to change in the mid-nineteenth century where a distinction was made between delusions and hallucinations. This involved a differentiation made between a hallucinated state, synonymous with prior discussions of hallucinations and delusions, to the notion of hallucination as being a particular convulsive condition of the brain, independent of the mind. Hallucination was to become viewed as a sensory by-product and evidence of somatic disorder, rather than connected to the errors of the mind. The split between delusions and hallucinations was to become a key differentiation in the constitution of hallucination as evidence of underlying biological deficit or abnormality. The following two quotes highlight the distinctions at play in this transformation.

> The insane man mistakes a windmill for a man; a whole for a precipice; and clouds for a body of calvary. In the last case the perceptions are incomplete; hence an error. The ideas and sensations are but imperfectly connected. In hallucinations, sensation and perception no more exist than in reveries and somnambulism since external objects do not act upon the senses ... In fact, hallucination is a cerebral or mental phenomenon, which is produced independently of the senses. (Esquirol 1845:106)

> He sees and hears, but these impressions do not reach the centre of sensibility. The mind does not react upon them. (ibid.:109)

We can see from the above quotes that hallucination was becoming specified as a pseudo-sensory product of the mental disturbance itself, located within a disordered brain. This shift did not simply result from advances in medical understanding and knowledge within the discipline of psychiatry itself. Although, as we saw at the beginning of this chapter, this is the predominant way in which transformations in knowledge are understood within traditional histories of the discipline. However to understand this radical rupture or discontinuity in the ways in which the 'problem of hallucination' was articulated and acted upon, we need to make use of some of the other analytic tools at our disposal. So far, we have been looking at some of the general explanatory structures and divisions through which the meaning of hallucination was made intelligible and differentiated from other kinds of experience which we might now define as signs of mental illness. In order to understand these shifts it is necessary to go beyond the discipline itself, and explore how the problems to which the 'psy' disciplines were responding were shifting and changing in relation to wider governmental strategies. We will see that specific social problems were transforming how questions and general explanatory structures were framed in relation to the problem of 'human nature' or exactly what 'makes us human'.

The conditions of possibility

As Gordan (1992:30) highlights when discussing Foucault's 'Histoire de la Folie' (1971), there was a significant shift in the object of governmental strategies and the way social problems were understood. In the eighteenth century, the focus was 'urban luxury and idle indifference', shifting in the nineteenth century to a concern with 'proletarian degeneracy and idle poverty'. The focus on 'urban luxury and idle indifference' in the eighteenth century, took place within an increasing problematisation of the habits of the poor, the 'moral' conditions seen as exacerbating madness, and a concern with the precariousness of sensibility. There were two divisions within which the mind was formed: one where its delicate structure was viewed as vulnerable and subject to breakdown (error), and the other where its breakdown, or developmental progression, was influenced by certain 'moral' conditions. It is important to reiterate that the notion of the 'moral' central to this discursive configuration was articulated through particular kinds of concepts and explanatory structures. It does not have a continuous meaning throughout history and is not a static category. In the next section we will begin to unpack some of the ways in which the notion of 'moral' conditions and 'moral insanity' were conflated within particular practices of government and regulation. The first distinction, central to the writings of Locke, became embedded within some of the theories and concepts within the discipline of psychiatry itself.

Within the first distinction, as we have seen, madness was viewed as a disease of sensibility linked to the mind in error. Although civilisation, with its focus on progression, stated that the capacity to reason was what made humans distinctly human, and different from animals, there was also a fear that this last acquirement would be the first to falter and sway. As Foucault (1971:217) highlights in *Madness and Civilisation*:

> Civilisation, in a general way, constitutes a milieu favourable to the development of madness. If the progress of knowledge dissipates error, it also has the effect of propagating a taste and even a mania for study; the life of the library, abstract speculations, the perpetual agitation of the mind without the exercise of the body, can have the most disastrous effects ... The more abstract or complex knowledge becomes, the greater the risk of madness.

Civilisation, although seen as providing a milieu favourable to the development of sensibility (the mind's ability to feel), also constituted what Foucault (1971:219) has termed an 'artificial milieu'. Discussing the epitome of this milieu, the novel, Foucault remarks that

> the novel constitutes the milieu of perversion, par excellence, of all sensibility; it detaches the soul from all that is immediate and natural in feeling and leads it into an imaginary world of sentiments violent in proportion to their unreality, and less controlled by the genteel laws of nature. (ibid.:219)

In this sense, as many authors have suggested, madness was viewed as a 'disease of civilisation' (Donnelly 1983:122), and within the Enlightenment optimism of the time, 'moral man' could be restored through habit and sympathy to his external relations with the world. In other words, the erroneous tricks of the mind and imagination could be anchored through practices orienting individuals to the external reality in which they existed. Drawing on Lockeian notions of 'moral man' and the mind as a tabula rasa, then within both a rational system of society (Owen 1836), and the deployment of 'moral therapy', madness was potentially curable. Sensibility if left within this artificial milieu would be at the mercy of its own laws of abstraction and combination, and if left unchecked would become situated within this imaginary realm; over-stretched and alienated. Reason thus needed a support through habit and a form of education inculcating the experience of rational moral influences.

Owen (1836:xii) who in Orwellian fashion, proposed the reconstruction of society and the formation of the human race within a moral world based on truth (science) and not error (religion) optimistically recounts,

> by the superior arrangements, which, through experience, man will be enabled to make, all will attain the best dispositions, habits and manners, and the most valuable knowledge that each can be trained, from infancy, to receive.

The construction of a moral world was not merely a transfer from faith to reason, but an attempt to reconceptualise how social problems of poverty, crime and misery were understood and acted upon. As Owen (1836:xii) proclaims, 'These evils will be known only, in the history of the past, or of the irrational period of human existence.' A particular form of sociality or individuality was presupposed within these strategies, where the capacity to maintain relations with the external world was viewed as centrally important. This capacity allowed a spirit of 'benevolence, confidence and affection' (ibid.:xxii) towards others, and was viewed as the key distinction between humans and animals. This moral feeling or sentiment however could be hindered by particular moral circumstances (environmental conditions such as the 'primitive' or intemperate), and one's inherent ability to develop the sentiment.

Within these sets of practices and understandings there was a concern with the habits and vices of the poor, who were seen to be less checked by civilising influences. Although moral explanations of madness were privileged within these formulations, the notion of simple and complex ideas (and madnesses) created a split between the sanities of the rich and poor. Some were viewed as simply uneducable and not able congenitally to develop the sentiment. Others were more at the mercy of moral influences, which produced intemperance, or if one was the right class, an over-stretched sensibility. There was then a mix of influences which could produce insanity – physical, emotional, physiological, financial, intellectual, accidental and the unethical. In relation to moral insanity, the notion of excess was central to an understanding of the mind-in-error, to include 'excesses of joy, grief, fright, fear, anger or love; religious fanaticism, intemperance, immoderation in food, gambling; vices of all sorts' (Rose 1985:28). As we have seen from Owen's proclamations, education was viewed as an important social practice to curb excess and facilitate the development of a moral sentiment.

Prior to the shift between physical and moral conceptualisations of madness in the late nineteenth century, the moral was the object of therapeutic and governmental strategies. It was the series of problems produced within this space, which was one of the conditions for the transformation of this domain. With the problem of demoralisation, where vice was seen to proliferate in the enclaves of society most removed from civilisation, the panic engendered by ideas of contagion became a target, both for governmental strategies, such as sanitary science, and for moral therapy.

It was these conditions which were seen to exacerbate madness, and to which those who were seen to congenitally lack the capacity to develop sensibility tended to drift.

The lowest elements were concentrated together into large and impenetrable masses, isolated from the beneficent influences of civilisation, losing what ever virtuous habits they might have had and contracting bad ones. (Rose 1985:47)

In these colonies and rookeries, vice and immorality flourished without check, leading to the degradation of the worker and the transmission of these immoral habits to their offspring who were brought up in an overcrowded, in-sanitary atmosphere, forced at a tender age into contact with sights and experiences of corruption and crime. (ibid.:48)

Moral therapy was offered as a strategy to help produce moral forms of character and strengthen moral habits. With the mind-in-error as target, the power of the doctor's imagination over that of the patient, and the rational ordering of the asylum, the notions of sympathy, error, and moderation were brought together within an institutional setting.

Moral education, moral reform and moral therapy

The deprivations of both minds and morals, which are effected by the vices of our education, by disdain for religious beliefs, and by the faultiness of public morals, exercises its influence, upon all classes of society. (Esquirol 1845:43)

The notion of an epidemic of madness became linked to particular moral conditions seen to produce insanity. This was a similar conception to the notion that atmospheric conditions linked to hygiene could produce disease. Asylums, once a form of exclusion and confinement, still bearing the legacy of rottenness expounded by the old horizon of leper houses, were transformed into therapeutic spaces designed to effect change. This was distinct from prior conceptions within the eighteenth century where asylums became sites of imaginary fears of contagion. As Foucault highlights (1971:206):

If a doctor was summoned, if he was asked to observe, it was because people were afraid, – afraid of the strange chemistry that seethed behind the walls of confinement, afraid of the powers forming there that threatened to propagate.

Within what Foucault (1971:244) terms a 'long phase of hesitation' where the 'problem of the mad' was surrounded by 'material difficulties' and 'theoretical uncertainties', a significant 'event' was marked in 1792 with the creation of the York Retreat. As Foucault highlights: 'At the Retreat, religion was part of the movement which indicated in spite of everything the presence of reason in madness, and which led from insanity to health.' The Retreat was an asylum run by Quakers and instigated practices and understandings in relation to the mad which worked with the notion of madness as 'error' or moral insanity. The retreat was like a large rural farm, which was constituted as a refuge and place of haven and safety from the outside world. As Foucault suggests, the Retreat was very different from previous asylums and their association with cruel, brutal, inhumane treatment.

> In some asylums which I have visited, chains are affixed to every table, and to every bedpost; in others, they are to be found within the walls. At the Retreat, they sometimes have patients brought to them frantic and in irons, whom they at once release, and by mild arguments and gentle arts, reduce almost immediately to obedience and orderly behaviour. (Stark 1810 in Bucknill and Tuke 1858:72)

By removing people from their homes and providing 'novel mental impressions' (ibid.:444), with suitable employment to relieve idleness and gloomy sensations, sanity could be restored. The error in madness, which forced the person into an estranged relation with the external environment, could be countered and realigned through the rational ordering of the asylum. The doctor, as the Father figure, could bring the notion of sympathy into the doctor–patient relationship, using the power of mind, to counter the error within the patients. This art, as opposed to a science, did not rely upon coercion, but by appeals through love, fear, consolation, compassion and kindness (ibid.:136). The asylum was to become something other than an enclave of moral contagion.

Moral treatment or therapy at the Retreat was also premised upon the principle of instilling self-prevention or 'auto-prophylaxis' (Tuke 1878:139). People were trained in particular ways of understanding and detecting prior signs of moral insanity, and also in strengthening the self-will to combat the 'mind-in-error'. According to Tuke, warnings of danger could include 'inability to sleep' (ibid.:157), and emotional warnings such as depression of general spirit, sense of exhaltation or buoyancy, as well as irritability of temper and fears about the future (ibid.:165). An economy of physical and mental regimens were practised, in order to keep the mind in check. Although moral therapy was developed primarily because 'medicinal treatment was seen to have its limits' (Bucknill and Tuke 1858:450), the 'physical' appeared within this discursive configuration in a specific way. The 'physical' did not relate to disease and illness, but a concern with keeping the body fit and healthy, in equilibrium with the mind, in order to strengthen self-will. Thus as well as recognising the importance of a cheerful disposition, rest and quiet, and physical exercise, diet and temperance were all-important. Resting the body was a practice which could then be translated into the importance of mental repose, which could again be influenced by stimulants, the use and abuse of alcoholic drinks and limiting starch and fats, for example. Tuke (1878:210) was attempting to produce an account of why insanity seemed to be linked to the poorer classes, in line with understandings and governmental practices at this time, and primarily viewed 'insufficient, inappropriate food and irregular living' as the excesses which could force the mind into 'error'.

As Castel (1988:74) argues, discussing the emergence of the asylum as a therapeutic site, within the late eighteenth century: 'the "normal" world was henceforth the place where disorder was reproduced, whilst the great cemetery of the asylum, became a site co-extensive with reason, in which the insane lived in the lucidity of the law and made it even more their own'.

Castel (1988:97) argues that what the asylum created was a 'well-packaged system' bringing together a theoretical code, a technical practice, and a relation of dominance between doctor and patient, within an institutional context. The asylum thus made possible a space where particular strategies, practices and problems could be addressed through a unified set of understandings, which were to accord the 'moral' particular diagnostic pertinence.

The hesitation

Despite the predominance of moral modes of explanations in the late eighteenth and early nineteenth centuries, there was resistance to these kinds of explanations. Mayo (1817) argued that mental aberrations were a result of physical abnormality. The so-called ravings of the mad were linked to a diseased brain. Madness was to be detected through physical symptoms and not through the manipulation of experience in relation to 'error'. It was not simply that there were different insanities (simple and complex for example), but that all madness was linked by degree. The degree to which the person had succumbed to disease would affect the particular manifestation of symptoms. Mayo (1817:45), for example, argued that the various psychic manifestations of insanity were related to the stage or course of the inherent disease. He rejected the division made by Pinel and Esquirol between mania and melancholia; rather than distinct entities, they were viewed as running into each other.

> We have witnessed madness counterfeiting inflammation of the liver, commencing with rigors, and with a secretion of bile as profuse as in cholera morbus. While the disease maintained this form, it was marked by a very desponding state of the patient, which might have supplied the means of detecting it.

Although Mayo championed a particular conception of the 'physical' the 'moral' was combined within this discourse in a particular way. Although he advocated that the mind was a function of the state of the brain, external 'moral' circumstances could act as exciting or constraining forces. In later writings Mayo (1838:2) cites Dr Butler: 'habit strengthens active principles, and weakens passive impressions'. It was this linking of the mind and brain via the concept of habit, which was to play a key role in restructuring the space of madness in relation to the will. Moral impulses were viewed as forming the will, which acted as the controlling power, over-riding the morbid predisposition which some individuals bore for madness.

> What do we notice as taking place, when we exert a power, which we certainly possess, of disengaging the mind from the influence of will, and allow the current of thought to proceed without interference? Let any person who has ever sat figuring to himself images and pictures in the embers of the fire, or in the passing cloud, answer this question. Why, in a short time, a tendency will be perceived by him rising in his mind, to give a real existence to these productions of the imagination – to give to its conceptions the force and truth of perceptions. (Mayo 1838:11)

Thus with the suspension of the power of the will, in relation to the imagination, madness becomes a disorder of the will. When the mind is passive then this deficient state provides the conditions for error so characteristic of madness. The 'whirl of insane associations' (ibid.:22) part of the creative 'vividness of mind' (ibid.:48) loses contact with external relations (sympathy) and the will loses its power.

> ... cases of intense excitements, in which the influence of the will may be regarded as wavering, and almost suspended, the power of sympathy is capable of readjusting the almost destroyed equilibrium ... Now, it would appear, either that the insanely predisposed are peculiarly deficient in this principle, or that insanity tends to weaken its efficiency, in those who are afflicted by the disease. (ibid.:33)

The above quote brings together the two divisions which were beginning to transform the relation between the moral and the physical. The moral sentiment was that which was characteristically human, and that which was also formed through experience. What was seen to differ in cases of insanity were differences in intellect and the ability to practice judgement and will. There were three general concepts which underpinned Mayo's formulations. The first is the state of mind from which develops moral and intellectual incoherency (error), which if left unchecked may pass 'into a chronic state of moral and intellectual perversion'. This perversion, through a notion of individual differences and heritablity was linked to the powerless state of the insane will.

In relation to vice and the role of education: 'Virtuous principles should be strengthened; vicious tendencies should be supplanted in favour of the cognate virtuous tendencies' (ibid.:85). The aim therefore of moral therapy, according to Mayo, would not merely be to counter error, but to strengthen the influence of the will. This could be hindered by the physical state of the brain, such as inflammation, which may also influence the mind. The mind and brain were to run in sympathy, the disequilibrium either due to temperament or predisposition, or the vice of certain moral conditions.

The mad within this space were still to have a degree of reason or moral sense to which reform could be directed. The limits of this sentiment were still the 'brutes' or idiots who have no kernel of reason and sense at all. This distinction between brutes and those with a perverted moral sense is elucidated in the following quote: 'In the latter case, the patient cannot hear the voice of conscience; in the former case (the brute), he has no conscience to hear' (ibid.:132).

The important mutation in relation to the moral domain I will argue is that those in error were eventually to become related to idiots, in that the insane predisposition was viewed as a recapitulation towards this state of abolition. Perversion and deficiency were to become related by degree and not type. 'Brutality and idiocy have been arranged in the category of mental disease in reference to a deficiency or abolition of an essential property of the human mind' (ibid.: 149).

It is the above themes which culminate within the writings of Esquirol (1845), who as I suggested earlier, exemplifies this co-existence of the moral and the physical in explanations of madness. However, towards the middle of the nineteenth century, certain insanities began to be viewed as mainly organic/physical. As Esquirol (1845:21) suggests, 'Insanity, or mental alienation, is a cerebral affection, ordinarily chronic, and without fever; characterised by disorders of sensibility, understanding, intelligence and will.' It is the linking of the will, the notion of a moral sensibility, ideas and the imagination, which form the elements of this moral/physical discursive space.

> In some cases of mental alienation, man, deprived, in some sort, of the control of the will, seems no longer to be master of his determinations. The insane, controlled by the predominant ideas and impressions, are drawn away to the performance of acts which they themselves disapprove. (ibid.:25)

It is within these divisions that simple (constitutional) and complex (error, sensibility) madnesses could co-exist, and which opened up a conception of the 'physical' to co-exist in relation to the 'mind in error'. The dichotomy of simple and complex constructed a developmental account within which degrees of reason were linked by a process of recapitulation.

> The different forms of insanity terminate in each other. Thus, mania terminates in dementia, or lypemania; and mania with fury, terminates critically by dementia, when the latter is the product of too active medication, at the commencement of mania or monomania. All forms of insanity degenerate into dementia, after a more or less brief period of time. (ibid.:59)

The cure in this account will depend upon how far the subject is seen to have succumbed to the course of disease. This is reflected in the following quote:

> Mania and monomania, are much more frequently cured than lypemania. We never cure idiocy nor senile dementia. Mania is cured more promptly than lypemania. There are many insane persons, who can be restored only to a certain point. (ibid.:63)

Dementia operated at the limits of rationality; as a cerebral affliction affecting the sensibility, will and understanding. Not man in error, but man in a state of degeneration, unable to reason and connect ideas. Progressing up the scale of ascendancy was the notion of monomania, a partial insanity related to the mind-in-error, the complex insanity.

> The patients seize upon a false principle, which they pursue without deviating from logical reasonings, and from which they deduce legitimate consequences which modify their affections, and the acts of their will. (ibid.:320)

It was within this discursive shift which brought together an interplay between the 'physical' and the 'moral' that hallucinations radically shifted in the way they were specified and made sense of. The experience was constituted as one which differentiated the heritably mad (those who were seen to have inherited a predisposition for madness), from the moral (deluded) mad. Hallucinations began to be constituted through particular biological and physical frameworks of explanation. The ability to maintain relations with the world was individualised and understood through explanations which saw inability as a function of disease rather than experience.

The interplay between the 'moral' and the 'physical' was to finally shift in the mid- to late nineteenth century. It was this decisive shift from the moral/physical to theories of degeneracy which definitively transformed the meaning of madness, and the eventual role that hallucinations were to play in administering madness. In the next chapter we will explore in more detail some of the historical and political circumstances which led to the 'problem of hallucination' being specified through a particular set of biological and evolutionary discourses.

5
Conditions of Degeneracy

Writings in the latter half of the nineteenth and early twentieth centuries constituted a space within which madness was to become an expression of degeneracy. Madness was linked to biological inferiority and viewed as a sign of a diseased brain – dementia praecox. This disease was seen to be characterised by a state of volition and weakness of judgement seen to be an effect of a process of dementia. Madness was constituted as a gradual form of mental deterioration culminating in dementia. Kraepelin (1913:219) who coined the term 'dementia praecox', viewed as the modern precursor to schizophrenia, argued that it was 'the name provisionally applied to a large group of cases which are characterised in common by a pronounced tendency to mental deterioration of varying grades'.

Within this discursive configuration the body, and what were taken to be its psychic peculiarities and physical stigmata, played a key role in the identification of the signs and symptoms of this process of mental deterioration. The person became a 'case' study where a particular way of specifying the 'psychic' and the 'physical' became the object of psychiatric practice. Through particular concepts and explanatory structures, persons were judged and surveiled to determine the degree to which they had succumbed to this degenerative process. Madness had been individualised within a domain of disease and responsibility. The 'weakened will' had been transferred to a field of clinical discourse, where it became linked to a diseased brain. The ability to maintain 'sympathetic' relations with the external world, once characterised through a notion of the 'mind-in-error' (moral insanity) was now viewed as a predisposition or inherent capacity which could be affected by disease processes. The moral sentiment or sensibility which had become a key definition of humanness within the eighteenth century, linked to experience, had now transformed into a biological capability whose limits were set by prior inherited dispositions to dementia.

This disposition was viewed as 'written on the body' and also found within particular manifestations of conduct and behaviour. These were all clues to the course of the disease process and the rate at which the body and its character had deteriorated. Thus what were constituted as 'expressions of degeneracy' revealed the extent to which the biological and psychic constitution of the person had decayed and reverted to earlier, what were taken to be more primitive, modes of existence. Kraepelin (1919:235) argued that the manifestations and expressions of degeneracy were idiosyncratic and could be found in different combinations and patterns. The combinations of physical and psychic manifestations in patients diagnosed with dementia praecox could include 'all sorts of physical abnormalities (which) exist with striking frequency, especially weakliness, small stature, youthful appearance, malformation of the cranium, and of the ears, high and narrow palate, persistence of the intermaxillary bone, abnormal growth of hair, strabismus, deformities of the fingers or toes, polynastia, defective development and irregularity of the teeth and like' (ibid.:236).

Similarly 'psychic' manifestations could include 'a quiet, shy, retiring disposition, made no friendships, lived only for themselves. Of secondary importance, and more in girls there is reported irritability, sensitiveness, excitability, nervousness, and along with these self-will and a tendency to bigotry' (ibid.:236). With this shift to a particular way of specifying the 'physical' linked to biological deterioration or decay, the 'moral' also mutated. Rather than being constituted through concepts which linked it to excess and error, the 'moral' was made intelligible as a set of 'exciting conditions' which could only facilitate madness in those who had inherited a prior disposition. With the reconfiguration of the 'moral' as a set of conditions which could only affect those who had succumbed to degeneracy, it was a particular rendering of the 'physical' which was to become the target of psychiatric intervention and practice.

This radical mutation in psychiatric understanding took place within a broader set of historical circumstances which began to understand particular social problems as problems of degeneracy. Psychiatric knowledge and understandings became intertwined with broader strategies of social regulation which sought to understand crime, poverty and misery, for example, as problems of biological decay, deterioration and reversion to the 'primitive'. Eugenics governmental strategies emerged as the solution to these problems, incorporating the knowledges of psychiatry and psychology to understand, conceptualise and map this 'domain of degeneracy' (cf. Rose 1985). Specific ways of differentiating psychic normality and abnormality became linked in a unified strategy to target those who were unable or incapable of practising particular forms of individuality and sociality. Rather than the assured development of scientific understanding which could be posited as an explanation for these shifts in psychiatric knowledge, particular ways of being and acting in the social had been problematised and marked out for governmental concern and attention. Psychiatric knowledge, in its transfer of particular kinds of experience to a clinical field, had become an important conceptual practice for understanding, intervening and acting upon particular people's experiences and conduct which were viewed as troublesome in some way or another.

The naturalisation of responsibility

This mutation also highlights a central argument which runs throughout this book. We have seen the terms moral, physical and biological appearing in different ways throughout our discussion of the 'problem of madness', and specifically how the concepts which articulate these objects differentiate and make intelligible hallucinatory experience. They are not continuous static terms, which are simply more or less privileged depending upon the particular set of historical circumstances we focus upon. They mean very different things, and are constructed and constituted in very different ways within allied discursive configurations. As we saw in the last chapter, the notion of the 'moral' had mutated from a philosophical concern with 'what makes us human', to a way of understanding particular conditions of life through concepts of excess. These were conflated in understandings of moral insanity which championed particular practices to return the person to particular ways of relating to themselves and the exigencies of their lives. A notion of the 'physical' also appeared within these understandings, where a differentiation in psychiatric practice in the early nineteenth century was made between the simple and complex insanities. A version of the moral and physical co-existed in the taxonomies of madness at this time, where the physical referred to the limits of those who were viewed as simply incurable and uneducable. Within the biomedical understandings to emerge towards the end of the nineteenth century, a notion of the moral still appeared, but had mutated to refer to those 'exciting conditions' which could act upon those with a prior hereditary predisposition. Education was still viewed as a useful strategy not simply to produce the moral sentiment generally, but to strengthen the character of those children who were

> born of insane parents. It will be proper to give to these children a peculiar education, to exercise them much in gymnastics, to inure them to external impressions; in fine to place them in a condition different from that of the authors of their being, according to the precept of Hippocrates; who recommends that the constitution of the individual should be changed, to prevent those maladies, to which, by hereditary descent, it is liable. (Esquirol 1845:50)

Krafft Ebing writing in the early twentieth century also posited (setting the foundations for what was now mental disease) the notion of a particular inferior constitution being acted upon by particular environmental factors. These were conceptualised as a range of exigencies of life which could act upon a 'bad seed'. We can see again, in the following statement, the divisions of simple and complex, moral and physical mutating in relation to a particular evolutionary way of thinking about disease and illness. Here we can see the beginnings of the dichotomies of the natural and social, individual and environment which are central to the tapestry of understandings within contemporary psychiatric and psychological discourse:

> The exact physical and mental condition of the patient; the habitual state of health; any possible abnormal dispositions and previous diseases; the original disposition; the development under education; the inclinations, tendencies, and circumstances of life of the individual; the form of reaction to external influences and injuries. (1904:137)

The notion of 'inherited disposition' or hereditary taint also became further differentiated through gendered divisions. In some writings, women were constituted as presenting an inherently weak constitution owing to their sex. As with the iconography of the figure of Ophelia, who combined childlike innocence with wild, untamed emotional expressions, such as shouting, dancing and singing, she came to signify the immanent vulnerability of a feminine constitution. In Showalter's (1987:91) engaging discussion of what she terms the 'female malady', there are many

references to the ways in which these discursive constructions circulated within the paintings and photography of the time. These
depictions of the wild untamed woman were also used in medical
portraitures to denote particular forms of disease.

> Medical textbooks sometimes illustrated their discussions of
> female patients with sketches of Ophelia – like maidens; as one
> historian notes, the descriptions of these 'Ophelias whose
> delicate and refined sensibilities had been wounded and
> maddened by a disappointment in love' were often 'affectingly
> drawn'. And when young women in lunatic asylums did not
> willingly throw themselves into Ophelia-like poses, asylum
> superintendents with cameras imposed the conventional
> Ophelia costume, gesture, props, and expression upon them.
> Diamond dressed one young woman in a black shawl and placed
> a garland of wild flowers in her hair. (ibid.:91)

Women were not able to be responsible because they were unbal-
anced by an impulsive passion. Women were viewed as closer to
nature and as having animalistic expressivity. This had far-reaching
effects beyond psychiatry, and was used as a justification for
women's long and continual denied access to education. Maudsley
(1879:163) echoes this view in the following quote about the value
of education as a moral influence for women:

> The common system of female education, which is now falling
> fast to pieces, was ill-adapted to store the mind with useful
> knowledge, and to train up a strong character; had it been
> designed specially to heighten emotional sensibility and to
> weaken reason, it could hardly have been more fitted to produce
> that effect. Its whole tendency has been to increase that pre-
> dominance of the affective life in woman, which she owes
> mainly to her sexual constitution.

In many writings men and masculinity were equated with the more
complex forms of madness, linked to the notion of an over-
stretched sensibility. There were conditions of life seen to be peculiar
to a man such as work, wealth, business and family responsibilities,
which could disturb the fine-tuning of this reasoned sensibility. For
women, the simple counterparts, passion and desire, constituted
their physical and psychic apparatus. Maudsley (1879:166) again
champions this view in the following set of statements:

It must not be supposed that it is because of anything in the constitution of men which renders them more liable to such derangement; on the contrary, there are obviously disturbing conditions peculiar to the female constitution which are more fitted to be occasions of mental disorder.

Passion thus was to act as the violent wind, upsetting an already disturbed sail, and in Maudsley's words 'sinks the ship' (ibid.:159). The simple and complex, overlaid by notions of femininity and masculinity in relation to the idea of inherited disposition, allowed for the emergence of an Affective insanity which was viewed as instinctive, from Insanity without Delusion which was viewed as moral (Maudsley 1879). These different kinds of madness linked by degree allowed for certain people to be placed higher up an evolutionary scale, closer to reason than nature.

It was argued in the previous chapter that Esquirol represented some of the hesitation and shifts that were beginning to appear in psychiatric practice and understanding in the mid-nineteenth century. These shifts were related to a mutating of the terms 'moral' and 'physical' with those explanatory structures which articulated their meaning. With the reconfiguration of the 'physical' as a domain of degeneracy, the notion of 'moral insanity' shifted and changed in meaning, linked to a partial insanity known as monomania. This was a more complex insanity which was not simply the 'mind-in-error' but a reasoning insanity based on a disorder of will. The mind was not in error, but was unable to determine its own thought. Esquirol (1845:320) describes this insanity in the following way, highlighting the newly emerging link between error and will within this configuration:

the intellectual disorder is confined to a single object, or a limited number of objects. The patients seize upon a false principle, which they pursue without deviating from logical reasonings, and from which they deduce legitimate consequences which modify their affections, and the acts of their will.

The Enlightenment optimism in relation to the ability of psychiatrists and others to restore the individual through habit to the external world had begun to dissipate. With the institutionalisation of madness within asylums attempting to cure patients through moral therapy, the notion of the mind-in-error as the target of the clinical profession had been put into question.

Through bringing together large groups of people in a therapeutic space where a range of experiences were understood as moral in nature, people were seen to differ in their ability to acquire or re-acquire this moral sentiment. A new concept appeared within this set of explanations which saw the 'moral' as a function of the will. The will was seen to be the capacity which would allow persons to develop the ability to practice sympathetic relations with others. The will was to become the fulcrum for discussions, centring upon the relation between insanity and responsibility. The moral/physical split was beginning to transform, whereby the notion that 'man' was formed through his experience was put into question. It would appear that not all men were born equal, and that there were those who could not or would not develop their intellect to produce a relation of self-control and sympathy. Moral therapy was set by the limits of an individual's core of rationality, and not by the limits of rationality per se. This capacity had become naturalised and linked to biological inferiority and disease. Maudsley (1874:320) realises this late nineteenth-century idea of a heritable constitution underpinning madness in his argument for the function of education:

> But great as is the power of education, it is yet a sternly limited power, it is limited by the capacity of the individual nature, and can only work within this larger or smaller circle of necessity. No training in the world will avoid to elicit grapes from thorns or figs from thistles in like manners, no mortal can transcend his nature; and it will be ever impossible to raise a stable super-structure of intellect and character in bad natured foundations.

Crime and responsibility

With the shift from the formation of man through experience, to those devoid of the sensory and intellectual apparatus to acquire the moral sense, discussions became focused on the relationship between crime and insanity. The problem of crime and those who drifted to it was to be one of the main social problems to which psychiatry provided the terms and concepts through which crime and the criminal were to be understood. With the transfer of the problem of mind to a clinical field, psychiatry emerged as the knowledge to judge and adjudicate responsibility understood through concepts of disease and biological inferiority. This is one place in which eugenics strategies and 'psy' knowledges became interlinked in strategies of social regulation.

The hereditary predisposition viewed as underlying both crime and insanity were viewed as an expression of decay. It was those types who had failed to acquire the sentiment who according to this view represented a form of atavism. This was a term central to evolutionary discourse to denote a regression to so-called pre-civilised modes of conduct. The concept of monomania, the partial insanity, played a key role in Maudsley's discussions of responsibility, and was to create a borderland of confusion and ambiguity. There was no straightforward division of the insane from the sane; it would take the expertise of a clinical field to unravel the hidden intelligibility of unreason. Despite the ambivalence represented in the nosographies of the time, the particular 'psy' configuration of truth and meaning emerging at this time, primarily constituted 'problems of mind' as a function of the diseased brain.

> Insanity is, in fact, disorder of brain, producing disorder of mind; or, to define its nature in greater detail, it is a disorder of the supreme nerve centres of the brain – the special organs of mind – producing derangement of thought, feeling and action, together or separately, of such degree or kind, as to incapacitate the individual for the relations of life. (Maudsley 1874:15)

This statement from Maudsley emphasises how a particular form of sociality and individuality, characterised by the propensity to be responsible towards oneself and others, was presupposed within psychiatric discourse, and also underpinned definitions of legal responsibility. These definitions centred around individuals' ability or power to control their own actions. This capacity was viewed as part of the biological make-up of individuals and was linked to the will, which became that aspect of an individual psychology which could be worked upon and developed.

> The formation of a character in which the thoughts, feelings, and actions are under the habitual guidance of a well-fashioned will, is perhaps the highest effort of self-development. It represents the attainment, by conscious method, of a harmony between man and nature; a condition in which the individual has succeeded in making the best of himself, of the human

nature with which he has to do, and of the world in which he moves and has his being. (Maudsley 1874:300)

These new terms – will, hereditary taint, responsibility and the brain – set the parameters through which this biomedical discourse was to transform the 'problem of hallucination'. Insanity was constituted as a core of unreason; its psychic and physical manifestations altered by its varying courses in the body. The patient was to become the distorting factor; the degree of hereditary taint producing the boundaries of the various clinical groupings of the disease entity. It is the notion of individual differences which underlies Krafft Ebing's (1904:xiv) writings. Viewing mental illness as a 'disorder of the vasomotor system' producing disturbances of mental functions, or as he terms them, 'Anomalies of the Cerebral functions' (ibid.: 45), he lists a whole range of disturbances from the rapidity of ideation to the rapidity of apperception. It is within this cerebral space that hallucinations come to signify as manifestations of a disturbed or convulsed brain. They are prior to delusions and pertain to a diseased sensory apparatus:

> The nosological significance of an hallucination is that of an elementary disturbance of the psycho-sensorial functions. It always indicates an abnormal condition of the central nervous system. It occurs most frequently in insanity, but is not, in itself, a criterion of mental disease. (Krafft Ebing 1904:108)

Hallucinations are not part of the vividness of imagination as within previous 'epochs' and are differentiated from dreams, daydreaming and vivid imagining. Delusions have become synonymous with judgement and interpretation; hallucinations are part of the disease process itself. The presence of hallucinations has become a sign in relation to other elementary disturbances revealing a state of decay. They are a function of an underlying disease process, the intelligibility of which is only available through the close examination of an individual's history, and physical and psychic abnormalities. The corporeal and psychic space of the individual, constituted through particular understandings of the biological, became the object and target of psychiatric practice. Thus, the degree of madness would depend upon the state of the brain: the neuropathic constitution.

As we have seen from the preceding discussion of some of the ambiguities and contradictions within psychiatric discourse from the mid- to late nineteenth century, the moral and physical were beginning to mutate, but still appeared within psychiatric discourse in particular ways. It was in the late nineteenth century that a particular set of historical events and circumstances led to the notion that madness was a 'disease of degeneracy'. As we will see one significant event was in population statistics and how crime and insanity were linked within growing populations. Although crime and insanity presented a threat to the smooth running of the social order, it was thought that insanity would eventually die out, as it was seen to be passed from generation to generation, eventually destroying certain family lineages. With the advent and inception of Darwin's theories of evolution, the unit of analysis was to mutate from the family to the population. Within this topographical space, it was those of the lower classes – the 'dangerous classes' who were viewed as reproducing at a faster rate than the middle classes (Blackman 1996, Blackman and Walkerdine 2001). The fear was that if madness was passed on through 'insane' families its characteristics would be passed to the population at large. With a statistical conception of the population, deviations from the average or norm would over time actually shift the norm. Deviations thus posed a threat to the selection of characteristics across generations, destabilising the civilising process.

This had a profound effect upon enlightenment thinking; not only could one produce the beauty and perfection characterised by the fully self-conscious 'self-regulating' individual, it was also possible to produce the monstrosities of pre-civilised modes of conduct; sensibility was not merely threatened, but the nation itself. Thus with the linking of time, history and change, the self-assuredness of civilised experience could not be guaranteed or maintained. As Darwin (1909:252) warns: 'Specific forms are not immutable creations.' This was one set of fears which made eugenics strategies and the newly emerging biomedical discourses partners in administering and targeting those who were viewed as degenerate.

Conditions for degeneracy

Castel (1988), Rose (1985) and others cite the 1860s as the time of the crucial shift to theories and strategies of degeneration in relation to the formulation of particular social problems and the kinds of strategies and governmental intervention produced on the basis of these understandings. The conditions of possibility for these decisive shifts will now be reconstructed, paying particular attention to the specific role hallucinations came to play in these transformations.

The asylum

Foucault (1971) made the statement that madness was born out of the asylum. How could such an absurd statement be made, when asylums were resurrected as therapeutic spaces to deal with the delirium of a mind-in-error? Foucault (1971) argued that the moral space of madness which brought together certain experiences within an institutional context, although fated, made possible one of the fundamental conditions for the modern experience of madness. This was the notion of 'individual differences'. Within the homogeneous, rationally-ordered architectural space of the asylum, lived a variety of species of madness, distorted, and lived through the idiosyncratic pathways of individual bodies. It was the visibility of the asylum space which produced a naturalisation and clarification of the old themes of the moral and the physical, which had more or less co-existed before this event. It was this new restructuring of the relation between the moral and the physical which was to shift so dramatically the object of psychiatric practice.

> The conditions of asylum practice further, were specifically endorsed for the opportunities they allowed of systematic observation and comparison of inmates. The ultimate promise of asylum confinement was that large numbers of inmates, carefully observed through the course of their disorders, and compared as statistical measures, would provide the basis for a new science of mental disorders. (Donnelly 1983:154)

Clinical medicine

The rise of clinical medicine is usually cited as the epistemological event from which modern scientific understanding has developed. Curiously though, the kinds of arguments we are beginning to consider cite the emergence of particular institutional sites as being 'surfaces of emergence' (Foucault 1972) through which 'moral' understandings of madness as 'error' became problematised. The general divisions between the moral and physical and simple and complex madness, did not seem to tie together all the contradictions and incoherencies found when observing groups of people together. This was further compounded through the new site of the hospital in the late nineteenth century, which through changes in the theory and practice of clinical medicine, allowed increasing opportunities for observing and judging individual differences, allowing comparisons to be made, charted and norms constructed. As Donnelly (1983:145) argues:

> Under the conditions of the new clinical medicine in hospitals, such observation of differences became more comprehensive and systematic; the gradual diffusion of uniform procedures and standard methods of examination and record-taking also allowed, in time, the establishment of broadly-based 'norms'.

It was not simply that advances in medical understanding required new spaces within which to enact psychiatric practice, but that there were certain shifts in historical and social circumstances which enabled the hospital or clinic to emerge as the key site for the practice of clinical medicine. Rose (1985:32) argues that some of the key conditions of possibility for these shifts were increasing urbanisation and industrialisation and changes in laws of assistance. These changes in laws of assistance made institutionalisation a condition of medical treatment for those on relief. The doctor–patient relationship had gone beyond the art of bedside rapport and was to create different kinds of relationship between the doctor and patient. The doctor's expertise was no longer his rapport and persuasion, but his ability to detect the signs and symptoms of disease through comparing each individual case in relation to a general knowledge of disease processes. It was the body and its life history known as 'the case', which was to mark this intersection, and become the diagnostic tool of psychiatric practice from the early 1900s onwards.

As Rose (1985:32) argues:

> The case was unique but intelligible, for its individuality could be charted in terms of its conformity to, or deviation from the general standards of functioning, which were now available for comparison.

Within these formulations the notion of disease itself had radically transformed. The notion of moral insanity was more equated to a dis-ease with life; a kind of going off the tracks which could be gently corrected through habit and persuasion. The 'physical' related to those who were seen to congenitally lack the ability to reason at all. These were the brutes and idiots who were viewed as incurable and uneducable. Within these newly emerging explanations, people could be at the mercy of disease processes which were linked by the degree to which they had succumbed to decay and deterioration. Thus, symptoms became the means to identify the course of the disease and compare individuals with each other. Symptoms had become evidence of disease itself, and were not necessarily written on the body as with earlier physiognomical conceptions of madness.

Unemployment, poverty and conditions of life

From a concern with the formation of 'man' through his moral environment, to the interaction between the individual's natural endowment of reason and his conditions of life (Maudsley 1874), the problem(s) of pauperism, crime, and unemployment were to transform. Earlier governmental strategies such as sanitary science, in the early to mid-nineteenth century, targeted vice and those conditions of life seen to produce moral insanity. The 'problem of demoralisation' was framed through an understanding that there were certain environmental conditions which would produce excess and error. There were seen to be certain enclaves which the lower classes drifted to, which both separated them from the humanisation produced through the influences of civilisation, and breeded intemperance and excess. The problem was thus posed within a moral domain, in Rose's (1985:47) words: 'the loss of moral values engendered by the conditions of existence of this class'.

Within this formulation, strategies such as the social hygiene movement developed, aimed at breaking up these localised territories and allowing the lower classes to receive the beneficent influences available to the middle classes. However, these strategies were seen to fail in their optimism, actually worsening conditions of life and promoting further overcrowding. The problem of vice and intemperance became linked to the problem of unemployment. Idleness and employment were key concepts structuring the moral experience of madness. Within Tuke's asylum at the Yorkshire

Retreat, as we saw in the last chapter, regular employment was one of the techniques through which people learned to strengthen their will, thus protecting themselves from vice and immorality. Unemployment was socially undesirable, leading to the excesses characterised by a mind out of harmony with external relations. Habit and will were to be formed through regular ordered, monotonous work. These links between unemployment, poverty and madness transformed within a changing economic horizon in the late nineteenth century. The key division operating within this strategy was the notion of 'want of employment' (Rose 1985: 48). There were those, according to Booth (1892), who were maintained in a relation of dependence on public assistance, as the casual labour they relied upon was variable, seasonal and unpredictable. However, merely changing the conditions of life of a particular milieu would not eliminate this stratum of employment, as wealth could only be maintained through differing levels of access to work.

Booth conceptualised these levels by delineating eight classes within the population. It was classes A–D which represented the proportion of the population in poverty. Classes D and C were the small earners, regular and intermittent respectively. Class B represented the casual labourers, those who were still viewed as wanting employment, dictated by a calculus of pleasures and wants. They would play when they wanted and work when they wanted. Class A represented the residuum, the unemployables who acted at the limits of morality; they were savages beyond morality and hence a desire for employment. With increasing fears concerning race decay, the 'unemployables' took on a distinct social constitution, seen as less endowed constitutionally, unable to acquire the capacity to operate sympathetic relations with the external world. Vice became linked to this distinct group, viewed as closer to the 'primitive' and actually threatening the assured development of civilisation. Moral contagion was seen to spread from a particular grouping of people and not merely a particular social milieu.

This reformulation of the 'problem of unemployment' introduced a number of schemes of decasualisation. Their aim was to lessen the gap between the employed and unemployed, by removing casual labour and forcing those within this hinging class to either go up or down. As Rose (1985) highlights when discussing a key strategy at the time embodied within a report by Beveridge (1905), the division made was between those who could and wanted to work and those who could not. Those who constituted this class of unemployables, a large number of pauper lunatics (Donnelly 1983), were to be removed to labour colonies and denied the right to reproduce. These eugenics strategies understood this class of people through particular biological discourses which understood one's character as linked to inherited dispositions or 'hereditary taint'. The problem was shifting to a concern with character and tainted constitutions which could not be reformed simply through changing conditions of life. The decisive shift, however, was when all these modes of explanation became linked within broader eugenics strategies. This was made possible by a certain conception of biology and population statistics, which systematised the links into a central apparatus for detecting and preventing the degeneration of the race within an evolutionary framework of explanation. This was to finally sway the balance in favour of heredity and a particular understanding of biology, restructuring the meaning, division and constitution of madness in a far-reaching way. It was within this field of discourse that the 'problem of hallucination' came to be rendered in its contemporary form, in relation to a number of key explanatory concepts.

Madness as an expression of degeneracy

> Mental disturbances that affect individuals of robust brain may be called psychoneuroses. Those developed upon a defective foundation may be called degenerate insanities. (Krafft Ebing 1904:279)

Through a complex interweaving of 'events' major shifts were occurring within psychiatric discourse. As we can see, these shifts cannot be explained by a process internal to the discourse itself, nor solely by external factors. There is rather a complex and 'polymorphous interweaving of correlations' which have combined and recombined to produce present understandings (Foucault 1991a:58). Within these shifts the importance of disposition and degeneration had entered the very constitution of madness. The aim of psychiatry was to chart the various manifestations of this process of decay in order to detect and prevent the thwarting of civilisation. The posing of the decay of mental functions as a threat became significant within increasing attention to a whole range of social problems, which became linked within this unified system of explanation. Madness was to represent one of the forms of regression to previous forms, along with crime, unemployment, idiocy and vice, amongst others. With the premise that species are the modified descendants of other species, then the various classes within the population, as outlined by Booth, were constituted as representing differing forms of atavism. The classes were naturalised as forms of the differing 'races of man'. It was these differing races in relation to a notion of 'differential reproduction' which were to threaten this form of individuality and sociality which had been thoroughly naturalised within Darwin's writings.

The imagination

Darwin (1871) introduced a range of concepts seen to differentiate 'man' from lower ancestral forms. One such differentiation was between imagination and reason. Drawing on Lockeian notions of the combining and selecting of ideas, imagination was naturalised as part of the creative process of 'man'.

> The imagination is one of the highest perogatives of man. By this faculty he unites, independently of the will, former images and ideas, and thus creates brilliant and novel results. (Darwin 1871:45)

Dreaming was viewed as part of the poetic visionary process, producing novel connections of ideas. If unchecked, reason would err, resulting in what Darwin (1871:68) termed 'the strange superstitions and customs' characterising religion. It was the moral sense which was viewed as the 'highest psychical faculty of man' (ibid.:71), formed through habit and producing a relation of responsibility towards the community.

> Man thus prompted will, through long habit, acquire such perfect self-command, that his desires and passions will at last instantly yield to his social sympathies, and there will no longer be a struggle between them. (ibid.: 91)

Darwin was therefore taking themes which had existed in the previous century and combining and recombining them, naturalising a particular form of individuality and sociality. Difference in relation to this conception of 'what it means to be human' was presented through an evolutionary trope which understood deviation as degeneration. 'The difference in mind between man and the higher animals, great as it is, is certainly one of degree and not of kind' (ibid.:105). 'We must trace a perfect gradation from the mind of an utter idiot, lower than that of the lowest animal, to the mind of a Newton' (ibid.:106). I will argue that the construction of imagination as one of the highest psychic qualities of 'man', naturalised a division which had already emerged: that hallucinations were not part of the imaginative process, but simply pseudo-sensory by-products of a diseased brain.

Darwin (1871) also had much to say about previous, what he described as philanthropic governmental strategies, which had sought to break down demoralising influences. By extending sympathy to those less fortunate, philanthropists were actually maintaining those who were seen to be a threat: 'We build asylums for the imbecile, the maimed and the sick; we institute poor laws; and our medical men exert their utmost skill to save the life of every one to the last moment' (ibid.:168). This philanthropic process was seen itself to present a threat to civilisation and was 'highly injurious to the race of man' (ibid.:168). Thus eugenics, in the name of social salvation, should take over from the social hygiene movement to deal with the new problem of degeneracy. Let us see how this particular way of framing social problems and producing particular practices of individuality and sociality became constituted within psychiatry itself as a new science of mental disorder.

The science of psychiatry

> Family physicians, again, can often help to prevent the marriage of the insane, or of those who are seriously threatened with insanity, and to secure a proper education and choice of education predisposed to disease. (Kraepelin 1913:3)

Kraepelin, as we have seen in previous chapters, is credited with discovering dementia praecox, which is viewed as the modern precursor to schizophrenia. Less is written about his eugenics views in relation to madness and criminality, and how dementia praecox was viewed as a single morbid disease process which revealed a core of degeneracy. Kraepelin (1919:249) viewed those who drifted to criminality and vagrancy as bearing the seeds of their own destruction within their constitution. A different way of specifying the moral was contained within his nosography, in relation to the 'partial insanities', such as paraphrenia which still show evidence of rationality. Making links with the courts, Kraepelin (1919) discusses the concept of dissimulation. This concept marked the borderland between wilful deception and individuals not being responsible for their actions due to biological inferiority and inability. In relation to the will or volition, these individuals are seen to retain elements of control, where the end-point of dementia had not been reached. This twilight zone was to endure within contemporary explanations of madness, where hallucinations have come to represent this borderland. The case of Peter Sutcliffe, also known as the Yorkshire Ripper, is a case in point (cf. Blackman and Walkerdine 2001).

Within what were seen as a veritable range of symptoms, including sensory disturbances, sexual sensations, association experiences, incoherence of thought, stereotypy, negativism, judgement errors, delusions, ideas of influence, exalted ideas, emotional dullness, loss of sympathy, weakening of volition, waxy flexibility, catatonic excitement, mannerisms, autism and stupor, to name some of the candidates, was also a range of clinical pictures from hebephrenia, dementia simplex, silly dementia, simple depressive dementia, delusional depressive dementia, circular dementia, agitated dementia, periodic dementia, paranoid dementias and so on through to the terminal states seen as the 'last period of the development of the disease' (ibid.:205).

In an American rewriting of Kraepelin, Defendorf (1902) presents these forms within an ascendancy scale from the most civilised, complex and male such as Infection psychoses and Exhaustion psychoses at the pinnacle, through to Dementia Praecox and at the bottom end, general neuroses including epileptic and hysterical insanities: those born from a constitutional psychopathic state. These were peculiarly gendered, showing how differentiations between masculinity and femininity were also central to these formulations.

> Hysterical insanity is a psychosis arising from a psychopathic constitution, characterised by great instability of the emotions, defective will power, and heightened self-consciousness. (Defendorf 1902:353)

Family history was an important tool to calculate and identify what were taken to be defective physical constitutions. As Kraepelin (1913:97) advises:

> It requires a detailed inquiry into the habits, traits and physical illnesses of all the members of the direct branches of the family, laying particular stress upon mental peculiarities, alcoholic and other addictions, and criminal tendencies.

The detailing of 'family history' also included attention to birth traumas, possible early emotional anguish, evidence of onanism (the practice of masturbation), religious experiences, vices and employment record. Present symptoms were also observed (status praesens), paying attention to 'psychic' and 'physical' abnormalities to identify the degree to which the person was seen to have succumbed to degeneracy. States of degeneracy could therefore be expressed psychically (through what we might now understand as psychological states), physically (inscribed on the surface of the body) and through particular social acts such as criminality. Homosexuality also at this determinate period was viewed as an expression of degeneracy and was given a psychiatric diagnosis termed 'Contrary Sexual Instincts'.

> The contrary sexual instincts are far more prevalent among men. It is an uncommon condition, the cases reported to date numbering but a few 100, although homosexual patients maintain that it is by no means rare. It is more prevalent in certain employments, such as among decorators, waiters, ladies' tailors; also among theatrical people. Moll claims that women comedians are regularly homosexual. (Kraepelin 1913:510)

Thus a range of what were considered as socially undesirable behaviours were problematised through particular biological concepts and viewed as expressions of degeneracy. Psychiatry was increasingly becoming part of a project to chart degeneracy, reposing problems of social existence within an evolutionary framework of explanation. It was within the practice and conceptual basis of psychiatry that specific problems were understood and acted upon in particular kinds of ways, unifying psychiatric explanations with broader governmental strategies such as eugenics. As we have seen, within the shifting conceptual basis and practice of psychiatry, the 'problem of hallucination' was divided from the imagination and viewed as a pseudo-sensory by-product of a diseased brain.

Archaism in the twentieth century

Despite the constitution of hallucinations as pseudo-sensory products of a diseased brain, there have always been resistances to what William James (1902:12) terms this 'medical materialism'. James argued that ecstatic states of consciousness produce certain psychic phenomena such as trances, hearing voices, reverie and so on and so forth. These are not pathological and easily reducible to a biological core of degeneracy represented by a diseased brain. Rather he viewed them as being expansive and as having deep psychological significance. Mystical states of consciousness are the foundation for the experience of personal religious experiences. Within an existential framework, James defines religion as the relation an individual may have to whatever he may consider divine. With a reverence and fascination for certain states of consciousness, such as the hallucinated, James (p. 18) argues that these psychic phenomena should be judged along a spiritual dimension: i.e. for what they do, their utility; their 'immediate luminousness, philosophical reasonableness and moral helpfulness'.

In a similar vein, Parish (1897:291) speculates on why hallucinations are only ever considered as fallacies of perception. He argues instead that hallucinations are an example of a different state of consciousness; a disassociation of consciousness – 'perception in the state of dissociation' (ibid.:324). Within this dissociative state, images and ideas are allowed free play; much as the mind in delirium, there is a continual stream of consciousness. As he argues: 'there is absolutely no distinction, either theoretic or practical, to be drawn between the sense deceptions of the dream-state and those of "waking-consciousness". This represents a reversion to what psychiatry would term an out-moded explanation. Parish (1897) argued that this is a psychic experience of consciousness; a different experience from normal waking consciousness, but no less pathological.

> For while, of course, there is nothing to prevent us from giving a name to each and every state of consciousness, labelling it in fact, it is obviously impossible through words or any other medicine, to make anyone else share our psychic experience in all its fullness and intimacy, to make it the same experience for him. (ibid.:330)

Inverting the theme of decay and degeneration, these states are actually viewed as part of the development of the human psychic potential. These modes of explanation were not accorded any diagnostic significance within psychiatry but still existed in different spaces and places as possible ways of articulating the 'problem of hallucination'. Despite this philosophical conception of the mind as a psychic space of ecstatic consciousness (where dreams, hallucinations, trances and religious ecstasy were all linked in relation to the fantastical action of the imagination – a psychosensorial state or condition), biomedical modes of explanation dominated the concepts and techniques of psychiatric practice.

Beyond the corporeal

In this section I want to concentrate on the writings of Hack Tuke, the son of Samuel Tuke, the founder of the York Retreat, which as we saw in the last chapter was the first charitable county asylum in Yorkshire in 1777 to impart the practice of 'moral therapy' in an institutional context in relation to the 'problem of madness'. Hack Tuke was committed 'to the abolition of mechanical restraints' (Bucknill and Tuke 1858:vi) in interventions with madness and proposed moral treatments to restore the individual to sanity. In the last chapter we looked at some of the elements which constituted the 'moral' within these practices and the relationship between the doctor and patient which was engendered through these understandings. Hack Tuke in his writings in the nineteenth century revisited some of these practices and understandings, in relation to some of the terms and concepts now central to psychiatric practice. I want to focus particularly on these critiques of clinical psychiatry and the kinds of concepts and explanatory structures which mapped what was increasingly understood to be a psychological space.

Tuke published two books in the nineteenth century, in the midst of theories of degeneracy, which recount the 'psychophysical principles' (1892:x) which he argued should be part of clinical practice. His book was not simply an account of the virtues of moral therapy, but a thorough elucidation of the principle and basis of imagination that he suggested was the psychological mechanism through which moral therapy had its affects. Tuke (1872) aimed his earlier book specifically at the medical profession who had outlawed in the early 1900s the practice of hypnosis which shared similarities with his conception of the 'psycho-physical'. Revisiting the Retreat in his writings, he wanted to subject the underlying principles of moral therapy to systematic medical analysis to remove it from its enduring legacy of quackery.

> There are two classes of readers to whom I wish more especially to address myself. The medical reader who, I hope, may be induced to employ psychotherapeutics in a more methodical way than heretofore, and thus copy nature in those interesting instances, occasionally occurring, of sudden recovery from the spontaneous action of some powerful moral cause, by employing the same force designedly, instead of leaving it to mere chance.

Tuke saw the basis of a 'New Science' in his explanation of the 'principle of the imagination', which he used to explain mesmerism, hypnotism, the effects of emotion in producing disease, the effect of the intellect on the health of the body, to induce anaesthesia and so forth. This was not simply the championing of the 'moral' over the physical, nor the reflection of the imparting of religious beliefs in the practice of medicine, but a way of understanding and constructing human subjectivity which was radically different from the kinds of evolutionary understandings incorporated into psychiatry. Although some of the terms also set the parameters through which psychiatry understood particular mental processes – will, imagination, mind, body and so forth – these terms articulated very different concepts and explanations in relation to those connected to the discourses of psychiatry. These terms had shifted in meaning due to the place they now occupied in a discursive field which was in discord with Tuke's 'psycho-physical' principles.

Tuke presented a series of experiences which he felt were inexplicable from a materialist perspective. 'The whirling dervishes of India, the serpent-eaters of Egypt, the second-sight men of the Highlands, all knowing how to excite convulsions, or delirium, or spectral illusions and somnambulism in themselves or their dupes, by mental acts or drugs' (1872:7). He felt that approaching the mind as a function of the brain was problematic and moved to a notion of the imagination as a capacity which had a quasi-magical power. This capacity could be switched, rejoined or channelled through the focusing of the will. Tuke (ibid.:82) argued that the mind and body were in an 'inseparable union', and could affect each other through the sympathetic action of one with the other.

In the contents pages of his first manual – the *Dictionary of Psychological Medicine* – 'The Influence of the Mind Upon the Body' – he outlines the 'action of the imagination upon voluntary and involuntary organs, upon the organic and vegetative functions to include the blood, sweat, bile, skin, hair, urine and gastric juice, the action of the emotions upon the body', and then a second section outlining the influence of the will within this process. The focusing of the will was due to what Tuke termed 'expectant attention'. Discussing a seminal physiologist of the time, Unzer, Tuke (1872:5) illustrates the beneficial or enchanting effect of developing this focusing capacity. He claims, 'I am confident that I can fix my attention to any part until I have a sensation in that part.'

The intellect could be utilised not only in relation to intellectual powers, such as mental application or hard study, but to focus the mind in a state of volition to create certain images, sensations, experiences at will. By focusing only upon certain states of mind grounded in experience and sensation, i.e. the intellect, man was excluding a whole 'other side' of potential and expansionary experiences, which despite their invisibility still exerted a massive force. Tuke (1872:35) offers numerous examples of this action of the imagination, from the effects of swallowing a placebo, to the effect of producing insensitivity to pain or heat, an artificially induced anaesthesia produced by 'physical means'. Tuke develops this notion of sympathethic action through drawing parallels with spiritual phenomena and the importance of mesmerism in relation to the idea of 'expectant attention'. He accords the success of mesmerism, not to the elusive properties of a magnetic force inhering within the individual, but to the combined effects of the action of the imagination and expectant attention.

> The state of the mind – the condition of the cerebral hemispheres – may play upon the ganglia of the senses so as to produce certain sensorial phenomena, and also that it may so affect the sensorium that impressions upon the senses received from the outer world may be modified in various ways. (ibid.:37)

Within this discursive complex hallucinations were constituted as markers of the intensity of action upon the sense-organs. Hallucinations were allied more to ecstatic states which were viewed as states of mind where images and internal reverie command the experience and behaviour of the so-called mystics.

> It would be much more difficult to believe in the credulity of the saints and mystics, if we did not see ample physiological reasons for believing that the senses were really acted upon by their intense thought on certain spiritual subjects. (ibid.:37)

Thus the imagination can actively influence both the sensory and auditory senses, producing sounds, voices and images which are produced by 'expectant attention' and are not merely pseudo-sensory by-products of a diseased brain. Hallucinations are therefore viewed as a reflection of the intensity of the imagination, and restructured alongside other twilight states such as sleep, day-dreaming, reverie and ecstasy where the mind has the power to create its own peepshow. Illusions and hallucinations once more become linked with the creative potential of the fantastical imagination.

> In some conditions of the encephalic centres, such a powerful excitement of the sensory ganglia occurs, that the effect is identical in sensory force – in objectivity – with that which results from an impression produced upon the peripheral termination of the nerves, causing hallucinations or phantasmal. (ibid.:35)

Tuke (1872:82) discusses the 'psycho-physical' principles of the stigmata and the healing properties of prayer, linking the relations between the imagination, will and the mind without recourse to the action of a divine entity. In the following quote we can see the reconceptualisation of spiritual phenomena, through the union of the mind with the body, that Tuke seeks to instigate as the basis of a materialist psycho-medical practice.

> The periodicity of Stigmata is a further interesting illustration of the influence of Attention and Imagination upon the direction and localisation of the cutaneous circulation. On saints days and on Fridays, the seat of the marks became more painful, and a brighter colour indicated a fresh influx of blood to the part. The mystics' thoughts being specially concentrated upon the passion.

The 'suffering of Christ' invoked by the idea of the passion is central to the psychical process according to Tuke (1872), through which an idea becomes represented or experienced physically in the body. Thus, the action of the imagination and the invoking of particular emotional states, such as fear, hope, and agitation, are central to the process through which ideas or concepts induce sensations or changes in the body. It is this principle which Tuke argued was central to the doctor–patient relationship at the Retreat which was founded upon the subtle process of persuasion. As well as the habit-forming effects of work and monotony which were seen to strengthen the will (by making the action of the will involuntary rather than voluntary), the doctor's imagination was practically utilised to appeal to the imagination of the patient by gently arousing their will and inducing expectation or hope. This was seen to be especially important where patients were suffering mental shocks sending the mind away from its habitual paths of association. Again Tuke (ibid.:375) draws parallels with the healing properties of prayer and the inducing of hope with its sympathetic affects of mind with body – through agitation and calm – in the cure of mental and physical dis-ease.

> Those who have visited the continental churches will remember the large number of crutches, sticks, splints etc. which have been left by those who have been cured or relieved of contracted joints, rheumatism, and palsy, by prayers offered up to some saints, or by the supposed efficacy of their relics.

Discussing the site of the Church for the performing of miracles and faith-healing produced through the technique of prayer, he proposed that the principles underlying so-called religious phenomena could be applied within medical practice for psychotherapeutic means. Moral therapy was discussed as the site through which these techniques had been localised within the doctor–patient relationship. Moral therapy's target worked through appealing to the imagination as a persuasive force which could excite not only hope, but could arouse certain mental states through the methodical application of this art of existence. Thus:

> The principle may be carried out, in a general way, by calming the mind when the body suffers from its excitement by arousing the feelings of Joy, Hope, and Faith, by suggesting motives for exertion by inducing regular mental work, especially composition, by diverting the patient's thoughts from his malady; and thus, in these and other ways, influencing beneficially the functions of Organic Life through the Mind. (ibid.: 416)

The underlying basis of 'moral therapy' as practised at 'The Retreat' was, for Tuke, an exemplar of the effective development of this art through its methodical application in the restoration of health. Interestingly the 'insanity' of the patients made them more amenable to this process because of the 'suggestibility' produced through the suspension of the will. This state Tuke viewed as being akin to a dream state, where the mind would lose its anchoring with external relations and create its own representations, feelings, perceptions, images and emotions (1892:35). This dream state was allied to ecstatic states, hallucinatory states and trance where the body would undergo physiological changes, the will would become suspended and the mind would become more 'automatic' and receptive to the commands of others. This was the ideal state for hypnosis to successfully occur and was also integral to the inducing of anaesthesia with an associated loss of bodily and psychic sensation.

It was this 'ecstatic state' through which Tuke also discussed the status and significance of hallucinations. A hallucinator was literally somebody who 'wandered in mind' and who created images and sensations without accompanying perception of any external stimuli. Tuke drew similarities with states of religious exaltation where through the focusing and absorption of the mind upon an idea, fantastic images and voices were credited with divine illumination or supernatural character. Tuke (1892:565) defined hallucination as 'a sensation perceived by the mind, whether through the sense of sight, hearing, smell, taste, or feeling, without any external cause capable of producing it'. He was clear that hallucinations per se were not signs of insanity; the problem arose when under certain conditions, voices or visions were credited with the status of reality and would therefore have a dictating force on subsequent action. In line with the emerging shifts occurring in clinical medicine in the late nineteenth century, voices and visions were a 'risk' because of the threat of irresponsible behaviour that may ensue.

Despite this resistance to 'medical materialism' from diverse sites and writers (James 1902, Parish 1897, Tuke 1872, 1892) it was psychiatry's intimate involvement with wider strategies of population management which privileged its knowledge of degeneracy, as being the set of understandings through which people were rendered and administered along its normalising axis. The dominance of biomedical modes of explanation was governmental, not philosophical.

They were linked with wider strategies of government concerned with governing individuals in relation to particular ways of understanding sociality and individuality. These 'truths' were established and circulated well beyond the practice of psychiatry itself, and were made possible by allied systems of explanation posed in relation to more general problems of social regulation.

It could be argued that this is why the 'problem of the will' was inserted into a clinical domain, and linked to notions of clinical and legal responsibility. The decisive debate within psychiatric practice was not so much how to divide the mind/brain, but how to adjudicate responsibility for criminal actions. This was especially pertinent in relation to the McNaughton case (1843) which stimulated intense discussion around the 'knowable subject' – how far did perpetrators know what they were doing? It was within this governmental problematic that the 'test of insanity' (Henderson and Gillespie 1927:502) created a space where psychiatric discourse intervened as the knowledge to adjudicate the 'mad' from the 'bad' (cf. Blackman and Walkerdine 2001). Madness was viewed as a disease of the will, estranging persons from sympathetic relations with the external world, thus destroying the moral sentiment and the ability to control one's behaviour, thought and conduct. Responsibility was explained in relation to a particular conception of human nature, where the phenomenon of volition, the choice to focus one's will, was viewed as essential to Enlightenment conceptions of man. The pinnacle of this humanisation process was the ability to self-govern; the highest form of will being self-control. Thus discussions around legal responsibility invoked these images where the 'other side' of the will, diseases of the mind, were seen to erase this capacity for self-governance and hence to render the perpetrator irresponsible for his/her actions.

Within this discursive complex voices were viewed as pseudo-sensory products of a diseased brain and were beginning to take up a privileged place within twentieth-century discussions concerning responsibility and risk. 'The 'problem of hallucination' was viewed as posing a problem of will. The diseased brain was viewed as releasing certain phenomena, such as voices and images which would come to dominate the person's behaviour and conduct. To hear voices was to present the potential risk of threatening and irresponsible behaviour that may ensue. Voices could 'take over' one's will, acting as a mandate for action. Tuke (1892:566) raises these concerns when discussing voice-hearing.

Voices are the most common, and when they assume the character of a mandate they become exceedingly serious. They are a fruitful source of homicidal and suicidal acts.

It was not until the inter-war years that these kinds of critiques of psychiatric understanding and practice were to play a part in the restructuring and reorganisation of the discipline. Miller and Rose (1986:4) argue that critiques of psychiatry 'have been of crucial significance in strategies for its modernisation and transformation'. These specific critiques were to be crucial in psychiatry's reflection on the categories it used to explain mental distress when confronted with forms of distress which did not seem to be amenable to biomedical intervention. In the next chapter we will begin to look at the rise of what was termed 'social psychiatry', and the new kinds of concepts and objects which were to create the possibility of a psychological space through the kinds of terms we now recognise.

6
The Invention of the Neuroses

This chapter will examine how the themes of degeneracy, and the particular kinds of biological explanations which underpinned them began to transform during the inter-war years. We will explore how the discursive field and the objects and concepts which articulated it, began to mutate, creating the possibility of a new territory of psychiatry. One of the main themes underlying this historical investigation of the 'problem of hallucination', is that there has always been a dependency between what we might term 'hard' (some version of the physical or biological) with 'soft' (some version of a psychological/psychic space) (Miller and Rose 1986). The interrelationship between these two shifting terms, and the allied discursive fields which give them meaning, has been a central focus of our examination. In this chapter we will begin to explore some of the internal restructuring and reorganisation which created the possibility of new objects and concepts, different relationships between the doctor and patient and different sites claiming the authority to intervene in relation to particular mental processes. These transformations are not made possible solely by processes internal to the discourse of psychiatry itself, nor solely by external factors, but as we have seen in the last two chapters, by a complex interweaving of both. This chapter will specifically focus upon critiques of psychiatry which, as Miller (1986:4) argues, 'have been of crucial significance in strategies for its modernisation and transformation'.

One of the most significant objects to emerge as part of the new psychiatric territory during the inter-war years, according to Rose (1986) and Armstrong (1983), was the 'Invention of the Neuroses'. It was the entering of the so-called 'normal mind' into the clinical domain, which restructured the dichotomy of the biological/environmental in relation to a division made between the psychotic and the neurotic. It was within this division that the concept of 'reaction types' or a different specification of the concept of 'individual differences' emerged. A popular text of this discursive formation was Henderson and Gillespie's (1927) *Textbook of Psychiatry*, which problematised the notion that madness was related to a core of degeneracy localised as a pathological lesion of the brain. These shifts were creating a new set of conceptual instruments for examining the individual, which no longer saw the 'case' as merely a way of detecting to what degree the individual had succumbed to a disease process. Rather the notion of the 'case' itself was used to raise questions about previous disease categories and why such varying clinical symptoms could arise from the same apparent cause (for example, dementia praecox). Henderson and Gillespie (1927:19) rethought degenerate modes of explanation in relation to a concept of 'types of reaction', which although retaining a notion of 'inherited disposition' was concerned more with how particular individuals reacted to their environments.

Reaction types

The concept of 'reaction types' brought together the notion that mental disorders were a complex manifestation of how an individual reacts to his/her environment. Within this conception there were varying degrees and types of reaction(s), which wove together the psychotic/neurotic distinction within which the problem of mental health was to be rethought psycho-geographically. Rather than environmental conditions only acting upon those with a prior degenerate constitution, the 'problem of mental health' was located within a space between the prior disposition of the individual and a set of environmental relations.

The examination of individual cases was still an important diagnostic tool, but was less about comparing individual symptoms with a general knowledge of disease processes. The Method of Examination shifted to an interrogation of an individual's prior vulnerability: family history, personal development and history of associated 'strangeness', to include a history of the present illness. As Henderson and Gillespie (1927:71) state: 'The date of the first deviation from the normal should be stated as accurately as possible, and then the development of the symptoms should be followed step by step.' The concept of 'bad' or 'tainted stock', which underlay theories of degeneracy was replaced by a notion of inherited disposition which could be inherited genetically or be a result of various 'accidents', such as birth traumas or problems in gestation. This was not a notion of inheritance, which viewed the individual as having a biologically inferior constitution, but as inheriting a vulnerability or 'risk' for particular kinds of reaction –

how well they can adjust to particular exigencies of life. Bleuler's (1923) conception of schizophrenia as a disease process becomes a type of reaction:

> The earliest of these may have begun in the unfertilised germ-plasm, another may have operated in utero, and the rest may be the reactions of an organism thus handicapped to the aids and obstacles which it subsequently meets in the environment in which it finds itself. (Henderson and Gillespie 1927:25)

Although the notion of heredity is still important, conceptually it does not maintain its privileged position in explanations of particular mental processes. The so-called reactions of the 'normal mind' (the neurotic) were related to psychotic reactions both quantitatively and qualitatively producing differing degrees of reaction. Both neurotic and psychotic processes were viewed as particular 'types of reaction to environment' (ibid.:397). These could include Affective-Reaction Types, Schizophrenic Reaction Types, Organic-Reaction Types as well as the psychoneuroses. The mind was to become a key object within this framework, signaling the fragility of this finely tuned apparatus, which could break down under certain stresses and strains. Its capacity to adjust to these relations was related to its inherited predisposition where 'psychotic reaction type(s) were still linked to diseased biological processes'. Neurotic reaction types were viewed more as exaggerations of the normal variants of behaviour. Armstrong (1983:31) argues that this enabled psychiatry to 'embrace variations ranging from gross madness to inconspicuous peculiarities of disposition'. In other words, it allowed for more and more aspects of behaviour, thought and conduct to be constituted as problems amenable to psychiatric intervention and explanation (cf. Rose 1988, *History of the Human Sciences*).

Psychiatry now had a new conceptual apparatus through which to address problems that had previously been constituted as 'diseases of civilisation'. We saw in the nineteenth century, prior to the sedimentation of eugenics strategies within psychiatric practice, the 'mind-in-error' had been the target of moral therapies. These practices targeted those whose reasoning processes were seen to have gone off the tracks. The concept of 'types of reaction' allowed for a way of addressing the precariousness and fragility of the mind in relation to the stresses and strains of the environment.

Although the individual case was to play a key role in detection, eugenics modes of explanation still underlay the psychotic reaction types. The fundamental conceptual distinction between neuroses and psychosis was the level of contact with the environment. The neuroses were a 'part reaction' where relations with the external world are still maintained. The ability to be responsible for oneself and others still guides conduct and behaviour.

Psychotic reaction types were quantitatively different. They signalled a progressive maladaptation of the individual to his/her environment, which could end in a state of dementia. This maladaptation could take a slow and insidious form, eventually regressing to a state where the moral sentiment – the capacity to maintain relations with the external world – is erased. Schizophrenic-reaction types could lose this intellectual and moral capacity, therefore no longer only signifying maladjustment but a constitutional defectiveness. This way of specifying sociality and individuality was one which had begun to be naturalised within the evolutionary theorising of the nineteenth century, as we saw in the last chapter. It was also embedded within the legal apparatus and had become a key distinction for judging criminal culpability. Losing this capacity subjected 'psychotic reaction types' to the domination of their own internal ravings and delusions. Signs of 'hearing voices' became a key concept to adjudicate the person's level of involvement with the external world.

> The schizophrenic patient no longer seeks to commune with his fellows, but lives instead in a world of his own. There is then no need for clear definition in thinking, and the very lack of clearness itself helps to make possible another of the conditions mentioned – that as much as possible his introverted world may be as his wishes dictate. (Henderson and Gillespie 1927:195)

The significance of 'hearing voices'

The 'problem of hallucination' had become a key test of insanity in the adjudication of the distinction between the neurotic and the psychotic reaction type.

> For a time, they may not exercise much influence, but often they dominate the patient so that the hallucinatory suggestions may be acted upon. It is frequently in response to such commands

that impulsive and violent acts are perpetuated. (Henderson and Gillespie 1927:192)

The 'problem of hallucination' was not merely a biomedical problem, but a problem of government and regulation. The experience of hearing voices was to take on a more and more privileged role in establishing the limits and boundaries of what is considered normal experience. Taking on a central role in adjudicating responsibility, hallucinations began to become more finely differentiated. It was not merely the 'hearing of voices' that presented an inherent 'risk'. As we will see it was necessary to more finely discriminate the experience in relation to a number of explanatory concepts. These included the 'soil' or foundation of the voices or images, which was seen to influence their organisational form. This division was operated through a simple/complex dichotomy, where 'toxic states' such as the effects of fever or alcohol were viewed as producing more simple forms, such as flashes of light. More complex forms were seen to be organised according to a delusional system seated within the mental state of the individual. This was seen to determine the content of the hallucination, and in turn to produce a reality status for the individual concerned. This was referred to as the 'colouring' of the hallucination and could take on a grandiose, persecutory or accusatory tone, with the risk of becoming mandatory.

Vividness was another concept through which the 'pseudo-hallucination' was differentiated from the hallucination (seen to signify an inherent risk). Vividness was another measure of how well a person was oriented towards the external world. Thus, paradoxically, as madness became located within an internal subjective space, it was the observation of certain behaviours which was to provide a measure of the person's contact or involvement with the external world. Psychiatrists were to attend to so-called evidence of this through observing the person's listening attitude, whether he or she talked aloud, and were to make active responses to hallucinatory commands. Despite the increasing differentiation of hallucinations, the fundamental distinction was the level of recognition, i.e. how able were they to pronounce upon their own condition, and recognise their own madness. Pseudo-hallucinations were those which did not command a reality-status for the individual, thus: 'The patient has the vivid sensory experience, but realises that it has no external foundation' (Henderson and Gillespie 1927:93).

As we can see, hallucinatory experience was to cross the divide between 'physiogenic' and 'psychogenic' explanations (ibid.:90). 'Psychogenic' explanations viewed hallucinatory experience as repressed wishes forcing their way into consciousness, appearing to come from outside; 'assuming an external sensory appearance', as opposed to 'physiogenic' explanations which viewed hallucinations as pseudo-sensory products of a diseased brain (ibid.:91). Within 'psychogenic' explanations hallucinations were allied with altered states of consciousness such as sleep and other dream-like states, such as somnambulism, twilight states, trances, stupor and delirium; a state of dissociation. This space was constituted as a psychological space related to the mental processes of the normal mind. The concept of the neurotic was the term used to distinguish this space from more biological explanations. As Rose (1986a:47) highlights, the neuroses 'were mild mental disturbances that were sufficient to cause social inefficiency and personal unhappiness, although they did not disable the individual completely'.

However, the fear was that if the neuroses were left untreated they could develop, as they were quantitatively and qualitatively related to the psychoses. Rose (1986a:43) argues that this created a new role for psychiatric discourse, penetrating further and further into the lives of individuals, where 'it is increasingly in psychiatric and psychological terms that we think and talk about our personal unhappiness'. As we will see, this created new sites claiming authority to act upon experiences now understood in psychological and psychiatric terms, as well as new objects and ways of understanding these objects as psychiatric phenomena. Armstrong (1983:66) makes a similar argument about the role and function of psychiatry in the twentieth century.

> The new psychiatric gaze was not so much concerned with the examination and celebration of the individual case but with the ever-changing limits of normal variability within the community.

The constitution of the neuroses as a psychiatric and psychological object took psychiatry beyond the asylum walls and into a social community space. Psychiatry became interlinked with a set of newly emerging governmental strategies concerned less with the targeting and detection of degeneration, and more with identifying those who could not adjust to their environments. The 'mental hygiene movement' targeted for example, 'problem children' and the 'feebleminded'. These terms were those used to denote people who were not efficiently and effectively adjusting to their environments (usually institutional such as schools – cf. Rose 1985). These 'problems of maladjustment' were viewed as minor disturbances which were treatable.

> Psychiatry should not focus upon the confinement of the small number of psychotically deranged persons. To fulfil the task that society required, it needed to shift its attention to the detection and treatment of those large numbers of the population who were now known to be liable to neurotic breakdown, maladjustment, inefficiency and un-employability on the grounds of poor mental health. (Rose 1986a:62)

With the extension of psychiatric knowledge into more and more practices of the social, new sites emerged to deal with these more minor disturbances of mental health. These were to include the 'mental hospital', as opposed to the clinics of the nineteenth century, and institutions such as the Tavistock, which provided for both the psychoses and neuroses. The notion of the clinic was not simply that people suffering from mental distress should be confined within biomedical settings. It was argued that people should be able to gain knowledge about mental disturbance and be educated and educate themselves in the detection of those signs of mental disturbance, which were considered curable. Rose (1986a:52) argues that this shift in the conceptualisation of mental distress, and shifting governmental strategies targeting the population, articulated mental health as 'a personal responsibility and national responsibility'. These shifts also accorded a more privileged role for psychological explanations and expertise. As we have seen throughout the last two chapters, the notion of a psychological space has existed, articulated in different ways and producing the possibility of particular kinds of self-understanding and practice, throughout the historical period we have been exploring. What was important within this set of historical circumstances was the ways in which new objects were created which were viewed as amenable solely to psychological intervention. These objects, such as the neuroses, then became the target of different kinds of theories, explanations, interventions and professional groupings. These objects were then distributed across a range of practices and professional groupings, some of whom were at odds with biological explanations, and some of which struck up new alliances with the psychiatric profession. So far we have looked at the tapestry of some of these explanations. Now let us turn to some of the events and exigencies which led to the problem of mental health, and particularly the 'problem of hallucination', being posed in a radically different way.

Psychoses and psychoneuroses in war

Rose (1986a) and Armstrong (1983) both argue that the First World War was a significant 'event' for producing the possibilities of a reformulation of the mind as a psychological apparatus to re-enter the clinical domain. Psychoanalytic concepts and theories became important techniques and practices for conceptualising this space and working with particular kinds of mental processes. Even though Freud had been writing in the early 1900s, in the midst of theories of degeneracy, the kinds of concepts and explanatory structures central to his theories had not been deployed within psychiatric knowledge and practice. It was to take a particular experience, the experience of 'shell-shock', following the First World War for psychoanalysis to be considered a possible effective treatment for some forms of mental disturbance. Before discussing how this transformation was specifically made possible, I want to consider the ways in which a particular kind of psychological space was created through psychoanalytic structures and concepts.

In 1900 Freud wrote his first edition of *The Interpretation of Dreams*. This book brought together his conceptualisation of the mind, and various techniques through which it could be identified and made intelligible. As Freud proclaims:

> If I were asked what is the theoretical value of the study of dreams, I should reply that it lies in the additions to psychological knowledge and the beginnings of an understanding of the neuroses which we thereby obtain. (Freud 1932:15, 3rd edn)

Freud argued that the neuroses were a manifestation of the normal mind and its devious workings. Freud related dreams to other psychic phenomena such as delusions and obsessions, which were linked to 'more comprehensive problems of psychopathology' (ibid.:15). It was this linking of various psychic formations within a psychological space which opened up an ethereal space beyond the imagination, within which to think about the problem(s) of mental disorder.

The 'dream problem' prior to Freud was made intelligible either within a supernatural framework, where the dream was a message from a Divine source, having inspirational or prophetic qualities, or within a biological framework. Biological explanations posited the dream as a release of unwanted impulses and energies collected through the course of a day; a 'superfluous reaction' (ibid.:88). Freud accredited the dream with personal significance and meaning and identified it as 'the royal road to the unconscious' – the psychic space existing beyond the contingencies of time and materiality.

Freud conceptualised a whole 'other realm' of life, beyond the waking state, which could even break through, in the form of other 'dream-like phenomena' such as hallucinations and slips of the tongue. For Freud, the 'waking state' oriented the mind towards the operations of reason and intellect. It was through dreaming that these conventions were relaxed, and the workings of the unconscious came into play. 'The imaginative life, already relaxed from the control of reason and intellect, was seen to be no longer held together by psychical and physical stimuli, but is left to its own uncontrolled and confused divagations' (ibid.:56). With a relaxing of the focusing of attention, the unconscious takes centre-stage, assuming fantastical forms. The will, being the voluntary power which in the so-called normal waking state guides the flow of ideas, is suspended, and the unconscious redirects the mind. We can see here that Freud is drawing on some of the terms and concepts which were central to the ways in which the mind was conceptualised at the time, for example, the will, intellect, imagination and so forth. However, the fundamental differentiation Freud was making was in the relative autonomy of this psychological space independently of the workings of the brain.

> Everything that might show that the psychic life is independent of demonstrable organic changes, or spontaneous in its manifestations is alarming to the contemporary psychiatrist, as though such an admission must mean a return to the old-world natural philosophy and the metaphysical conception of the nature of the soul. (ibid.:56)

Rather than dreams being a gateway to a metaphysical realm, the dream is viewed as freeing the mind from the chains of sensory life, producing strange, absurd, illogical and incoherent associations. This was a very different way of articulating, what had been conceptualised as the delirium and error of madness in the eighteenth and nineteenth century. Madness was constituted as a form of communication, a dialogue; albeit a different form of language to the reason and intellect of everyday life. An interesting and pertinent discussion in Freud's writings revolves around the ethical sense in dreams. The question that Freud addresses is concerned with whether the moral nature of man persists in dreams. This problem was posed in relation to ideas that the dream represented a primitive re-emerging of an earlier stage of mental life. Freud argued that 'the fundamental element of human nature, the moral essence is too firmly fixed' (1932:79). We can see here that Freud was reproducing a particular form of individuality and sociality as natural, tied to human nature, in line with some of the wider views incorporated into a range of practices of the social at this time. Although in dreaming, the ethical sense still persisted, Freud made a primary link between dreams and mental diseases. He argued that there was an intimate connection between dreams, neuroses and the psychoses. As stated, dreams were viewed as a form of delirium. Freud went so far as to say, ' We may say that we are working towards the explanation of the psychoses when we endeavour to elucidate the mystery of dreams' (ibid.:102).

The neuroses and psychoses were viewed as dream-like phenomena, insanity viewed as a waking dream. These symptoms had hidden meanings, the analysis of which could lead one to the origin of the disturbance. This was a psychic problem, which through a process of interpretation would relieve individuals of their symptoms. Hallucinations related to transformations of ideas, originating within the psychic realm of the individual. Hallucinations were therefore, according to Freud, distortions or displacements of unconscious wishes and memories. However, despite the radical rethinking of the mind that Freud produced, and the possibilities it provided for the blurring of the distinction between abnormality and normality – the blending of the psychic with the biological – Freud's theories were not incompatible with evolutionary theories. He suggests that,

> dreaming is on the whole an act of regression to the earliest relations of the dreamer ... Behind this childhood of the individual we are then promised an insight into the phylogenetic child-

hood, into the evolution of the human race, of which the development of the individual is only an abridged repetition influenced by the fortuitous circumstances of life. (1932:506)

The problem of psychopathology for Freud, although linking the neuroses and psychoses through his formulation of the mind as a psychological apparatus, was still linked to evolution, through the ways in which these experiences harped back to earlier forms of existence. Although this conceptual apparatus blurred the boundaries between normality and pathology it still did not take on a diagnostic pertinence in nineteenth-century psychiatric practice. The transfer of the mind to a clinical field was to occur in relation to the problem of shell-shock or what was also known as wartime neuroses.

Traumatic neuroses

The late War taught several valuable psychiatric lessons, although it produced no novel type of mental disorder. It proved with great prodigality of example, that purely psychological factors can produce mental illness. (Henderson and Gillespie 1927: 464)

The hysterical phenomena associated with war neuroses posed particular problems for the specific kinds of biological explanation embedded within biomedical psychiatry. Hysterical symptoms within these conceptualisations could only be viewed as signs of a progressive brain disorder. 'Certain types of illness appeared in unexpected forms. Of special note was the occurrence of dementia apparently without residual deterioration' (ibid.:464). The notion of 'individual reactions' restructured the way symptoms were understood. One could react to life circumstances in a variable number of ways. 'In many cases "dementia-praecox" is the psychological reaction of an individual to his environmental differences, rather than that which regards it as the mental manifestation of some obscure "metabolic" disorder or structural degeneration' (ibid.:465).

Even though the notion of different kinds of psychological reaction became part of psychiatric theorising, the problem of shell-shock still centred on whether certain men were more constitutionally predisposed to shell-shock, and was it this core of vulnerability which determined the degree and type of reaction? Henderson and Gillespie (1927) operate this distinction when discussing the psychoses in war. They offer some explanations, which articulate notions of prior vulnerability: 'Insane heredity, psychopathic predisposition, previous mental illness, mental deficiency, moral imbecility and excessive alcoholism' (ibid.:468). Those who exhibited psychotic reactions according to Henderson and Gillespie were not likely to benefit from psychoanalysis, the technique which became increasingly important in relation to the neuroses. The use of suggestion and persuasion could act upon a space of suggestibility, but psychotic reactions producing a greater detachment from reality could not be 'readjusted'.

The psychoneuroses were exaggerations, minor variations, whereas psychotic reactions were of a more fundamental nature. Although they were linked it was the nature of the link which was to set the terms of debate of contemporary psychiatric discourse. Within the ambiguities and contradictions to structure this intersection, 'hearing voices' crossed the normal/pathological divide, being both psychogenic and biological in origin. Although the 'normal mind' had entered psychiatric discourse, there increasingly became a greater concern with the brain as an inefficient instrument effacing the capacity to be a competent citizen. The space of the psychological was a space of infinite possibilities of reaction, where the person still maintained external relations with the world. Because of the blurring between normality and pathology, it was difficult to maintain the notion that there were distinct disease processes, rather than 'types of reaction'. However, a concern grew with those who were not able to manage themselves, to self-govern; as Bleuler (1923:171) suggests; 'As far as the concept of insanity has become at all practical, it rests not on medical or psychopathological criteria, but on the idea of social incapacity.'

> A slight disturbance in the psychic mechanism can change the strongest man into a pitiable object of care or into a dangerous enemy of society. It is for this reason that the psychoses attain their social importance much more than other diseases. They spread their harm to wider circles and thus rob the patient himself of his independence in all his relations to his fellowmen. He can no longer maintain himself and he loses his qualifications as a legal subject. (ibid.:226)

Despite psychiatric concern with minor instances of mental disturbances it was not until after the Second World War and the 1950s
and 1960s that psychiatric techniques for acting upon the 'normal'
mind proliferated. A social psychiatry emerged with an increasing
concern with an individual's ability to cope with the stresses and
exigencies of the environment. It will be argued that the very critiques of psychiatry which flourished in the Fifties and Sixties made
possible a whole new set of objects and ways of thinking and acting
upon them. As Rose (1987:57) highlights:

> The post-war modernisation of psychiatry was a positive
> strategy, not a mere victimisation for financial savings. What
> was at stake was a new way of thinking about mental distress, a
> new way of linking it to social ills, and a new way of practising
> in relation to it.

In the next section we will begin to examine the nature of some of
these critiques, which played their part in the transformation of the
practice, laying the conceptual terrain for the psychiatric and
psychological landscape we now recognise in the present.

Beyond sensibility – a journey to enlightenment

> Everyone exists in an environment, the most important part
> of which consists of other people, so psychiatry encompasses
> relations between people. (Crown 1970:1)

The post-war period involved another significant shift and transformation in psychiatric discourse. The concern was with a new
object, normality, and its variations in relation to one's exigencies
of life. Psychiatry was to become an apparatus for managing the
normal individual as well as what were seen as gross instances of
abnormality – 'how and why things go wrong for people' (Crown
1970:1). The conceptual distinction between the neurotic and psychotic was to become more blurred. The concept of 'types of
reaction' shifted to the concept of personality. This was articulated
as the site of the expression of an individual's reaction to a set of
environmental relations. The personality was the locus of possible
breakdown in functioning, which included the expression of this
breakdown, and the subjective or phenomenological experience of
that breakdown for the individual concerned.

'Breakdown in functioning' was still linked to a person's inborn potential. The notion of personality and its predisposition to breakdown was linked to prior vulnerability; for example, whether the personality would merely become exaggerated or disintegrate altogether. The terms of the debate through which 'malfunctioning' was made intelligible was articulated through a dualism between the individual and the environment. Genetics and particular biological explanations were deployed to understand prior vulnerability.

Psychoanalytic ideas had taken up a place within psychiatric discourse allowing for a phenomenological approach to symptoms. Symptoms were not viewed as expressions of distinct clinical pictures, such as dementia praecox, melancholia and so on and so forth. Psychoanalytic concepts created a psychological space which was constituted as a space of infinite possible reactions, each intelligible only in relation to the person's own psychic reality – their own experience of 'symptoms' which could be conscious, or exist below the conscious threshold of awareness. The disease model of psychiatry was problematised. People were not merely automatons, but interacted in a social world of meanings. Human subjectivity was viewed as far more complex than the kinds of understandings of subjectivity which underpinned biomedical psychiatry. The focus was on understanding a person's constant struggle to adapt to this social world of meanings and people. As Crown (1970:9) argues,

> But psychology and psychiatry are not physiology. They take over where physiology leaves off. The light impulses activate parts of the cerebral cortex of the brain, but we see a landscape of trees, fields, light and shade. No conceivable combination of light impulses can be used to compare my experience, as a town dweller when I look at an exquisite view in the Lake District, with that of the reader who has lived there always and to whom such a view is familiar.

'Malfunctioning' could be expressed in a number of ways. The distinctions between the neurotic and the psychotic were deployed as measures of severity. Neurotic reactions were seen as mild personality disturbances, importantly still maintaining full contact with reality – the disrupted personality. However, there were other types of personality, which under stress would disintegrate – the schizophrenic type. They were viewed as more likely to break down under minor stress, and for the reactions to be more severe and chronic.

This greater potential for breakdown was viewed as originating in the 'inborn potential' – the genetic vulnerability, which was viewed as setting the limits of their functioning.

> A young person with considerably genetically determined potential will break down under a relatively minor stress, while a person with less schizophrenia potential will not do so; he or she will need considerably greater stress to precipitate this condition. (ibid.:98)

Ironically, although the psychiatric apparatus was concerned with coping – the ways people were resilient in the face of adversity, and those conditions viewed as facilitating breakdown, such as the family, a central focus was still with those types who were not equipped biologically with the capacities to deal with stress. The schizophrenic type was constituted as one who was not equipped with the capacity to maintain contact with external relations. This 'lack' was constituted either through genetic discourses, or with a focus on those conditions of life, which had not allowed them to develop a 'healthy ego'. Here we can see psychoanalytic concepts being incorporated into some of the language and explanatory structures of psychiatric discourse.

> It seems possible that at least part of the disturbance in schizophrenia for example the terrible auditory hallucinations, are related to the permanent inability of the weak ego to distinguish what is within from what is without, i.e. to 'test reality'. (ibid.:60)

The key distinction of 'insanity' was to become a person's capacity to judge between internal and external reality. It was in relation to this capacity that hallucinations were to act as 'tests of insanity'. The hearing of voices was not considered a symptom in and of itself of madness, rather the test was whether persons believed in their reality. Howells (1968:230) argues for a subtle redefinition of psychiatry's definition of hallucinations, a 'belief in a reasonably vivid, integrated perception that occurs in the absence of appropriate stimuli'. The conceptual apparatus shifted and changed in relation to this new problem, of how to distinguish the reality-status of voices from those which a person knew were not 'real'. A key concern therefore was with differentiating a person's belief or relation to the voices. Voices and images were not essentially pathological, and as will be discussed could be produced under a number of conditions.

Let us now look at some of the historical circumstances which played a key role in the restructuring and reorganisation of psychiatric discourse following the Second World War. As well as broader debates about human subjectivity, and how to understand the subtleties of what it means to be human, there were also sustained critiques of the role and functioning of psychiatry, particularly in its biomedical mode, which played a part in its transformation. Rose (1987) argues these critiques were launched at four levels: therapeutic, political, theoretical and juridical. Some of these critiques especially in relation to the phenomenon of hearing voices will now be examined to show the contingency of the 'new' postwar social psychiatry.

The making of a mystic

Within a particular set of historical conditions, what might broadly be termed a 'humanist and existential vogue', the 'schizophrenic reaction' was viewed as an attempt to adapt to an alienated environment. The schizophrenic types were viewed as those who had successfully adapted. These reverse discourses or counter discourses argued that the 'hearing of voices' was part of an experience of expansion – signs of a 'new world'. Enlightenment, the process of humanisation, was seen to have excluded a whole range of other experiences, which were viewed as part of man's evolutionary development. Man's ability to estrange himself from the external world was the key to this development. Within this reverse discourse, hallucinations became allied again with other states of consciousness such as somnambulism, dreaming, trances and ecstasy. The hallucinated state was an ecstatic state of consciousness, the soil to free the imagination to explore an illusory, expansive space. It was this state of consciousness which was viewed as one of the highest forms of human experience and not merely an atavistic return to a 'precivilised' mode of existence. Within this discursive configuration, 'schizophrenic types' were viewed as possessing an exceptional gift or sensitivity, not 'schizophrenic types' but 'sensitive types'.

Wallace (1959:58) echoes some of these understandings when considering varying cultural responses to hallucinatory experience(s). He similarly argued that hallucinations were not pathological in and of themselves. He argues that although hallucinations were viewed as a symptom of mental disorder, this was 'neither a necessary nor a sufficient condition for such a diagnosis'. He argued that the psychiatric definition was over-inclusive. It conceptually included other forms of imagery and perception, such as dreaming and hypnogogic imagery. He also cites a whole range of conditions within which the hearing of voices or seeing of visions occurs: 'Sleep, Fatigue, Hunger and Thirst, Prolonged Physical Pain, Extreme Physical Illness, Social Isolation, Special Exercises (breath control, posture, sensory restriction), Drugs, Emotional Stress in normal persons, Mental Illness' (ibid.:62).

However, as has been discussed, it was individuals' relationship to their voices which was deemed crucial within psychiatric discourse. For Wallace (1959:58) it was the psychiatric definition which caused specific responses to the experience which may lead to other forms of mental distress. He suggests:

> It is likely that in some cultural sub-groups in our society the nature of definition and response to hallucination entertained by hallucination and his associates may aggravate or precipitate other mental disabilities indeed, the mental patient may suffer from added anxiety precisely because of the nature of the definition of hallucinatory experience which he entertained prior to experiencing it himself.

The subjective experience of hearing voices or seeing visions was thus seen to be circumscribed by a negative societal attitude to distortions in sensory or auditory experience; a determined cultural response. Within this reversal of psychiatry's modes of explanation the hallucination produces the madness and not vice versa. The 'Western attitude(s)' is thus one which conveys contempt, pity, anxiety, shame, fear and self-doubt, rather than as Wallace (1959) describes, the positive emotional responses within other cultural settings. Wallace (1959:67) asks

> how much anxiety, self-appreciation, and cognitive distortion are added to the miseries of mental patients by the circumstance that they have learned to fear waking hallucinations in the course of living in a society in which waking hallucinations experience is almost uniformly negatively valued.

These criticisms were being made in the context of a more general critique of psychiatry as 'culture bound'. Within this framework, the key concept differentiating the hallucinated state from other states of consciousness was the psychiatric definition. This was viewed as an arbitrary judgement, which had profound consequences for the person hearing voices. The hallucinated state was realigned with other ecstatic states whose common feature was a loss of sensibility (Laski 1961), a moment of internal reverie. This state was exalted and revered, viewed as providing access to a whole range of creative experiences. Texts such as Gowan's (1975) *Trance, Art and Creativity* argued that the pejorative term 'hallucination' actually related to a protataxic mode – a trance state which was necessary for creativity.

> Hallucinations appear to occur under all types of trance experience, spirit possession, mediumship, shamanism, hypnosis, psychoactive drugs, and sensory deprivation. They also appear to occur rather uniquely outside of trance to 'normal' persons where there is sufficient psychic pressure (such as the death of a friend or relative). Whether one is dealing with the voices of spirit possession, and mediumship, the magical lights and other out-of-body experiences of the shaman, the induced hallucinations of the hypnotist, the psychedelic colours of the drug-user or similar visual imagery in sensory deprivation, the diversity and universality of such imagery is evident. (Gowan 1975:128)

The weakening of ego boundaries – the loss of sensibility – was thus given a positive evaluation, and not viewed merely as a sign of pathological functioning. It was viewed as a gift which can be developed and which is viewed as the next step in evolutionary development. Laski (1961) redefines Virginia Woolf's writings as accounts of ecstasy, where she is viewed as having an extra-special sensitivity. These states are merely altered states and not pathological states of consciousness. These ecstatic states were thus linked to forms of mystical experience, which previously within psychiatry had been constituted as 'abnormal phenomena'. Rejecting this view of the normal subject underpinning psychiatric discourse, these reverse discourses argued that the goal was to become something 'other' than Enlightenment man. As Greeley (1974:7) argues:

> If mystics are not complete madmen if they are not raving lunatics, then there are other dimensions to life than our commonplace, commonsense everyday technological world view would be willing to concede.

Developing ecstatic states of consciousness was not only expansive, part of one's personal development or self-actualisation, but was part of a broader despair with the materialism seen to surround both psychiatry and the nature of society. There was seen to be a general dissatisfaction with the promise of modernity; science actually producing some of the worst atrocities of inhumanity rather than the humane truths it concealed under its banner of progress.

> The release of atomic energy in 1945, the discovery of the environmental crisis in the middle 1960s, the ethnic, religious and racial wars that have ravaged the world for the last quarter century have all shaken the faith many of us shared that salvation would be achieved through the scientific methodology and technology. (Greeley 1974:113)

This malaise was seen to provide the setting for a new model of ethics or salvation based on neither religion nor science, but an ethics of 'personal development'. This 'mystical revival' was associated with the voice of Timothy Leary – 'tune in, turn on and drop out' – and was viewed as a despair with changing the world – a feeling of alienation and powerlessness. These reverse discourses promulagated particular techniques and practices for producing ecstatic states of consciousness central to this ethics of 'personal development'. One condition of possibility for this transformation of selfhood came from the use of psychedelics or mind-expanding drugs such as LSD or mescaline. According to many proponents such as Weil (1973:13) the use of mind-altering substances was part of a 'positive psychic development'. It was actually processes of socialisation which were seen to constitute these experiences as anti-social. Ecstatic states were again viewed as one of the highest forms of experience, where drugs provided one of the most direct means of access. Psychosis was viewed as one such state, which was realigned to other 'doors in the wall'.

> Sleep and daydreaming are examples of altered states of consciousness as are trance, hypnosis, meditation, general anaesthesia, delirium, psychosis, mystic rapture, and the various chemical 'high'. (Weil 1973:31)

Weil (1973) divided waking or so-called normal consciousness from ecstatic states, by invoking a reversal of the usual modes of evaluation. Normal consciousness was part of 'straight land' and 'stoned thinking' or 'stonesville', was the natural part of our consciousness which 'straightland' excluded. 'Stoned thinking' involved going beyond the intellect, i.e., relinquishing self-control to an internal or non-ordinary reality; the realm of the psyche or the unconscious mind. The neuroses were viewed as a normal phase of this psychic development, the channel through which the corporeal body could be influenced.

> If the subject in a good trance is touched by a finger represented to him as a piece of hot metal, an alternative blister will develop at the point of contact. The blister is real. It is produced by an enervation of superficial blood vessels. And this channel between the mind and body is wide open whenever we are in an altered state of consciousness that focuses our awareness on something other than our ego and intellect. (Weil 1973:160)

'Schizophrenic-types' were those who possessed the secret or potential of creative genius through which to achieve these states. The gift was viewed as exceptionally strong – ironically the hospital setting providing a totally disenfranchising condition within which to integrate the experience. This notion derived its intelligibility from the 'LSD experience'. Drugs such as LSD had been seen to provide only the potentialities of certain experiences, what was deemed important was the 'guide' and 'setting' for how these experiences were experienced. The psychedelic experience was viewed as a journey which was influenced by the guide – a person who could stimulate feelings of trust, stability and emotional serenity, and the setting – an environment which would positively influence the experience (Masters and Houston 1966).

Hospital and clinical settings were viewed as drab and antiseptic; what was needed was a home-like setting to evoke desired responses. Anti-psychiatric drugs and psychiatry as an institution were viewed as obstacles to harnessing this creative potential of 'schizophrenic-types'. As Weil (1973:181) expounds, 'every psychotic is a potential sage or healer and to the extent that negative sychotics are burdens to society, to the extent can positive psychotics be assets'.

Doors in the wall

The discussions surrounding the uses and abuses of chemical substances such as LSD brought together some of the pertinent questions of the time, raised within a scientific framework. The question of whether there was a realm beyond sensibility, or were certain experiences merely by-products of a disordered and abnormal brain, was posed within some of the terms and concepts we have just been discussing.

As Stevens (1993) writes in a historical drama charting the role of LSD, questions which had been persistently raised within different texts and sites about the nature of the mind, for example, different ways of mapping a psychological space (i.e. Tuke 1872), were now being addressed through very different terms and categories. Questions which Stevens (1993:17) illustrates were now linked to man's potential to consciously evolve himself. Questions such as: Can we consciously evolve ourselves? Does a magic trigger exist that is capable of shooting the species forward a few increments? Is there a door in the mind we can pass through? And if there is, does a key exist capable of opening that door?

The notion of another world, a realm existing beyond materiality and corporeality, has of course always been the province of religious and mystical frameworks of explanation. However the dialogue between religion and science, the physical and psychological, has always been consititued through very different terms and concepts, given meaning through allied discursive fields. Were visions, voices, trances, etc. evidence of the 'self' transcending itself to 'another realm', the realm of mystic life, or are these experiences simply signs of a bodily disease? Underhill (1911:320) asks, 'would St Francis of Assisi show the marks of a saint or marks of physical abnormality?' As she decries:

> The beautiful reveries of Suso, the divine visitations experienced by Francis, Catherine, Theresa, and countless other saints, have been degraded in the course of their supposed elevation to the sphere called 'supernatural' – a process as fatal to their truth and beauty as the stuffing of birds. (ibid.:321)

Voices and Visions are signs of this ecstatic state, to be contemplated and translated. Voices and visions are within this framework of paramount importance, and part and parcel of the mystical life. Hallucinations are the veil through which the 'other realm' commands to be known; as Underhill (1911:321) suggests: 'The messengers of the invisible world knock persistently at the doors of the senses.'

It was the themes which had circumscribed these mystical modes of explanation which were to be reinserted and translated into a psychological space. A key concept associated with the seminal writings of Huxley centred around the door. The brain was viewed as a safety valve, reducing the flow of possible activity. However, beyond this valve of so-called normal consciousness lay a whole other world akin to Buckes' (1901) cosmic consciousness (in Shortt 1986); the world of Jungian archetypes (Jung 1978) and the Freudian unconscious. Bringing together psychoanalytic concepts with psychiatric terms and concepts, Huxley (1961) claimed that certain experiences may be doors to higher states of consciousness, which were not only life-enhancing but encompassed an evolutionary potential for changing man and the societal space in which he was immersed.

Stevens (1993) argues that Huxley was an important figure because he made links with research within psychiatry in the Forties and Fifties, which was investigating the apparent links between the model psychosis seen to be induced by LSD and the nature (aetiology) of schizophrenia. Huxley argued in relation to his own experience of mescaline intoxication which he believed produced a state of 'oneness', or cosmic consciousness. Through the concatenation of psychoanalysis and psychopharmacology he argued that LSD should be viewed as a psychedelic tool and not a psychotimimetic (a model of psychosis). It could be the key to these veiled higher states, providing a door to these scientifically uncharted states of mind.

The counter culture

It was within the widening context of the Sixties that Huxley's peripheral ideas were taken on board, within an emerging counter-culture. As Stevens (1993) argues, with sociological studies in the Fifties of the desire to conform, and its renegades – the disenchanted rebels portrayed by James Dean and Marlon Brando, a space was created for an alienated youth who understood themselves through psychological modes of explanation. These discourses operated within a discursive field where the concept of self-actualisation was declared positive for one's psychological health (Greeley 1974). The 'normal' mind was capable of actualising beyond the exigencies of its immediate environment and needs (Maslow 1968). The 'normal mind' thus became a problem to be worked upon and transformed. Within the psycho-sciences an oppositional discourse was in play which relied upon a rethinking of human nature. Man was no longer an automaton, a mere product of his environment. Rather there was viewed an essential part of man which had been repressed and neglected by the rigidly defined lifestyles of the immediate post-war years. This core of the person became an object of a range of discursive explanations within the psycho-sciences (cf. Kelly 1955). It was linked with two concepts: growth and development, whereby a person's subjectivity became something to produce, discover, understand or utilise, to move beyond immediate environmental constraints. Maslow as early as 1954 had suggested that persons were primarily motivated to move beyond immediate physiological needs. Within his conceptualisation of a 'hierarchy of needs', the pinnacle and ultimate aim was to move towards self-actualisation. This embodied an attitude of attending to one's creative talents and aspirations, an inner directedness which would allow one to achieve one's full potential.

These modes of explanation were embodied by humanist theories within psychology, where the person was viewed as governed by self-fulfilling tendencies (Rogers 1961). Rather than conformity, individualism was celebrated. Each person spoke from his or her own experience of the world, thus subjectivity was specific and needed to be understood as such. These notions, which came from a phenomenological understanding of the person, entered psychological discourse in various ways. This occurred within a broad theoretical problematisation of positivism within psychology which within social psychology came to be known as the crisis (Armistead 1974) (cf. Chapter 3). Within these critiques individuals and their understandings of the world were placed centre stage, demanding alternative methodologies and modes of psychological inquiry. These critiques culminated in a new paradigm in the Eighties, where the specifics of human inquiry produced a range of alternative methods of inquiry (cf. Reason and Rowan 1981).

Within the area of personality theorising Rogers (1961) published a text entitled *On Becoming A Person*. Rogers' theories centred around the core 'real' or 'true' self, which for many people, he argued, had become estranged due to societal pressures. He offered a therapeutic system through which a person could facilitate and nurture this core self, thus becoming a person. The healthy and well-adjusted personality was one which was self-realising and self-actualising. To adapt, develop, grow and become oneself was a life-enhancing process. These modes of explanation became known as the 'third force' in American psychology and became incorporated into a human potential movement (Maslow 1968). This movement became linked into a set of oppositional discourses ranging from critiques of psychiatry's repressive and custodial functioning, the medical model within psychiatry (Laing 1960, 1967), ethnocentrism within Western psychiatry (Cochrane 1977), as well as a broader cultural movement made up of different groups attempting to resist 'straight' or mainstream society.

It was within this constellation that LSD research had brought these wider themes into a scientific laboratory context. These questions, as has been illustrated, were being asked in relation to a set of chemical agents, which by some were viewed as providing a portal into this underdeveloped human potential – a state of consciousness beyond self-consciousness. The mystical religious framework had been reworked within a psychological landscape. The contours of this space were to play a key role in the transformation of psychiatric discourse in relation to the new objects made possible within these broader reverse discourses.

The emergence of a psychological space

There had been significant events throughout the history of psychiatric discourse that had provided the conditions of possibility for the entering of the 'normal mind' into psychiatric discourse. From the writings of Freud (1900) to the phenomenon of battle neuroses, and then to a widening interest in the cultural specificity of Western psychiatry's claims, certain experiences which had previously been viewed as signs of degeneracy and organic malfunctioning were becoming viewed as part of a spectrum of possible human experience. These spaces, as we have seen, are not continuous, and are created through very different kinds of concepts and explanatory structures.

However, despite the new philosophy of the mind to come out of the psychedelic movement it was only on the fringes that these techniques and modes of understanding were deployed in relation to those suffering mental distress. For these radicals such as Laing and Cooper, madness was a journey, a trip which a person must travel through in order to integrate certain experiences into his/her world. One such account of this journey is *Journey Through Madness* (Barnes and Berke 1971) where Mary describes her journey from darkness to light, a rite of purification, which enabled her to 'come up' from her psychosis. Her psychosis was viewed as a reaction to a set of circumstances which had alienated her 'real self'. As Berke proclaims when discussing the specifics of Mary's journey(s);

I don't think the label 'mad' does justice to Mary or for that matter, to any person who may manifest himself in a way that a stranger would consider peculiar. Nothing that Mary experienced, nothing that she went through is far removed from what we all have to cope with in ourselves. That Mary confronted her physical, psychic or spiritual demons may mean that she was just more in touch with them than most people. (ibid.:349)

In relation to the questions proffered at the beginning of this section regarding the existence of a meaningful and enhancing space beyond the body, one can see that the parameters of the debate are set within divisions which have mutated from the early physical/moral dichotomy, to the contemporary bio–social–psychological jigsaw (see chapter 2). Biomedical psychiatry and its charting of a domain of degeneracy viewed ecstatic states and experiences as pathological reactions of an abnormal or diseased brain. Paradoxically this division had set the boundaries for a dispersal of reverse discourses, which claimed that these experiences are actually part of a range of possibilities for experience. Hearing voices and seeing visions fluctuate across this division and at the extreme limits may either be first-rank symptoms of schizophrenia, or evidence of an ecstatic state, or even of spirit possession (Lewis 1971).

In relation to the role of LSD or other agents which are actively sought out to induce certain states, such as hearing voices, the following quote raises the concerns which were made by many in relation to this view. Discussing the relation between certain drug-induced states and the visionary experience of ancient Middle Eastern cults, McDermott warns (1971:xii):

The question for serious consideration is whether drug taking and similar techniques may not represent both an atavistic return to the cults of primitive societies and an irresponsible reawakening of primitive faculties – and whether they may not be liable in modern life to be destructive both to society and to the individual.

To conclude

We can see from this chapter that the 'problem of hallucination' was to act at the intersection of differing biological, social and psychological explanations of the experience. Although the experience was not considered necessarily pathological, the hearing of voices was taking on a more and more privileged role in discussions of legal responsibility, and of how to adjudicate the boundaries of so-called normal experience. Contemporary psychiatric discourse has incorporated the 'normal mind under strain' into its formation, where the psychiatric apparatus is now spread across a range of sites, incorporating different professional groupings (such as social workers, housing workers, psychologists, occupational therapists and so forth) and different understandings and techniques of cure. The contemporary 'problem of hallucination' within this apparatus is framed through the problem of how to differentiate the hallucination from the pseudo-hallucination, and the problem of non-compliance and treatment-resistant symptoms. In relation to these problems, psychological understandings are taking on a new role, seen as useful adjuncts to biological and drug therapies. Within this discursive framework, as we saw in Chapter 1, the phenomenon of hearing voices has become more and more finely differentiated. Despite the combining and recombining of psychological, biological and social explanations, contemporary psychiatry is still committed to finding the exact biological, neurological and genetic aetiology of mental distress.

One may ponder how the psychiatric apparatus of the Sixties and Seventies was able to incorporate the various attacks on its theoretical, institutional, technical and juridical basis (Miller and Rose 1986). It has already been shown how psychiatric discourse had been transformed by the war by what has become known as the 'Invention of the Neuroses' (Armstrong 1983). However, the Fifties and Sixties marked a significant shift in the psychiatric architecture. The concept of individual reactions and personality types had brought together the notion of 'prior individuals' reacting to a set of environmental exigencies (Crown 1970). The following quote encapsulates how psychiatric discourse wove the organic and psychological together, when discussing the nature of schizophrenia:

> An organic cause for such illnesses has not yet been found and psychological factors often play a part in the aetiology of these illnesses and are prominent in their clinical syndromes. There is some reason, however, to consider these functional psychoses as likely to be due to biochemical disturbances. (Merskey and Tonge 1965:3)

Despite the enigmatic nature of the concept of schizophrenia, with the so-called miraculous discovery of certain pharmacological drugs, which alleviated 'symptoms' in the Fifties, and the relationship between 'LSD psychosis' and certain signs of psychopathology, the psychoses were viewed as having a probable base in a biochemically disturbed brain. As has been discussed earlier, the distinction between psychosis and neuroses was in the level of contact with reality. Those symptoms, viewed as having a psychological origin, were characterised by 'no loss with reality' (Merskey and Tonge 1965:3). 'The 'neurotic predicament' was primarily a disturbance of adaptation inhering within the social matrix in which the individual was located. These modes of explanation extended beyond the individual, locating these signs of disturbance within wider social relations, primarily the family.

> The person with least tolerance is usually the one who first shows signs of distress. The family tensions may be arising from an emotional disturbance elsewhere in the family circle, and so on occasions it may be true to say that the patient is showing the symptoms of someone else's neuroses. (ibid.:54)

The environment was also viewed as a set of stresses and vicissitudes, such as various traumas, relationship problems and support networks which all exerted an influence on the delicate equilibrium of the mind. The mind was subject to breakdown and would become distorted and exaggerated in response to environmental pressures. Mental health was fragile, and despite the alternative modes of explanation discussed, where the dissolution of the mind was the first step to attaining mental health (Gowan 1975, Huxley 1961, Leary 1968, 1973, Ouspensky 1968), psychiatric discourse provided a space within its discursive formation for the 'normal mind' to break down.

Within this division between the neurotic and psychotic, 'hearing voices' could cross these psychological and biological boundaries. It was recognised that 'hearing voices' was a possible experience, due largely to interest in other ecstatic cultures (Sargeant 1973), and the emotional stresses which could produce the experience. As Merskey and Tonge (1965:75) iterate: 'other psychoses, some hysterics and even perfectly normal people in states of drowsiness may have very vivid hallucinations'.

Such hallucinatory experiences can of course occur when consciousness is clouded, perhaps due to drugs or simply in the twilight state of falling asleep or waking up, when their significance is as trivial; their occurrence in clear consciousness, however, almost always indicates the presence of Schizophrenia. (ibid.:76)

The problem had been sown; if the boundaries between normality and pathology were blurring, if hearing voices were part of a variant of possible experience, then conceptually how was one to distinguish between the normal and the abnormal? It is this problematic which structures the dispersal of contemporary concepts articulating the 'problem of hallucination'. As we saw in Chapters 1 and 2, the contemporary psychiatric discourse is highly differentiated However, the key concept is the individual who hears voices, the Enfeebled Personality, and their relation to the voices. It is this relation, calibrated in terms of risk and responsibility, which gained its significance from the eugenics modes of explanation within which psychiatry emerged. Its historical heritage circumscribes its legacy: to play a part in administering normality according to a presumed knowledge of the normal individual. Despite the shifting and mutating of the apparatus from its inception, the government and management of the individual is its central aim. An historically specific form of individuality underpins the contemporary psychiatric discourse; one where the notion of sympathy enters into its very specification and constitution.

As Sargeant (1973:21) argues:

A normal person is responsive to other people around him, cares about what they think of him and is reasonably open to their influence. If the great majority of people were not normally suggestible, we could not live together in society at all, we could not collaborate in any undertaking, we could not marry, and bring up families happily.

The history undertaken within the last three chapters shows how there is no simple, single lineage within which to trace and understand the constitution of hallucinatory experience. Its emergence and contemporary formation has been made possible by a polymorphous and heterogeneous set of 'events'. The formation of the object cannot be tied either to a realist causation of one origin or factor, nor to the steady and assured march of scientific knowledge. Its contemporary articulation has been made possible by a complex set of changing conceptions of 'man'; theories of the mind and madness; certain events such as the two world wars; the 'discovery of psychedelics'; changing sites where 'hearing voices' were problematised and specified and changing conceptions of biology and population statistics to name but a few of the disparate elements. All of these concepts, objects, and surfaces of emergence have become linked within a wider system for governing a particular conception of individuality and sociality.

This conception of individuality is defined by a set of pre-discursive capacities, such as sympathy, suggestibility and responsibility, which underpin how hallucinatory experience is specified, differentiated and made intelligible. These capacities are those which are also embedded within the psychological sciences, and a range of practices of the social through which we are shaped and integrated into society. They are also presupposed capacities of citizenship within modern liberal societies. To become only suggestible to one's own will, to lose sympathetic relations with the external world, will accord one a subject position within psychiatry where one is viewed as losing these capacities of citizenship: the ability to self-regulate. It is this 'lack' which is recognised, specified and governed as such through the psychiatric apparatus. This archaeology of 'hearing voices' is intimately bound up with a genealogy of the modern subject, and is an example of the localised ways in which this conception of the individual is managed, governed and regulated. It highlights the complex way(s) in which psychiatric discourse is bound up with wider strategies for managing and governing the population.

In the next chapter we will begin to explore how actual voice-hearers negotiate and engage with the concepts and explanatory structures which make the voice-hearing experience intelligible within the 'psy' discourses. Although the history we have followed in the last three chapters is important, to show the contingency of the current terms and categories which map the psychological and the psychiatric, it does not tell us how these concepts may be translated and embodied through the strategies people develop to deal with and manage their voices. Let us now turn to the issue of embodiment in relation to the 'problem of hallucination'.

7
Techniques of the Hallucinatory Self

In the last three chapters we explored how it has become possible for the 'problem of hallucination' to become specified, classified and made intelligible through a particular set of explanatory structures and concepts. The psychological sciences and the ways in which they frame and problematise human conduct and experience are important to analyse, because they claim the authority within the Western world to 'speak truthfully' about particular kinds of experience and understand them as signs of underlying mental pathology. Although people who hear voices in certain contexts may become subject to biomedical and psychosocial understandings, it is not clear to what extent these kinds of understandings and practices determine people's experiences of their voices. Many critiques of Foucault's historical work argue that you cannot read off from these analyses how people actually understand, engage with and experience their own possible mental and biological processes. The kinds of historical work explored in the last three chapters did not explicitly engage with this problem – of how the kinds of concepts and explanatory structures promulgated within the 'psy' disciplines become techniques of self-understanding and practice. We saw however in Chapter 3, the ways in which many analyses of contemporary practices of the self, such as 'self-help' (Rimke 2000), new age practices (Ross 1992), and practices in relation to HIV and AIDS (Kinsman 1996), rather assume that these kinds of discourses and the psychological and psychiatric concepts which underpin them tend to determine the ways in which people understand their own distress and suffering. These analyses, though, tend to remain at the level of textual analyses of the kinds of concepts and languages which construct selfhood in particular kinds of ways. These practices are then linked to wider governmental practices such as liberalism or neo-liberalism and viewed as part of the way in which we become the kinds of citizen which modern societies rely upon for their reproduction and maintenance.

In his later work, Foucault raised this problem, of how to analyse the ways in which we understand and act upon ourselves in light of particular understandings and explanatory structures. He was particularly interested in the ways that selfhood shifts and changes over time, such that there is no stable constant self which can be offered as the basis and recognition of what it means to be human. This shift in his work was important to attempt to move beyond the implied determinism of some of his earlier work, and to explore the kinds of strategies and understandings people engage in, in relation to those aspects of being they find troublesome or disturbing in some way. Rather than the idea of individuals meditating and reflecting on their inner selves, this methodology directs our attention to the places in which aspects of being become marked out for attention, and the ways in which these aspects of existence are made intelligible and amenable to particular kinds of intervention. In this chapter I want to draw on and develop some of these arguments to explore the 'voice-hearing experience'. I will argue that this work is also important in considering the difference between some of the practices and understandings developed from cognitive behavioural techniques and those of the Hearing Voices Network. I will say more about the network later in the chapter, but some of the mutations and developments within psychiatric understanding and practice on the surface look remarkably similar to the practices of the HVN. We will see that they are radically different, and make possible very distinct and different kinds of voice-hearing experience. Before we move on I first want to locate some of this work on 'practices of the self' in relation to social and cultural theory. I will then give you an idea of the methodology and show how it can be deployed to examine the practices of particular voice-hearers trying to experience and manage their voices away from biomedical and psychosocial understandings.

Move to consumption

Social and Cultural theory has increasingly turned to consumption as a topography of the social (Drotner 1994, Fiske 1992, Shirato 1993, Wolf 1993). Arguments concerning the diversification and commodification of the market are said to have produced concomitant changes in identity and its formation (Featherstone 1991). The more postmodern accounts suggest that culture is made up of a collection of packaged styles organised around taste and aesthetics in the arenas of fashion, music, relationships and so forth. The subject is now a consumer; free to choose, fashion and style their own identities from the cultural resources on offer (Chamber 1986, Crook et al. 1992, Kellner 1995, Polhemus 1994, Shields 1992, Strinati 1995). More sociological accounts, although stressing the exclusion of certain people from participation in this form of cultural activity (Lury 1996), suggests that a lack of economic resources of course prevents consumption from being a universalised process of identity formation), still tend to focus upon consumption as one of the key sites and practices through which individuals enact their identities. Lury (ibid.:7) argues for example that even though economic status prevents everybody from participating, 'its dominance is felt to the extent that people's aspirations, their hopes and fears, vocabulary of motives and sense of self are defined in its terms'. This is an interesting assertion and one that indeed needs investigating through analysing specific practices and the ways in which individuals define and construct their aims, hopes, aspirations and desires. McRobbie (1998) has recently argued that the 'ideology of excellence' (Du Gay 1991) and image of the 'entrepreneurial self' (Rose 1990), whose values were central to the cultural reforms of the Conservative Party in the Eighties, needs investigating for the ways in which it has informed and produced the possibilities of particular kinds of relations of self to the self (Foucault 1988). Through the vocabulary of choice, freedom and self-reliance, of 'going it alone and fending for yourself without the support of the "Nanny State"' (ibid.:2), she suggests that the current parameters of social and cultural theory are too deterministic. She argues that individuals are not taken in hook, line and sinker by 'Thatcher's ideology'. Through naming this as a 'subjectivising' discourse she argues that the outcomes of these discourses can never be known in advance because of their intersection with race, sexuality, gender, class and even family background.

As I argued in Chapter 3, even though the production of a rational, autonomous subject has been central to practices of government within liberal democracies, we must be wary of seeing these discourses as all-determining. We need to explore how actual people embody and struggle with the fiction of autonomous selfhood in their everyday lives. For example, it is clear that we are increasingly required to understand self-transformation as a key issue in relation to how we manage the circumstances of our lives. This painful necessity of self-invention and self-transformation may also create in its gaps, silences and contradictions, new forms of subjectivity, new forms of sociality, and new ways of coping which offer testimony to the ways in which ordinary people struggle with the necessity of self-invention in a rapidly transforming world. It is in the gaps, silences and contradictons of 'psy' discourse that the practices of the HVN have been made possible, and yet also show how the production of autonomous subjects who 'can cope with change and are self-motivated' (Walkerdine 2001), can also produce forms of subjectivity and sociality which cannot be contained by these discourses.

For example, McRobbie's (1998) analysis of the fashion industry is interesting because it shows how the fiction of the 'entrepreneurial self' has not only infused popular culture, but has produced the possibility of new cultural producers. These are young fashion designers, who 'choose' to be self-employed in order to maintain their artistic integrity. This attention to 'situated practices' and the ways in which people maintain and construct particular relations to themselves and others is a central focus of this chapter. However, I depart from these analyses in their prioritisation of consumption as the key object for analysis. Mort (1996) argues cogently in his analysis of the emergence of 'new man' imagery in the Eighties that consumption as a generalised way of thinking about identity and its relation to popular culture is inadequate. He does however argue, that consumption is one of the key sites and must be analysed in its specificity, as his analyses of retailing, fashion and the rise of men's magazines show. Foucault's later work on 'techniques of the self' (Foucault 1985, 1987, 1988, Martin 1988) has become one of the theoretical perspectives drawn on by scholars investigating these relations (McRobbie 1998, Nixon 1996). Miller and Rose (1997) have examined through detailed case studies the ways in which the knowledges of the 'psy' disciplines have played a key role in the construction of 'consumption technologies since the post-war rise in mass objects of consumer culture' (ibid.:2). In these analyses Miller and Rose develop one of Foucault's key insights concerning the relation between truth, power and subjectivity which seems to have been overlooked in the aforementioned analyses.

As we saw in Chapter 3, Foucault suggested in his earlier archaeological work that veridical discourses, those which 'function in truth', such as the human sciences, play a key role in the processes through which humans come to see themselves as particular kinds of subject. His work has been instrumental in the development of a large body of work, known as 'critical psychology', which we explored in Chapter 3 (Parker and Shotter 1990, Potter and Wetherell 1987, Rose 1985, 1990, Walkerdine 1990, 1996). This work has largely been ignored by social and cultural theory (cf. Blackman and Walkerdine 2001). As Rose (1996a) and Miller and Rose (1997) have argued, the social domain is made up of a range of heterogeneous practices, which address the subject in different ways according to different concepts. However, there are also 'family resemblances', such as the vocabulary of choice, freedom, independence and autonomy which organises social and cultural practices, such as schooling, therapy, the penal and legal systems, practices of consumption, leisure and advertising and even new communication technologies (Blackman 1998). Rose (1996a) makes the argument that the 'ethic' or 'fiction of the autonomous self' which organises these practices is one which is embedded in those knowledge/practices such as psychology and psychiatry which claim to be based upon the supposed truth of selfhood. He extends his analyses in specific ways, exploring how people are incited or invited to 'enfold' or relate to themselves through this fictional image across a range of practices such as consumption, leisure, advertising, the mass media (television documentaries, news, drama and soap opera) and so forth.

I want to develop this body of work by exploring how groups of voice-hearers are attempting to enact their identities in opposition to what I will term 'psy' modes of explanation and understanding. We explored the tapestry of these understandings in Chapter 1. The focus in this chapter will be on the subjective experience of actual voice-hearers and the kinds of strategies and understandings they develop to engage with particular somatic experiences. We will look at the possibility of this kind of work for exploring embodiment and the production of experience within cultural theory and critical psychology. In the next chapter we will explore some of the broader debates within which the concept of embodiment has emerged to bring 'the biological' back into social theory in a radically revised way. In line with one of the central arguments made throughout this book, debates about embodiment refuse the notion that 'biology', 'psychology' and even the 'social' are static entities which can be used to causally explain phenomena. As we saw in Chapter 3, moves to a 'social constructionist' position, where human thought, behaviour and experience are understood through appeals to the social and the workings of language and discourse, tend to ignore, negate or silence the realm of the biological. The following two chapters will attempt to explore the intersection of the psychological, the biological and the social in relation to the 'voice-hearing' experience in a radically revised way.

This approach to embodiment explores the way that certain knowledges and discourses have become privileged techniques of social- and self-formation. Many writers have argued that historically the 'psy' discourses have played this role offering an image of life and health which shapes and informs the way individuals understand their own subjectivities (Blackman 1994, Rose 1990, 1996a, Walkerdine 1990). Foucault termed this relational dimension of practices of the self, ethics, and was interested in the historical contingency of such practices (Martin et al. 1988, Foucault 1991b). I am interested in the *situatedness* of such practices; the differing ways phenomena are classified, constituted, visualised and imagined producing the very possibilities of experience. Cultural practices address the subject in differing ways, according to different criteria and concepts shaping the ways subjects live, feel and enact their existence (Rose 1996a). For example, there are many different ways of 'hearing voices' and associated feelings of joy, shame, guilt, fear and revelation contingent upon the differing ways voice-hearing is conceptualised. In this chapter I will give some examples of such practices of the 'hallucinatory self', to illustrate how these experiences can never be understood or reduced to the subject who has renounced or lost control (Clement 1994:xvii). Nor can they be seen as evidence of the autonomous subjects making more reflexive choices about their identity as voice-hearers. Neither of these perspectives can adequately engage with the psychological complexity of subjects engagement with these practices and the process of change, which may occur. This set of theoretical concerns will be exemplified through my work with the 'Hearing Voices Network' – a group of voice-hearers who are attempting to rethink and relive their experience of voice-hearing outside of the frameworks of the 'psy' disciplines.

Technologies of the self

Foucault (1988:18) defined 'technologies of the self' in the following way:

> (4) technologies of the self, which permit individuals to effect by their own means or with the help of others a certain number of

operations on their own bodies and souls, thoughts, conduct and ways of being, so as to transform themselves in order to attain a certain state of happiness, purity, wisdom, perfection or immortality.

This approach to the production of subjectivity explores the kinds of practices, understandings and aspects of existence which become marked out as problems to be worked upon and transformed in some way. In other words how it is possible for individuals to assign meaning, make judgements; to constitute experience in particular kinds of ways, and in a dialectical manner to act upon themselves on the basis of these sets of understandings and ways of problematising. There were four aspects which Foucault suggested would be useful to explore, to map and analyse these processes of subject-formation (what he also termed 'subjectification'). These four domains are not an analytic machine, but rather the kinds of areas which need exploring; these include what Foucault in the *Use of Pleasure* (1987:37) termed the 'ontology, deontology, techniques or practices of the self and teleology'. Foucault used these different broad categories to 'determine the moral experience of sexual pleasures' from Greco-Roman times to Christian times. The 'ontology' is the term used to refer to that aspect of being which is marked out for attention, what he also termed the 'ethical substance', or the 'what' of one's self-forming activity. Part of Foucault's concerns in his later series of the three volumes of the *History of Sexuality*, was to show how our modern conception of sexuality did not exist in different times and spaces. Rather in Greco-Roman times, 'sexuality' was made intelligible through sets of concepts, which articulated a notion of aphrodisia as being that aspect of experience to be problematised and worked upon. The aphrodisia were particular behaviours, desires, acts, sensations and images, which together constituted the practice of sexual pleasure. The 'ethical substance' is then that aspect of being marked out for attention as a domain of moral, ethical or even medical or psychological concern.

The 'deontology' relates to the kinds of concepts which make this aspect of being intelligible. Through what kinds of discourses, concepts, explanatory structures and authoriatative institutions does the 'ethical substance' become constituted and differentiated from other kinds of experience? For example, is it divine law, legislation, the life sciences, the human sciences, popular discourse and so forth? In the third volume of the *History of Sexuality*, the 'Care of the Self' (Foucault 1990), Foucault charts how the management of sexual conduct shifts and changes from pre-Christian to Christian times. The 'ethical substance' shifted and mutated from the practice of aphrodisia to the decipherment and elimination of evil. The deontology or 'mode of subjection' also changed to concepts based on the so-called universal principles of nature and God's law. The third aspect, related to the above two, includes the actual practices or techniques of the self. 'The forms of elaboration of ethical work that one performs on oneself, not only to bring one's conduct into compliance with a given rule, but to attempt to transform oneself into the ethical subject of one's behaviour' (Foucault 1987:27). These are the ways and means through which subjects act upon themselves and make judgements; the ways that subjects calculate, manage and organise their worlds. Although language plays a role within techniques, it is but a component or dimension of the apparatus. What this directs our attention to is the 'situatedness of practices'. There is no one transhistorical stable self which is the focus of our self-forming activity, rather there are many different ways of constructing relationships with the self. These techniques might be intellectual techniques – reading, memory, writing and numeracy. They might be different bodily or corporeal techniques, i.e. walking, sitting, digging, marching or different ways of knowing the self: self-reflection, self-knowledge, self-examination, deciphering the self and so forth. As Rose (1996a:32) suggests:

> To master one's will in the service of character through the inculcation of habits and rituals of self-denial, prudence, and foresight, for example, is different from mastering one's desire through bringing its roots to awareness through a reflexive hermeneutics in order to free oneself from the self-destructive consequences of repression, projection, and identification.

In the *Use of Pleasure* (1987:125) Foucault described the practices through which the relationship to the aphrodisia was inculcated. The three major techniques were dietetics, economics and erotics. Dietetics focused upon the 'right time' for acts to occur in relation to states of the body and climactic changes. Economics focused upon the mutual faithfulness of marriage, and erotics on the renunciation of pleasures in relation to 'boys'. The aim or strategy of these practices were moderation, timing, quantity and opportunity. These were the concepts which made the practice of pleasure intelligible. Nikolas Rose (1990) also introduces the notion of 'ethical scenarios' in a development of this work, to consider those places where practices are given some form of institutional support, for example, the therapeutic encounter, the doctor–patient relationship and so forth. Ethical scenarios are those places where the focus of one's attention is intensified in relation to those aspects of being marked out for attention, 'in the school and courts, in the practices of social work and medicine, in the private consultation, in the radio phone-in, in the solitary act of reading or writing' (Rose ibid.:241).

The fourth and final element is the teleology or aim or goal of the self-forming activity – to lead a beautiful life, to become a pure, immortal being, to become a free, autonomous being. Rose (1990:227) suggests that the goal or aim of much therapeutic work is to become a free, autonomous individual.

> And the rationale of psychotherapies – and this applies equally to contemporary psychiatry – is to restore to individuals the capacity to function as autonomous beings in the contractual society of the self.

The above quote is rather generalised and could lead to the kinds of conclusions drawn from many studies of practices of the self, that is, that they are ways in which individuals are governed and govern themselves in line with the requirements of liberal democracies. As stated earlier, one of the concerns in this chapter is to explore the kinds of practices of the self and new forms of subjectivity made possible in the gaps, silences and contradictions surrounding these discourses. One of the key things that comes up time and again in voice-hearers' accounts in the Hearing Voices Network, and also recognised within psychiatry itself, is that the drugs don't always work (the notion of 'treatment-resistant symptoms'). In the interstices of psychiatry, the necessity of self-transformation and the kinds of inequalities and oppressions created through the stigma of mental health problems, let us explore the kinds of possible relationships that one is invited or indeed in most cases, incited to construct with one's voices. What kinds of experience are made possible through the categories and concepts within the 'psy' discourse? How are voice-hearers likely to embody their voices through the explanatory structures embedded within these discourses?

History of psychiatry

As we saw in Chapter 4, conventional historiographies of psychiatry present the discipline as the pioneer of the modern stage of evolutionary development. This fiction of the emergence and functioning of psychiatry has been the object of criticism and resistance since at least the early Sixties, when it began to be viewed as a fortress of custodial management, segregating those who were distressed and attempting to eliminate their mental health problems through the application of medication. The irony exposing the governmental function of psychiatry is located in the language and terms which surround mental distress. Although psychiatry's edifice is built upon clinical discourse and the identification of certain signs and symptoms which act as ciphers for disease and illness (for instance, the hearing of voices is taken to be a first-rank symptom of a discrete disease entity, schizophrenia), the languages and terms through which mental distress is constituted revolve around *risk* and *danger*. As we have seen in recent controversies in Britain over the failure of 'care in the community' there is a perceived danger to the public based on the fear that the mentally distressed are not receiving adequate medical and custodial supervision. They are a *risk*, a timebomb waiting to go off. As with the symbolic imagery surrounding AIDS, the danger of the mentally distressed is that you can't necessarily see it, it evades bodily identification until it is too late. It inheres within an ethereal realm of voices, delusions and private imaginings. It is no longer written on the body.

However, as we have seen throughout the book, within contemporary psychiatric discourse the hearing of voices in and of itself, is not necessarily a sign of disease and inherent risk and danger (both to the individual and others). The 'psy' disciplines recognise that at least in terms of the voice-hearing experience, there is a range of conditions which may produce the possibility of voices and/or visions, for instance, hostage situations, trauma, bereavement, sensory deprivation and body mutilation. The problem is the relation the subject takes to these experiences, i.e. whether they are given a reality status or not. The hearing of voices has become one of the key limits or mechanisms through which *danger* and *risk* are adjudicated within both the legal and 'psy' apparatus (Blackman 1994). Voices may become a mandate, taking over individuals and commanding them to commit violence both to themselves and others. They have become a key hinge upon which individuals' level of involvement with reality and hence their ability to be responsible to themselves and others is articulated. They act upon the division made between the rational and irrational, the responsible and irresponsible so central to the maintenance and management of modern forms of citizenship.

The significance of hearing voices

The socially and historically produced meaning of the voice-hearing experience, embedded within the contemporary 'psy' disciplines, is intimately bound up with the discursive production and maintenance of a very specific image of human life and morality (Blackman 1996). This is a way of specifying individuality and sociality which understands human subjectivity as having instilled within its pre-discursive make-up the capacity to self-regulate and operate with a sense of responsibility and guilt. As I argued in the last chapter, it is this way of understanding human subjectivity and psychology where the hearing of voices can potentially act as a marker and 'test of insanity' – i.e. of how well the person is able to maintain contact with external relations. Let us explore how some of these presumptions underpin the ways that hallucinatory experience is specified and classified and in turn voice-hearers are invited to understand their experiences.

Within modern psychiatric discourse, a particular *relation* is engendered towards the voices or visions, where the voice-hearer is required to deny their existence and view them as meaningless epiphenomena, having no other function than as signifiers of disease and illness. One of the maxims operating within psychiatric practice, congruent with this mode of denial, is that talking to voice-hearers about their experiences will make them even more confused, and reinforce a reality which is the result of a diseased and troubled mind. The so-called curative process based on these views incorporates techniques of distraction, denial, negation and diversion, where the person is simply thrust into a mode of inattentiveness, both physically and mentally. The concept of 'insight' is viewed as the point of adjustment or state of normal psychological health where voice-hearers can relate to their experiences in a mode of denial. The 'psy' *relation* to the voices has certain consequences for the way the voices are embodied or lived by the voice-hearer, creating feelings of shame, fear, guilt, anxiety, terror and confusion, for the voices seemingly random, uninvited and uncontrollable assault on a person's psychological functioning.

Some of these practices and ways of understanding the 'problem of hallucination' are mutating within the discipline, particularly with the use of 'talking therapies' and CBT (cognitive behavioural therapy) for 'treatment-resistant symptoms' and the problem of 'non-compliance'. We will explore some of these practices in more detail later in the chapter.

The Hearing Voices Network

AIMS: To support a National Network of people who hear voices to better understand the experience alongside workers, family and friends.

- To set up self-help groups of voice-hearers to share experiences and discuss strategies for coping with voices.
- To educate society about the meaning of voices, to reduce ignorance and anxiety.
- To develop a range of non-medical ways of assisting people to cope with their voices.
- To bring together voice-hearers who have not been in contact with psychiatric services with people who experience distress through voice-hearing.

Coping with voices

- The Network exists to assist people to find their own ways to come to terms with their voices by showing:
- There are various explanations which have been shown to empower themselves and live with the experiences in a positive way.
- To find ways of coping other than by the use of drugs.
- There are people who cope well having found alternative explanations outside the psychiatric model.
- People who hear voices can be assisted in developing ways of coping better by participating in self-help groups where they can share their experiences, explanations and coping methods and benefit from mutual support (reproduced from the *Voices Magazine*, Hearing Voices Network.)

The 'Hearing Voices Network' (HVN) is an anti-psychiatric user group enjoining voice-hearers across Britain, Europe and Australia who are all attempting to live with and manage their voices. Most of the voice-hearers have been subjected to psychiatric treatment and indeed may still be struggling with amounts of medication or living with the threat of compulsory admission to hospital. One of the aims of the network is to provide the space within which people can adopt different *relations* to their voices, producing very different ways of being, thinking and acting. The HVN start from the premise that hearing voices is a normal variant of behaviour, much like left-handedness, and is not merely a sign of disease grounded in the biochemical reactions of the brain. There is an inversion from the 'psy' ethical system which denies the experience, to an expression of acceptance, where voice-hearers are invited to focus on the voices, recount what they are saying, to record them, document them and integrate them into their lives. In short, the style of living changes from one of denial to acceptance, through which individuals begin to transform their relation to the experience. As one voice-hearer comments:

> Because of the questions other people asked me I had to think about the answers. I had never thought about the voices in that way. I was surprised to find it all more logical than I thought. There is a structure to the voices. I know now that my voices appear when I think negative.

The voice-hearer in this context is explicitly referring to the 'self-help' meetings where voice-hearers meet together to talk and discuss their voices. The self-help meeting functions as a democratic space where each voice-hearer takes themselves as a subject and places themselves and their experiences within a specific frame of reference. Although one of the guiding maxims of the group is that each voice-hearer should be allowed their own framework of explanation, hearers who believe their voices are signs of disease, which renders their relation to the voices as one of passivity, are challenged by other members of the group. This positioning is one where voice-hearers are viewed as subjecting themselves to biochemical/biological explanations which are seen to deny them agency in their experiences of the voices. The following quote from a psychiatric user also highlights the emotional consequences of these explanations:

> Once when we had watched a television programme about depression, which argued that chemicals in the brain were

responsible for prolonged feelings of despair, John appeared exultant, triumphant even. He almost crowed, 'So that's it. It's physical; it's in the genes. There's nothing I can do about it.' (Casterton 1997)

The ethos of the HVN is that this way of living mental distress does not allow the voice-hearer to integrate the experience into his or her life. Within the meetings voice-hearers may give accounts of their own experiences and move away from psychiatric understandings. They may recall the act of transformation whereby they changed the way they thought about, and acted upon the experiences, and the consequences of these changed relations, i.e. less medication, more control, experience of less abusive voices. Therefore, the meeting is not merely a forum whereby the voices are validated and normalised, but requires what Foucault (1990:53) termed the 'help of the other', where the other members of the group offer guidance and counselling. The group meeting could be viewed as the institutional site through which these techniques of transformation take place.

Blackmind

I want to focus in this section specifically on a particular act of self-transformation of a voice-hearer who for many years has invested much in 'psy' modes of explanation. Despite her immersion in the ethics of the HVN she imagined herself as schizophrenic and her voices the random attack of a biological illness, for which a cocktail of drugs was her only hope. Sharon tells her story in one of the Hearing Voices newsletters signalling her move from fear, confusion, terror and passivity to one of anger and injustice at the pain and suffering caused through psychiatry's injunction, and her struggle to live this, in the face of racial abuse and trauma.

> I first began to hear voices at the age of about 13. I endured much racial abuse at school. As I lived in a white area people stared and I grew up paranoid and lonely. I had no friends to mix with. Other children's parents told them to keep away from me. I became withdrawn, confused, sad and suicidal. The first time I can recall hearing voices was when they ordered me to kill myself; they were so persistent. They called me 'nigger', 'coon', 'wog'. I was so depressed with all this going on that I finally

couldn't take any more. I took an overdose of 40 painkillers and was discovered and rushed to the hospital for a stomach pump. I did it to escape the voices. I wanted to die to make it all end. I'd had enough trauma. I had to leave the children's home at the age of 16. I enrolled at Harrogate College and found a tiny bedsit. I was hearing voices all the time and could not study well. I had no friends. They thought I was a bit 'crazy'.

I do have a theory about my voices. I believe that they are memories and recollections that return right back to my early childhood. Being the only black child at school I think I suffered much racial abuse – blame and abuse. But it is worse than that. This pattern has remained in my mind, and I am destined to hear constant reminders of terrible emotional trauma. What is the cure? There is no cure because I do not have a biological illness. I am bruised and hurt by earlier experiences, and this is part of my roots.

I met my husband, Mickey, in a drop-in some years ago. I feel wanted and loved at last. We have been married since 1987. I spend a lot of time helping out at the Hearing Voices Network. I have made many good friends at the group and at last feel accepted. Not as a mad, crazy nutter; but as a valid human being who has had a lot of SHIT in the past!

This testimony highlights the very real consequences, psychological and material, of embodying specific relations in our daily struggles to live, especially in the face of adversity, pain, oppression and suffering. The 'psy' relation promotes a relation of the *self to the self* where the subject is required to recognise that they have the capacity to be in control, autonomous and to choose. It promotes a relation of the self to the self, which suppresses, denies or projects certain experiences as 'other'. Particular responses to suffering are set up where conflict for example is individualised, hidden, denied, projected and/or experienced as failing and lack. This may then be experienced by the subject as evidence of personal failing or inadequacy, rather than the difficulties of living the 'psy' image of autonomous selfhood (cf. Blackman 1999b for a development of this argument in relation to women's magazines). This is especially pertinent given that, culturally, certain emotional experiences such as feelings of persecution and paranoia often signify as psychopathology. For example, feelings of guilt, shame, atonement, frustration, fear and anxiety repeatedly signify as individual failings to be corrected. The 'psy' technology is insidious because these 'practices of the self' allow for the co-existence of this emotional economy alongside a regulatory image, which confirms them as Other – as exceptional, regrettable phenomena. It is this self/other dynamic central to the 'psy' fiction of autonomous selfhood, which produces suffering either as pathology – evidence of cerebral disease – or simultaneously forms the basis of the subject's incitement to change. In many of the practices of self-help currently circulating within the cultural sphere, misery and suffering become objects or stimuli for self-improvement and change. The difficulties of living a specific image of life ironically becomes the key 'ethical substance' to be worked upon within an individual's practices of self-improvement. These practices work to confirm the 'psy' image of life as desirable, normative and natural (Blackman 1999b). This perhaps may give us some clues as to why psychological discourses are proliferating and increasingly taking on a privileged role in our self-understandings and practices. However, what I wish to show in the next section are the kinds of practices which are being created in the gaps, silences and contradictions within these discourses.

Techniques of the hallucinatory self

The following 'practices of the self', popular amongst members of the HVN, involve different relations to the self and the voices, based around an ethical theme of acceptance and control. The practices originating from these more mystical and esoteric ways of mapping corporeality will be explored for the territory they delineate as of ethical significance, the 'ethical substance' – what aspect of being is marked out and problematised to be worked upon and transformed – the specific forms of self-examination, judgement and valuation – the divisions made between the 'me' and the 'not-me', and the specific knowledges and concepts through which the experience is made intelligible. These techniques are structured according to an ethics of expansion where the voice-hearing experience is valued as a key site for spiritual development and transformation. I think they highlight what is at stake in thinking through practices of the self excluded from the 'psy' image of personhood. The specific technique examined involves those experiences of embodiment which view voices as a form of telepathic activity. Telepathic modes of explanation are popular forms of rationalisation of the voice-hearing experience in the HVN. The following account of such an experience comes from a voice-hearer talking about his experience at a Hearing Voices conference (September 1991).

> I've tried – I mean I've always tended to go for the telepathic explanations so I tend to kind of direct what I listen to and I'll listen in certain directions to try and hear certain people and sometimes I try and speak to my grandmother who's dead and usually – it doesn't always work, but usually if I direct if I get something from that direction like I can usually get my grandmother's voice, and I can sort of get to know things about people I want to know things about even if I can't actually speak to those people so it's – I must admit though it's not nearly as good as it used to be. I mean when I was off the depixol and on next to no medication I mean I could well I could almost go anywhere in my mind and hear almost anyone and you know, have no problem contacting anyone whatsoever. Now it's all a bit hit and miss and sometimes I just get tired of listening and fall asleep.

This voice-hearer had a relation with the voices which involved acts of listening, selecting and judging, ordering the experience as to who was speaking and what information could be judged from the voices. The ethical substance, the 'what' of the experience was not so much the voices, but the *quality* of the sensitivity. Techniques of attention were developed as a means to increase one's capacity for meaningful contact, a capacity which was actually viewed by the voice-hearer as being hindered or damaged by medication. The voices were viewed as the message; the aspect of being which was problematised was the actual quality of the channel whose levels of awareness could be affected by a number of factors. It was this level of awareness or state of consciousness which was the object of this voice-hearer's practices of the self.

Other voice-hearers who viewed their voices as messages and messengers, often from the dead (mediums), talked about some of the techniques they used to manage this channel of awareness or sensitivity. Many hearers in the group have joined what are termed 'circles for development', where they are instructed in specific practices that they can use to manage the gift. The idea of 'voice-hearing' as a gift seems to be central in the processes through which the actual relation to and experience of the voices is transformed. Many involve specific ways of changing one's mode of awareness involving meditative and visualisation techniques. The goal or telos of such activity is to develop a strong mind, so that the voices do not take over, and the hearer remains in control.

> It's got to be really strong ... entire mind. (I mean) you're stronger than her. She's using you as a vehicle and you're stronger than her, you can do it. (Get) your mind over it and get her away.

One hearer outlined one type of visualisation technique, which could be viewed as a practice of psychic isolation.

> I did once read a book about protecting yourself from evil, and to imagine that you have a triangle of light and to put that around you if you ever feel threatened. And I've tried that as well. I have done that.

The meditative techniques and practices of psychic isolation are used to enable the hearer to develop mental states seen to be expansive, in order to be able to control and master the experience. The end-point or telos of such practices is to be able to select from and channel the voices. The importance of this goal is emphasised in the following two accounts:

> I don't know about anyone else but actually if anyone could be channelling this in some sort of sensible you know how marvellous it would be ... but it's so rapid isn't it. It is like a telegram, and if this was pure fact if we were actually transmitting (say) intergalactic message you know it's just so quick.

> Not the speed, the speed is incredible. I mean, I couldn't speak it, I couldn't speak it now because it's just so massive. I mean it's lots and lots of things going on at the same time. It's not – isn't it, it's all sorts of complicated dialogues going on (upstairs). What I know (is it's awful) because you've got to keep quiet.

The techniques of psychic isolation are deployed as a means to structure the voices – to tune in or out – the goal of the practices an end-point of mastery or control. These strategies allow the hearer the capacity to make and exercise a choice over whether they attend to the voices or not. These practices may also employ techniques of symbolism whereby acts of judgement are made concerning the symbolic content of the voices i.e. are they good or bad, God or the Devil? This involves applying acts of division based upon theological conceptions of good and evil. These knowledges and the judgements they engender concerning the content of the voices construct relations to the voices based on faith and trust.

> At the very last moment before I tell I looked up to the heavens and said (God don't do this and he actually helped me to cope). So in that respect you've got to believe in the goodness of things. If you believe in wickedness you reap what you sow.

As well as the techniques of psychic isolation used to train or 'purify' the mind, there is also an economy of physical and mental regimens employed as a means of protecting oneself from psychic violence or abuse which may bestow a weaker sensitivity. These involve mental regimens such as praying and actual physical regimens such as diet and health management. One woman talked about the consequences of a lapse in certain physical regimens.

> Over the last years I've had experience of this noise harassment deliberate harassment through noise. And which has deprived me of sleep and making me suffer … kept me awake all night with videos and things but this has weakened me because of not sleeping so I know that and made me feel angry too so you're in a weak state to cope with it.

The lapse of an economy of physical regimens, resulting in leaving oneself open to what I have termed psychic violence is a common ethical theme within this system. Paradoxically, psychotropic drugs are also viewed as an agent which weakens the psychic constitution, such as are abuses of psychedelic drugs or acid:

> The way to deal with voices that wouldn't veridically say anybody in particular but might represent themselves as Satanists in fact by acid freaks say on Berkeley University. The way to react to them is to beat them. Terror California very hard strong bad guys at psychic telepathy.

Although the particular practices of psychic isolation, secular solitude, techniques of symbolism and the economy of physical and mental regimens do appear within other ethical systems, the relations between the practices present a pertinence not found elsewhere. This may be related to the mode of subjection, the 'why' of the experience and its consequences. Thus one woman who does not employ a telepathic mode of explanation uses a technique of psychic isolation: 'So what I've learnt to do is keep absolutely quiet in my mind, not a word.' Another uses a technique whereby a state of reverie is achieved which she equates with a mild form of epilepsy. She describes it as a different state of consciousness, bound up with relations to her *self* of intense self-containment and 'inward-looking'.

> I wasn't conscious of going out. (I was) kind of in a half state ... If you are going to become unconscious (but you don't) in that split second everything is very unreal and you just know that reality is somewhere else, it's not here. We're not existing as real in this body that we are in here.

However, although these types of techniques are used to control and manage the experience, they produce the possibilities of very different emotional experiences and relations to the voices from the telepathic explanation. The former is more bound up with the appropriation of stopping techniques, where the subject recognises them as false and desperately attempts to obliterate them. The mode of subjection, or the 'why', is bound up with scientific law which speaks a language of disease and deficit. Within the alternative knowledge practices underpinning telepathy as an ethical system, there is a radical discontinuity with psychiatric discourse. Telepathy does not appeal to scientific law, but to divine or natural law. The consequences of this differing address and incitement are that subjects are *not* passive recipients of a brain disease, but special persons who have a gift or sensitivity below the so-called normal threshold of conscious activity and communication. These alternative knowledge practices provide a language for the experience transforming the voices from a potentially chaotic and inexpressible experience to an ordered and intelligible form. They engender relations to the voices where the hearer is accorded agency. They embody techniques of acceptance and attentiveness through which the subject can transform their relations, judgement and understanding of the experience.

One of the most fundamental elements of the ephemeral ethics of telepathy is that the authoritative institution, the spiritual church, accepts, validates and offers guidance and instruction to those who hear voices. It offers an ethical context or scenario through which the elements in the system are brought into concordance. Although less rationalised as a form of discourse than psychiatry, i.e. it does not 'function in truth', it is institutionalised, and offers a body of knowledge and practices as an alternative to psychiatric modes of explanation. The art of expertise within the spiritual church is one of empathy, sympathy and compassion, not denial and denigration. Interestingly, the very kinds of experiences which are signs of mental deterioration within 'psy' knowledge practices, become signs of potentiality within those knowledges based upon an 'ethics of expansion'. They become objects or stimuli to work on and transform, but not as part of a practice of personal development towards normative goals of autonomy and independence. Rather, they are part of a micro-texture through which subjects transform the very ways they think about and relate to themselves as human subjects, whilst at the same time achieving the goal of control (especially of the mind) in a radically different way. The goal is not to overcome 'failings' but to integrate and incorporate specific experiences into a radically different mode of subjectivity and embodiment. These modes of subjectivity and embodiment connect up the mind, body, will and imagination in ways which question the very basis of the configuration underpinning the 'psy' ethic of autonomous selfhood. They also provide a means of living this ethic in a way which does not view particular ephemeral and emotional experiences as signs of personal inadequacy and lack.

Working with voices

Ron Coleman and Mike Smith, authors of *Working with Voices* (Coleman and Smith 1997) advance the acronym *CHANGE* to capture the 'Choice and Alternatives for Growth and Experience' being offered to voice-hearers through the publication of a 'self-help' manual designed to enable hearers and those professionals who can 'hear' voices to work with and transform their felt, bodily, lived experience of their voices. One of the central aims of the manual is to encourage hearers to *own* their voices rather than disowning and dismissing them as signs of disease and illness. As Romme and Escher state, 'voices are hardly ever interpreted as the messengers of the person's life history' (1997:3 quoted in Coleman and Smith 1997). They point to one of the over-riding issues which has been at the basis of this chapter so far, that it is not so much the voices that are the problem, but how they are embodied by the voice-hearer producing very specific emotional and bodily experiences. The following two paragraphs highlight some of the fundamental issues which these alternative knowledge-practices raise:

> Calling a person who cannot cope with the voices 'ill' is understandable when the voices and the emotions or behaviour they provoke are dominating the persons functioning and life. It is reasonable to call the person 'ill' when the voices are not an integrated part of the person but destroy one's free will. It is not right however to look at voices in itself as a symptom of an illness. No it is the coping with that experience that might give rise to the emotions and behaviour that can be called ill.
>
> Therefore a person who hears voices but cannot cope with them, needs support to overcome the powerlessness and to be able to begin living again. Support is needed in coping with the voices. Support is also needed in order to become stronger in one's own identity. Lastly support is needed in accepting that what has happened has happened and should not be felt as guilt, but rather needs to be placed back in the person's life history, placing the responsibility where it belongs with the activist not the recipient. (ibid.:4)

The relation to the voices and the emotional responses they provoke, is taken to be one of the key issues which voice-hearers and compassionate professionals need to heed in their own practices. I have used the terms active/passive to distinguish between psychiatric 'disembodied' practices and those such as telepathy, which encourage voice-hearers to integrate the experience into their lives in specific ways. However, I feel that these two terms do not differentiate what is at stake in distinguishing different practices from each other. The different practices encourage the voice-hearers to enact their identity as voice-hearers according to very different criteria and concepts. One encourages integration, whilst the other we could argue encourages disintegration and alienation from the body and its potentialities. The 'psy' ethical relation is potent because it functions 'in truth' and has a certain status and authority in making claims about the nature of the voice-hearing experience. This changes the question from whether the body is socially constructed, to how our experience of the body and its biological potentialities are always mediated through cultural signs and activity. It is not simply that we are either active or passive, but that certain practices encourage integration, whereas others can only recognise certain experiences as signs of disintegration and bodily/mental deterioration.

The workbook or manual I have referred to, produced by a service user, Ron Coleman, and a willing professional, Mike Smith, incorporates these elements into a strategic self-technology encouraging the voice-hearer to understand, contextualise, organise, accept and work with the voices. Paradoxically where the 'psy' ethical system encourages the hearer to work *against* the voices, the self-technology encourages the hearer to work *with* the voices. This reversal as I have stated before is one of the most fundamental transformative relations produced through the work of the HVN. I will now give you a sense of how the workbook functions as a technique for self-production and understanding to engender very different lived experiences of voice-hearing. The workbook is divided into sections that technologise the different elements – understanding, contextualisation, organisation, acceptance and working with the voices – into a systematic, routine writing practice. The manual acts much like a confessional tool, enabling individuals by their own means or with the help of a trusted friend or professional to rethink and relive their experience of voices.

Understanding your experiences

The first section of the manual invites voice-hearers to consider their emotional responses to the onset of voices and to write a description of their first experience of hearing voices. The hearers are encouraged to accept the reality of the voices and to consider the possibility that even if their initial experiences of voices were anger, fear and confusion there are other potentially more positive experiences to be had. The hearer is introduced to voice-hearers throughout history that have experienced their voices as sources of inspiration rather than as painful, isolated experiences. Hearers are also urged to consider whether one of their initial responses to the voices was denial, as this is seen by many service-users to be one of the main reasons people spend so many years within the psychiatric system. The next section of the manual encourages the hearers to write their life-history in order to begin to contextualise and integrate the experience into their lives. One of the most important aims of the writing is for the hearer to see if there are any links between the voices and significant, often traumatic events in one's life. The story-telling encourages the hearer to individualise the experience rather than view it as a meaningless epi-phenomenon of disease. As they urge the hearer, 'It is important to see yourself as an individual rooted in society and not as a patient rooted in psychiatry' (Coleman and Smith 1997:16).

The next section of the manual is a checklist which the hearer can use as a diary to record when the voices are heard over a ten-day period and the amount of time spent attending to the voices. The hearer is directed to the content of the voices, i.e. what they said or were talking about, and to the emotional response the hearer had at the time. Hearers are also asked to situate themselves in terms of whom they were with, where they were and the general conditions such as noise or quietness surrounding them. They are also asked to record what they were thinking about and what they were doing at the time. The checklist acts much like a document of the routine, mundane activities within which the voices are embedded. An important aspect of this recording is in a consideration of the felt, bodily, lived experience(s), which the voice-hearing produced, i.e. paranoia, heightened consciousness or feelings of being out of control, or omnipotence. This is in radical contrast to psychiatric discourse which views the above as signs of illness rather than as lived experiences produced out of the persons' relationship to their voices. The next section goes on to urge the hearer to organise and further integrate the experience through developing a frame of reference through which to explain and understand the voices. Each frame of reference involves very different ways of conceptualising and forming the object of which it speaks, i.e. telepathy views the voices as a gift and sensitivity rather than as lack and a sign of disease. Each of these ethical frameworks produces very different relations to and potential lived, felt experiences of voices.

A voice-profile

The last section of the manual pertinent to my discussion encourages hearers to compile a profile of each of the voices they hear, i.e. are they male/female, commanding/advisory, abusive/positive, and to begin to relate the voices to their own life histories. This way of classifying the voices is important for some of the proposed self-care techniques, where hearers are encouraged to confront the negative, abusive voices they may hear by building allies with the positive voices. Voices the person may find distressing can then be worked with through gaining help and support from positive voices. This is an important point as many people who hear voices are not troubled by positive voices and indeed describe them as providing support and guidance, much like a good friend. They may simply wish to choose when and where they listen to the voices, to be able to experience the voices in harmony and balance for example.

When symptoms persist

> More recently, the Zeitgeist has changed, such that, an increasing number of mental health professionals have become interested in talking to their patients, and attempting to understand their symptoms. (Haddock and Slade 1996)

In my collaborations with the Hearing Voices Network which have spanned this last decade, I have increasingly heard professionals claiming that the practices they engage in are the same as those created through the HVN. Some have even gone so far as to claim the HVN as the new 'science of hearing voices'. I am sure that much of this appropriation conceals a humanist aim, to make the conditions of those suffering mental distress less linked to a feeling of medical objectification and to feel that their symptoms also say something about their lives. Psychological techniques such as CBT are currently being studied for their efficacy and endurance beyond the therapeutic situation in relation to the psychoses (Tarnier et al. 1999). However, for the most part subjects included in such 'soft' studies are those who 'experienced distressing, medication-resistant auditory hallucinations' (Wykes et al. 1999:180). The 'problem of hallucination' is also a problem of non-compliance and resistant symptoms, both failing in one way or another to respond to medical treatment. Nurses are taking on a new role within medical practice in relation to these problems: being trained in some of these new psychological techniques in the treatment of psychoses. As an adjunct to the 'harder' edge of psychiatry, these techniques are viewed as useful to help address non-compliance, treatment-resistant symptoms and the risk of relapse (Jones et al. 1998). One of the main principles underlying the deployment of these practices is to help patients believe that they can be in control of their illness and therefore improve in an indirect way the efficacy of drug treatments (and therefore compliance). CBT involves practices which focus on the voices, rather than deny their reality. Techniques which include reasoning with them (although often telling them to go away!), asking the voices to come back later, distracting them (by listening to music for example), or recording them, documenting their physical characteristics, their loudness, tone, sex, accent and so forth (Haddock and Slade 1996). The deployment of these techniques recognises that despite the same apparent symptoms, i.e. the hearing of voices, people have different skills and levels of coping. These are seen to be related to some of the beliefs they have about their symptoms, and part of the therapy is to confront patients to help prevent withdrawal and passivity.

Although CBT is part of a set of psychological explanations which focus on the psychological mechanisms seen to underpin psychiatric symptoms, the therapy is very often used to help patients accept what are otherwise disturbing symptoms. This acceptance however does not necessarily work at the level of subjectivity. What I mean by this is that CBT attempts to train, convince, persuade and educate persons to relate to their voices in different kinds of way. It acts upon the 'beliefs' that individuals may have, such that they recast how they understand their voices and thus take on a more participatory role in their own recovery (where drug regimes are in most cases still part of the package). The HVN, as we have seen, is attempting to create spaces in which people undergo profound transformations in the experience and understanding of voices. Often, the very notion of disease and illness is rejected, and the experience of hearing voices can even become a marker of sensitivity, or even oppression. It is not just about changing 'beliefs', but radically transforming the ways in which voices are problematised and acted upon, often occurring within a particular dynamic of group processes. These processes work through confession and testimonial, transforming 'persons at the level of their subjectivity. Personhood is remade, producing new ways of being in the world, of experiencing and ascribing significance to that experience' (Miller and Rose 1994:35). This is perhaps one of the reasons why CBT is not seen to endure in many follow-up studies (Tarnier et al. 1999).

I am recognising the valuable role of these therapies in the treatment of the psychoses, but am remaining cautious about some of the radical transformations in the discipline which some are heralding. As Bentall (1996) acknowledges, there are but a few researchers studying their efficacy, funding is scarce and most research still focuses upon the 'hard' biomedical edge of psychiatry. Also I think it wise to resist appropriation by the 'psy' disciplines and instead focus upon the radical implications of this kind of critical psychological work for theory and practice. As I said in the beginning of the book, we need to engage in a dialogue with the human sciences; it is the nature of that dialogue which we need to flesh out and help to dictate.

The voice of reason

There is then, no one essential experience of hearing voices, as it changes within and across the different practices within which the human subject is addressed and located. These practices produce very different ways of classifying, ordering and giving meaning to the experience that cast or enjoin the relation of the self to the self in very different ways. However, the practices are not simply 'equal but different', but linked to wider moral, social and political objectives in differing ways. The 'psy' ethic of autonomous selfhood, as many writers have shown, forms the basis of many social practices such as schooling, education, the legal system etc. It is bound up with the government and regulation of the population in relation to desired images of selfhood. However, as we have seen there are different images of 'how to live' which work with and against this image, achieving a relation of self-mastery through very different concepts, i.e. sensitivity. The 'body' is connected or linked with different ways of specifying the mind, imagination, will and so forth, producing very diverse ways of being and living. As Rose (1996a:185) cogently highlights in relation to this point drawing on the writings of Deleuze and Guattari:

> Bodies are capable of much, at least, in part in virtue of their 'being thought' and we do not know the limits of what it is possible for such thought-body-machines to do.

Usually the analysis of practices of health and illness are confined to medical sociological inquiry (Lupton 1997, Peterson and Bunton

1997). However, increasingly cultural theorists are becoming aware of the limits of identity as an analytic account (Hall and Du Gay 1996), and the focus upon consumption as too generalised to make claims about processes of subjectification (Mort 1996, Miller and Rose 1997, Rose 1996a, 1995). Embodiment as a concept is useful because of its stress on the situatedness of practices of self-formation (Gatens 1996, Haraway 1997). There is much to say about those spaces and sites, which are organised and based around the supposed 'truth' of the human subject. These are spaces such as the doctor's waiting room, the psychiatrist's interview, the psychoanalyst's office, the chatshow, on the hospital ward and so forth, where people are problematised and problematise themselves through divisions made between the normal and the pathological. We need to explore the stories that are told, how they are told, how people problematise themselves, in relation to whom, to which imagined authority and according to which explanatory concepts and discourses. Work outside the canons of cultural theory, such as 'critical psychology', have much to say about contemporary forms of selfhood and the ways in which the 'fiction of the autonomous self' are embodied in local, everyday practices. This work is not only concerned with the reproduction of inequalities, but the ways in which new forms of subjectivity are being created in the gaps, contradictions and silences which surround the fiction of autonomous selfhood. We need to begin to develop theories which can engage with the psychological (and yet discursive) complexities of the ways the modern subject lives in the world.

Situated ethics

Rather than distinguish different modes of being as Western/Eastern, rational/irrational, material/ephemeral etc. we need to address what potency different relations play in transforming ourselves and our relations with others in our everyday lives. What potentialities do they open up for producing experiences which perhaps many of us can only ever imagine? How can we become something other and what role might the present historical contingency play in these transformations? What relation paradoxically do practices of transformation (such as the HVN) have to practices of regulation which exclude them as 'other' within the making of modern disciplined man? What relations do these practices have to practices of self-development endlessly circulating within the cultural sphere? How do the very general divisions that govern Western thought operate within specific discursive practices to produce ways of being which disturb these very dualisms in their everyday, local, embodied practices? What are the costs and consequences of taking ourselves to be very different types of subject? These questions need to be approached through an understanding that recognises experience as always *'being-in-relation'*. To advance this thesis may then allow us to go beyond the experience/language debates, and explore embodiment through attention to those situated practices which produce the various possibilities of experience. In the next chapter we will begin to explore debates surrounding embodiment, and assess their implications for rethinking those constituent elements which currently 'make up' human subjectivity.

8
Embodiment and Experience

We saw the way in Chapter 3, that the 'psy' discourses are viewed as a key link point between the ways in which authorities seek to govern individuals and how individuals understand and act upon themselves (Rose 1990). For example, psychological discourse, and particularly the 'fiction of autonomous selfhood', promulgated by 'psy' experts, is seen to produce citizens who are psychologically healthy inasmuch as they are 'governable, predictable, calculable, classifiable, self-conscious, responsible, self-regulating and self-determining' (Rimke 2000:63). In other words, the terms, categories, concepts and objects inscribed within psychological theories, and practices based on those understandings, become privileged techniques of self-understanding and practice. This is an interesting argument which links particular 'practices of the self' with practices of government, where the 'psy' discourses are seen to facilitate the development of forms of selfhood which modern neo-liberal governments rely upon for their functioning (Rose 1990, 1996b). This work considers the place of the human and life sciences in apparatuses of social regulation, such as schooling, education, social work, the law courts, the work place and so on (Rose 1990, 1996b, Walkerdine 1984, 1990). Those knowledges claiming to be 'sciences of the individual', rather than simply discovering some essential human nature, have, from their inception, become intertwined with broader, more general strategies of regulation. We saw clearly in the historical chapters, the ways in which the particular forms of individuality and sociality which have underpinned the 'psy' discourses have been presupposed within broader strategies for governing and managing the population.

As I argued in Chapter 3, much of this work remains at the level of concepts, exploring the kinds of languages and terms which make particular practices of the self intelligible. Let us consider an extended example, from some of Andrew Ross's work (1992), a cultural theorist interested in exploring the homologies between new-age practices and the philosophy and ideology of liberal societies. Ross (ibid.:531) begins by recounting a visit to the dentist where he is addressed as someone who should be willing and able to take on more personal responsibility for the maintenance of his dental health. As Ross suggests, 'this dentist's implicit suggestion that bodily maintenance was now my own economic, even moral responsibility took on ominous overtones for me'. We explored this theme of 'healthism' in Chapter 3, where increasingly, it is argued we are addressed in this way in relation to our own practices of health and illness. Ross begins to explore this theme of 'personal responsibility' across a range of practices, particularly those which have been constituted in opposition to materialist scientific author-ity, such as 'New Ageism'. These practices, he argues, extend the theme of personal growth and responsibility, extending and enhancing the body to enable it to be self-sufficient and self-regu-lating. Under the umbrella term of 'new ageism', he unites a range of different practices such as shamanic and magical techniques, biofeedback machines and so forth, arguing that they reinforce the dominant values of liberal ideologies.

> New ageism addresses and calls upon its adherents as active par-ticipants, with a measure of control over their everyday lives, and not as passive subjects, even victims, of larger objective forces. (ibid.:545)

He does draw attention to the forms of sociality and wider social and structural changes that would sustain these kinds of practices. He argues that these practices have emerged within the cultural reforms of the 'New Right' in the US, where the 'autonomous right to choose' has occurred within a space of decreasing social and welfare support. In the current climate, he argues that these prac-tices are regulatory, making health the personal responsibility of citizens, rather than developing socialised health-care systems which would accommodate these healing practices. He draws on Rosalind Coward's (1989) study of the alternative health movement, where she argues that 'health' has displaced 'sex' as the modern marker of identity. Reminiscent of Foucault's studies of the modern notion of sexuality, this argument suggests that 'health' has become a key expression of who and what we are as subjects, and to that extent is a regulatory mechanism.

   These are very generalised arguments, which link particular practices of the self with wider practices of government and regula-tion. If we consider the analytic tools which underpin Foucault's archaeological studies of the human sciences, then two are prioritised: concepts and strategies. These studies are mainly textual analyses, and do not engage with how actual people engage and transform these practices in their everyday lives. As Lati Mani argues (1992:551), 'some of these interventions come from marginalised groups in society'. bell hooks' most recent book (2000) *all about love*, champions the writings of Scott Peck, the American self-help guru, privileging the themes of choice and responsibility in the solutions we develop to deal with failing relationships, unsatisfactory jobs and childhood injustice. The kinds of ethics she develops, in relation to love and honesty, are offered as political strategies for those working and living in oppressed communities or dealing with violence and abuse in family settings. A black feminist writer, using the testimony of her own experiences of abuse, she is developing particular 'self-help' practices to transform relationships between men and women within her own oppressed communities. These are interventions which as Lati Mani suggests cannot be adequately investigated through 'disembodied theory'.

This calling should make us pause and reflect on how we might engage with science as cultural critics. Critical psychology, as we saw in Chapter 3, has developed a range of different positions in relation to the role of psychological discourse in our everyday lives. Some appear very deterministic, seeing the individual as being governed and regulated through those very qualities and understandings that we hold most private, subjective and unique about ourselves (Rose 1990). Others, see the 'psy' discourses as possible 'accounting repertoires' (Potter and Wetherell 1987), which the subject may draw on in understandings of their own selfhood, but which exist alongside other competing discourses. I am sure that both of these positions are pertinent, but neither are adequate in and of themselves, in adequately exploring contemporary forms of subjectivity. I hope that the last chapter showed the new forms of subjectivity being produced in the gaps, silences and contradictions surrounding, in this case, psychiatric discourse. This example brings to light how wary we should be of making generic and generalised claims about practices of the self. Similarly, there is much literature taking these kinds of arguments into cultural studies and arguing that the realm of the popular is a key mechanism through which conduct and thought is policed and governed (Miller 1998, Rimke 2000).

Talking about the mass-media for example, Toby Miller (1998:59), developing the work of Michel Foucault, argues that popular culture is an apparatus which creates 'truth effects'. 'These are telling technologies; they tell stories about who and "how" we are, in ways that make a difference to what they define and explain.' Miller is attempting to instigate a shift in cultural studies away from an understanding of audiences which links 'aberrant decoding' to transgression. This notion of audiences, as ideally made up of groups who can resist media influence, and transform the meaning of media texts, has been a popular argument in the 'culturalist' shift in cultural studies since the Eighties in Britain and America (Blackman and Walkerdine 2001, Hall 1981). In these shifts 'consumption practices' are now the focus of analytic attention, and the 'power of the mass-media' to shape and define the world has now dissipated. Miller is attempting to explore the 'conditions of possibility' for certain media texts to circulate particular meanings, and to explore the relationship between power and subjectivity. These are important moves, but must go hand in hand with attention to embodied practices.

> there is power, it is productive, and it works through the production and dissemination of truth, disciplining the citizen through a pursuit of the popular. (ibid.:267)

As we saw in the historical chapters, there are a myriad of conditions and circumstances which led to the 'problem of hallucination' being framed and articulated through a particular set of concepts and explanatory structures. The human sciences and the circulation of particular concepts within the mass-media, for example, are important sites where particular kinds of 'truth' are established about what makes us human (cf. Blackman and Walkerdine 2001). These 'truths' are regulatory in that they come to organise particular practices, such as the legal system, social work, the police and so forth, through which behaviour, thought and conduct are judged and evaluated in relation to psychological and behavioural norms. In many contexts, to confess the hearing of voices is to have your experience judged in relation to norms of health and disease, and may subject the person to compulsory admission to hospital and medication. However, as we saw in the last chapter, this is not all there is to say. The practices of the Hearing Voices Network, which are mainly constituted in the gaps and contradictions within 'psy' discourse, are making possible very different embodied experiences of voices. It is only by paying attention to 'situated practices' that we can begin to explore the complex processes of subject-formation, which constantly make and transform who we are as subjects. Let's now turn to broader debates about embodiment, which are beginning to address some of these issues. One of the main issues this chapter will address, is in light of some of the ideas we have explored in relation to the 'problem of hallucination': how can we begin to think about the status of 'biology' in processes of subject-formation?

Embodiment

Embodiment as a term generally refers to the 'lived body' – the notion that the body and one's biological or even psychological processes are never lived by the individual in a pure and unmediated form. The concept of embodiment is also often positioned as a way out of some of the problems with constructionism, as an analytic concept. In Chapter 3 I discussed the two poles of essentialism and constructionism which are often presented as polar opposites in relation to how we define humanness. To recap, 'essentialism' is a set of beliefs, which suggest that there are basic building blocks of human nature, which can be classified, compared and calibrated. Humanness is the product of pre-social and pre-discursive attributes or capacities, which can be measured through scientific means, i.e., psychometric tests. We saw in Chapters 1 and 2, the ways in which these kinds of beliefs underpin the huge mass of psychiatric and psychological research, attempting to discover the exact psychological or psychiatric mechanism producing the possibility of hallucinatory experience. Constructionism appeals to the workings of language, discourse and ideological processes in the construction of what it means to be human. There is seen to be nothing stable or pre-discursive which can act as the basis or recognition of humanness. Both Denise Riley (1983) and Diana Fuss (1989) argue that both sides of this dualism are unsatisfactory, and indeed are both forms of determinism. Essentialist approaches easily reduce to forms of biological determinism, and constructionist approaches present a more sophisticated form of discourse or social determinism. This is an example of the nature of some of the critiques, which have been made about the use of Foucault's work more generally (cf. McNay 1992, Sawicki 1991).

Are psychic upheavals rooted in nature, or are they socially constructed – or are these bad explanatory choices to settle on? For what do we mean by the natural, the biological, the social. (Riley 1983:1)

Constructionist approaches also generally negate the issue of biology altogether. Biological explanations of human life are generally rejected because of the ways in which biology has been used to categorise, administer and regulate the population, i.e., eugenics strategies. Even though I am sympathetic to these moves, what is often overlooked is that 'biology' as an object, shifts and changes in meaning and cannot pass as a stable, constant category, which we can simply reject. Nikolas Rose (forthcoming) also explores this argument in relation to the rise of molecular biology and how it is transforming how we think about and act upon ourselves as individuals. What is actually being rejected in most constructionist moves, is the notion that there is a changeless biology, which can explain social and psychological life (cf. Riley 1983 for further discussion in relation to developmental psychology). However, no revision or radical rethinking of the biological is offered in its place. The body becomes 'thought' as an effect of discursive processes, and studies of discourse are offered as places through which the body is formed and constituted. Woodward (1997:79) makes the following argument when considering the appropriation of Foucault's work on the modern penal system in *Discipline and Punish* (1977). In his study of the prison system Foucault developed the notion of disciplinary power; a form of power which he suggested was central to a range of modern institutions and practices.

This was not a form of power which worked through constraining or repressing individuals (we encountered this use of power in Chapter 2 in relation to role theoretical models). Rather, it is a form of power which incites or encourages people to regulate and monitor themselves, to discipline themselves. It acts on and through an individual's self-forming behaviour, such that individuals come to want or desire certain norms or ways of behaving for themselves. Power works tactically, Foucault suggests, through the instrumentalisation of certain techniques and practices, which transform people's relationships to their own bodies and sense of selfhood. For example, in the context of the penal system, he argues that there is a range of techniques employed, such as timetables, collective training, exercises, total and detailed surveillance (what Foucault described as the Panoptican) and so forth. The film *Beau Travail* (1998) directed by Claire Denis, is a beautiful and moving account of the use of discipline to instil a love of one's superior. Disciplinary power and tactics are deployed to create a sense of comradeship and solidarity in the context of the French Foreign Legion. This mode of power operates such that the men in the film do not experience this as something that is forced upon them in any way.

Foucault also argued that this form of power works most effectively in hierachical institutions, where people are continually monitored, assessed and compared with others in relation to norms of behaviour and conduct. The following quote from *Discipline and Punish* brings together some of the themes I have been discussing:

> procedures were being elaborated for distributing individuals; fixing them in space and time; classifying them; extracting from them the maximum in time and forces; training their bodies; coding their continuous behaviour; maintaining them in perfect visibility; forming around them an apparatus of observation, registration and recording; constituting on them a body of knowledge that is accumulated and centralised. The general form of an apparatus intended to render individuals docile and useful. By means of precise work upon their bodies, indicated the prison institution, before the law ever defined it as the penalty par excellence. (quoted in Rabinow 1991:214)

The notion of a 'docile body' has been used by many in studies of embodiment, arguing that this concept, and the work developed in relation to it, is an example of the ways in which the body is malleable; can be sculpted, moulded, altered and transformed. Woodward (1997:79) however argues that this work presents a tension, a tension that is characteristic of much of the work within social constructionism and studies of embodiment more generally. Her argument is that although Foucault is seeking to historicise the body, the body is actually given little attention except as being seen as an effect of discourse. The body is passive, 'always-already' waiting to be written upon by cultural discourses. The body simply becomes an effect of discourse.

> Once the body is contained within modern disciplinary powers, it is the mind, which takes over as the location for discursive power. Consequently, the body tends to become an inert mass controlled by discourses centred on the mind (which is treated

as if abstracted from an active human body). This ignores the idea of disciplinary systems of power as 'lived practices' which do not simply mark themselves on people's thoughts, but permeate, shape and seek to control their senuous and sensory experiences. (ibid.:79)

Her argument is that the body and its biological potentialities are foreclosed. The focus of much work on embodiment is on discourse and those knowledges and practices, which transform people's relationships to their bodies. The role of the 'biological' as a generative potentiality in this process is sidestepped. In a recent book, *Vital Signs: Feminist Reconfigurations of the Bio/logical Body* (Shildrick and Price 1998), the question of embodiment is posed along lines which reveal this underlying tension.

The beating of the heart, the pulsing of arteries, the flush of the skin, the intake and exhalation of breath, the reflex constriction of the pupil in light – these are the vital signs of the living body, the markers of an intricate interplay of dynamic forces which form what is known as the biological corpus. Though the discourse of biomedicine takes that model as its privileged theme, it is a foreclosure that must be resisted. The vital signs that are explored in this collection move into a more thoroughly discursive field in which texts and practices are every bit as important as, indeed inseparable from, the substance of the body. (ibid.:1)

Although starting with those biological processes seen as vital to the sustaining of human life, throughout the collection the kinds of bodies constructed through different knowledge practices associated with biomedicine are deconstructed, and alternative knowledges presented. The focus is more on how these practices do not contain subjects, rather than a simultaneous focus upon how we might revise biology, rather than simply view 'it' as an effect of discourse. The move to see embodied practices as effects of discourse comes from studies which explore how people relate to particular 'clinical' or 'biological' objects, such as the teeth (Vasseleu 1998), the heart (Birke 1998) and the dis/abled body (Price and Shildrick 1998). We will explore some of this work in more detail later in the chapter, but a privileged focus is on text, discourse and practice, rather than really developing and thinking through how to reopen dialogue with the biological and life sciences. This tension is most apparent in studies of emotion, which have become a sub-discipline of sociology and social psychology, in attempts to move beyond the idea that emotions are biological substrates of existence. We will explore this work in some detail in the next section.

How do you feel?

> Would we say we had experienced fear if our hearts did not race and our palms sweat; that we were in love if there were no sense of lightheadedness or elation, or that we were depressed or miserable without the feeling of physical drag, of everything being just too much trouble to bother about. (Burkitt 1999:116)

Ian Burkitt in his latest book, *Bodies of Thought* makes similar criticisms encountered in the last section in relation to constructionist perspectives. He argues that the key problem with these approaches is that they adopt a linguistic or discursive understanding of the construction of the body. In considering the body as a set of biological, as well as discursive processes, we must also be wary of resurrecting the emotions, for example, as biological universals or constants. This is the tension and one which Burkitt (1999) attempts to transcend in his formulation of the body and sociality as being inseparable. 'Emotions can be socially constructed while also having sensate, corporeal, components that are necessary to the lived bodily experience of that emotion' (ibid.:116). The conundrum is how to incorporate the lived experience of the body, of corporeality, without resurrecting aspects of the body as universal substrates of experience. The aim of this section will be to explore to what extent the sociology of emotions achieves this.

In conventional psychological theory, the emotions are presented as a set of variants, a universal set of characteristics, usually reducible to biology, which we all feel, but may simply interpret in different ways. This kind of body/cognition dualism allows for 'culture' to enter the equation as a set of narratives or discourses which we may use to interpret the bodily experience differently. This body/cognition dualism is often overlaid by other dualisms, such as innate/learned, nature/nurture, individual/environment and natural/social. These are the very dualisms that studies of embodiment are attempting to displace and overturn. William

Sargeant, a British psychiatrist writing in the 1950s, deployed these kinds of dualisms in his discussion of what we might term extreme emotional states, such as trance, ecstasy and hallucination. Researching religious festivals and practices, particularly those which incorporated some kind of ecstatic state, he argued that these practices, often understood in some cultures as 'spirit-possession', were actually abreactive reactions of the brain brought about by repetitive and rhythmic behaviour. These neurological reactions were then given different cultural interpretations the world over.

> The brain of man has apparently not altered in thousands and thousands of years, and we are often using similar basic methods of psychological healing and indoctrination in modern men as were used by our earliest tribal ancestors (Sargeant 1967:171)

Of course, although Sargeant is quick to recognise how cultural representations govern the meaning of experience, he is also equally ready to privilege some understandings, such as modern psychiatric understanding, as more truthful. We encountered this practice in Chapter four, where psychiatry in its representation of itself as the modern pinnacle of evolution, dismisses other cultures and past representations as ignorant, and tied to particular values and beliefs. Psychiatric understandings are linked to scientific progress and innovation. This view of biology as an invariant, static entity appears again and again when we talk about feelings and emotions. Weiss and Haber (1999:6) raise a similar set of questions in relation to the phenomenon of pain:

> Surely all human beings, whatever their culture or time, have felt pain. The more interesting question is how they have interpreted the experience of pain. And maybe, the experience of pain is so conditioned by the cultural-historical interpretations of it that there is little more that can be said about it other than it is generally aversive.

Weiss and Haber (ibid.) argue then that pain, along with other terms and categories we ascribe as having an invariant biological status, should be thought of in a nominal way. In other words, that these terms never have a continuous meaning, and that we can never simply separate the bodily experience from its interpretation.

The body as a 'lived body' is so bound up with culture and history that what we might see as the 'universals of experience', such as pain, emotion, feelings and so forth, are inseparable from historical and social processes. To take this a step further, to what extent is 'biology' a stable, invariant category, when through the embodiment of biological processes the experience itself is transformed? We saw this clearly in the last chapter where the embodied experiences of hearing voices revealed very different kinds of lived experiences of the voices. As a starting point, in order to hear voices, one must experience some kind of biochemical or neurological transformation, which provides the potentiality of the experience. As we have seen throughout the book, this is one of the 'problems of hallucination'. The experience traverses a range of conditions including reactions to traumatic events and potentially life-threatening situations (Belensky 1979, Comer et al. 1967); hostage situations; bereavement (Reese 1971); sleep deprivation; fasting, drugs; organic illness; and before falling asleep and waking up. However, the embodied experience of hearing voices is inseparable from the ways in which it is made intelligible and acted upon.

To illustrate how inseparable the process is, consider the following example relevant to the last chapter. The condition of coming to see and act upon your voices, as a special gift or sensitivity, may also be made possible to a certain extent by the kinds of voices one hears, i.e. are they positive or negative; advisory or abusive; experienced as coming from inside or outside one's head? However, even the characteristics of the voices are not stable enough criteria to determine the likely embodied experience of voices, as these can shift and transform through the different understandings and practices that voice-hearers engage in. In the self-help groups of the HVN that I sat in on, one of the key ways in which voice-hearers attempted to persuade those who understood and acted upon their voices 'as if' they were signs of disease, was through talking about their changed experience of less abusive voices, in their move away from psychiatric understandings. The relationship between biology and sociality is so complex that one cannot be untangled from the other, and championed as a causal mechanism.

This championing of either the biological or the social recurs throughout studies of the emotions. Within conventional psychology, and most of the language in Western cultures which surrounds emotional life, emotions are viewed as non-cognitive, bodily perturbations. Many studies within psychology attempt to define, describe and analyse the bodily/physiological states underpinning different emotions. This way of approaching the emotions as bodily, physiological states has been investigated by physiological psychology, for example, and is best summed up by the following phrase: 'we feel sad because we are crying'.

The emotion 'sadness', within this formulation, is simply a description of the bodily state or internal system of arousal. Rom Harré (1986) published a seminal work in social psychology in the Eighties, which attempted to create a new way of researching and understanding emotions in line with constructionist principles. This framework is an attempt to move away from physiological states and locate emotions within the context of social encounters and reciprocal exchanges. Harré suggests that emotions are not 'things', but are always about someone or something. We are mad at, angry at – in that sense they are intentional. Much of the literature in the sociology of emotions describes and delineates the social contexts in which emotional acts are lived and accomplished. This work relies on a different kind of metaphor; emotions are not what someone is (often relying on a hydraulic metaphor), but what someone does (a dramaturgical metaphor). These ideas have been explored in great length in a book by Arlie Hochschild (1983) called *The Managed Heart. The Commercialisation of Human Feeling*. This book is a study of the ways in which, more and more in the work-place, especially in the service industries (the airline industry for example), we are increasingly required to manage our emotions in particular kinds of ways. The idea of 'service with a smile' captures the kinds of 'emotional labour' and interpersonal skills we must develop in order to manage feeling in this way. She argues that not only are particular feelings brought into being by particular kinds of emotional work, but that we also can become estranged from ourselves and the context of our emotions when we continually have to engage in this kind of labour.

These kinds of study argue that emotions always involve some kind of cognitive work. The body/cognition dualism I discussed earlier underpins the shifts in constructionist work, which explore the kinds of 'emotional repertoires' or languages at our disposal. This is referred to by some as the weak end of constructionism (Harré 1986), the hard end are arguments which suggest that emotions do not exist unless there is an emotional vocabulary which makes the emotional experience a possibility. The focus within these moves is on how emotion languages are used in different contexts to position people in different ways, as with jealousy (Stenner 1993), or in a wider socio-political context, particular emotions are seen to endorse, sustain and reproduce certain systems of belief and values (Harré 1986). Much work in this area explores the cultural relativity of emotions. In medieval times for example, there used to be an emotion called accidie, which could roughly be translated as losing one's zeal for praying. It was a melancholy emotion, which, it is argued, simply does not exist any more (Harré 1986, Pfister and Schnog 1997). Nancy Schnog, writing in a book called *Inventing the Psychological* explores the ways in which mood has shifted and changed in meaning from the eighteenth to the twentieth century. In the eighteenth century it was linked to particular outlooks on life, such as courage, spirit, stoutness and so forth. In the twentieth century it is 'a basic unit and diagnostic measure of psychological normality and abnormality' (ibid.:85). She explores how mood has increasingly become lined to pathology and psychopathology by looking at how it becomes a marker of psychological instability in the *DSM III* (*Diagnostic and Statistical Manual*).

Most studies of emotion remain trapped within this dualism (body/cognition), shifting to the cognitive work that makes emotions possible, simply reversing the importance of the distinction, or ignoring or silencing the body altogether. Much of the criticism of this kind of work is that the emotions are reified as cognitive products without any attention given to bodily or sensate experience (Burkitt 1999, Turner 1992, Woodward 1997). On the one hand the study of emotions as embodied phenomena is offered as a way of bridging the natural/social divide, and yet much of this work simply privileges one side of the dualism over the other. Let us now turn to a related area, health and illness, and begin to explore the idea of biology as a set of potentialities necessary for the production of experience, but not reducible to experience.

Practices of health and illness

The concept of 'healthism', as we have already seen, is seen to relate to a set of shifts which have occurred over the last decade or so. These shifts have occurred within and outside health care disciplines where the customer or client (as opposed to the patient), is increasingly addressed as a subject who should be willing and able to take on more personal responsibility for the maintenance of their own health. We are seen to live in a society increasingly governed by 'risk', where health risks to the individual become more uncertain and unpredictable. These 'cultures of risk' include major epidemiological changes such as the spread of HIV and AIDS throughout populations, concern with food manufacturing processes, the use of additives, genetically modified food, the danger of inter-species disease such as BSE and CJD, and major changes in the structure of the economy and government since the 1980s through the cultural and political reforms of the Conservative Party in Britain.

Bryan Turner (1997:xvii) argues that these reforms brought quite dramatic changes to the health care system, where centralised mechanisms for the provision of social security and welfare have been replaced by 'a logic of internal markets, competitive tendering and devolved budgets'. The emergence of a risk society has been seen by some to have created a new set of problems for governments and a concurrent more intensive need for a micro-surveillance and disciplining of the population. This disciplining is seen to be based on more subtle and systematic forms of management and regulation, where 'healthism' is one such mechanism. As we can see these are very similar arguments to those of Ross (1992), linking particular practices of the self with wider practices of government and regulation. There are different interpretations of this shift within the literature. An interesting chapter by Deborah Lupton (1997) explores how sociological critique of the discipline of clinical medicine has moved away from what were termed 'medicalisation critiques' in the 1970s.

These critiques drew on Marxist perspectives and argued that the medical profession objectified people, turning them into medical objects, diminishing their own capacity for autonomy in dealing with the management of their own health. The photographer and writer Jo Spence (1995:207) produced a range of photographic images exploring the ways in which she was objectified by the medical profession in her experience of breast cancer. Her decision to undertake alternative health care treatments was understood by the medical profession as an act of ignorance and stupidity. She argued that her emotional experiences of the disease and her vulnerability and fragility were elided, and she was related to as a set of symptoms, rather than a person in a more holistic way.

Much of this critique came from feminist critics of medicine who argued that medicine used the categories of disease and illness to disempower people and render them helpless and passive. Doctors were viewed as agents of domination wielding their power in a coercive and violent manner.

> The answers to medicalisation, according to most critics, include challenging the right of medicine to make claims about its powers to define and treat illness and disease and encouraging the state to exert greater regulation over the actions of the medical profession so as to limit its expansion and 'deprofessionalise' it. Most critics also advocate the 'empowerment of patients' (consumers), encouraging people to take back control over their own health by engaging in preventive health activities, assuming the role of 'consumer' by challenging the decisions and knowledge of doctors in the medical encounter, joining patient advocacy groups and eschewing medicine by seeking the attentions of alternative health practitioners. (Lupton 1997:97)

Foucault's work on 'disciplinary power' became increasingly important for moving beyond the 'medicalisation critique'. This work began to explore the ways in which subjects did not simply accept medical authority, but subverted, challenged and struggled with and against medical discourse. The argument was, that if power was productive, then, especially with the decentralisation of the welfare system, and the rise of alternative health care treatments, a range of options was open to individuals in the management of their own health and illness. Doctors were not understood as coercive figures, but as facilitators in wider strategies of disciplinary power, 'through persuading its subjects that certain ways of behaving and thinking are appropriate for them' (ibid.:99). Analytic attention turned to resistance as well as investment in medical practice and a study by Bloor and McIntosh (1990) is often quoted in the literature as an example of resistance to medical authority. This was a study of a group of Scottish mothers receiving home visits from health visitors exploring the ways in which they responded to medical authority. These included direct rejection and attack on the legitimacy and value of the workers interventions, non-cooperation, silence, escape, avoidance and concealment. As Lupton (ibid.:103) suggests:

> Central to this new emphasis on self-discipline is a focus between the imperatives of bodily management expressed at the

institutional level and ways that individuals engage in the conduct of everyday life. Foucault articulated an interest in the local techniques and strategies of power, or the micro-powers that are exercised at the level of everyday life, and the ways that resistance may be generated at those levels by people refusing to engage in these techniques and strategies. In other words, he was beginning to devote attention to the phenomenology of power relations.

Lupton suggests that the move in Foucault's later work to techniques and practices of the self, which we explored in the last chapter, is a method for exploring how actual individuals experience, relate to and understand aspects of their bodies, rather than simply focusing on the texts and practices of clinical medicine, for example. We encountered the term 'phenomenology' in Chapters 2 and 3 which signals a move to focusing on the 'lived experience' of the body – a focus upon 'being in the world'. In the foreword to *Mental Illness and Psychology* (Foucault 1987b), Dreyfus argues that Foucault's PhD thesis takes up some of the themes which he later returns to in his work on 'techniques of the self', in the three volumes of the *History of Sexuality*. In this work he became interested in historicising experience and exploring how it becomes possible to have particular kinds of subjective experience of selfhood. Foucault had a direct lineage to phenomenological ideas through his teachers and mentors, Merleau-Ponty (1962) and Heidegger (1962). Dreyfus cites the following extract from Foucault's thesis as an example of these phenomenological ideas being deployed in relation to the experience of 'mental illness'.

> The way in which a subject accepts or rejects his illness, the way in which he interprets it and gives signfication to its most absurd forms, constitutes one of the essential dimensions of the experience. (1987b:47)

Foucault however rejected his PhD thesis, and as Dreyfus argues rewrote it as *Madness and Civilisation* (1971), his classic work on the historical emergence of the very idea of mental pathology. This work moved beyond situating personal experience in concrete social contexts, to study the historical and discursive practices that define a 'psychology' in which the notion of mental illness becomes thinkable as something that can be the object and target of scientific practice. Foucault wrote the *Archaeology of Knowledge* as a methodological exegesis of some of the tools he used in this work, and his other archaeological studies (1972, 1973), to explore the historical conditions of emergence of the human sciences. We explored the tools which underpin an archaeological approach in Chapter 3 – objects, concepts, strategies and subject-positions (cf. Blackman 1994). The problem with this approach and its development by many scholars is the reading off of embodiment, from textual studies of discourses, texts and practices. As we saw quite clearly in the last chapter, new forms of subjectivity are being made possible in the gaps and contradictions between and within the 'psy' discourses. It is only through attention to embodied practice that we can adequately explore the cultural and psychological significance of these practices in people's everyday lives.

The work in the 'sociology of health and illness' that we have explored in this section is interesting because it begins to engage with resistance to medical discourse and authority. Although this is important, we must also be wary of moving to a position of celebrating the agency of subjects who are now seen to be able to 'exercise choice' in relation to the management of their own health. The interrelationship between scientific discourse and our own understandings and practices is complex. Many argue, as we have seen, that the very 'exercising of choice' is itself a strategy produced through discourses such as the psychological sciences, which help to produce enterprising, healthy citizens instrumental to the workings of neo-liberal societies (Rose 1990, Kinsman 1996). Kinsman explores how notions of 'personal risk' and responsibility, for example, underlay how the Canadian government targeted people living with HIV and AIDS in the 1980s. A key governmental concern was with the transmission of HIV throughout populations. The solution and answer to this problem was framed and articulated through public health discourse, the legal system, and medical and expert advice, as a problem with those who were already HIV positive.

Particular groups within the population were targeted as 'risky', rather than using preventive and safer sex education to target the whole population. These 'risky' groups were further delineated through a guilty/innocent dichotomy where some were held personally responsible for their illness (those who had become infected through sexual activity were viewed as 'self-inflicted'). Those who were infected through blood supplies and transfusions were considered innocent and not morally and psychologically culpable. This unifying strategy evolved despite responses from AIDS activists and grassroots communities who emphasised the notion of high-risk practices, rather than high-risk groups. The guilty/innocent dichotomy was further overlaid by an irresponsible/responsible dichotomy, which differentiated those who were responsible and self-managing in relation to their HIV status, as opposed to those who were not compliant in taking action to inhibit the spread of disease. Psychiatric and therapeutic discourses were used to understand this recalcitrance. Kinsman (1996) argues that these strategies were normalising, premised upon a language of choice in a context, at least in the Eighties, where there were limited treatment options for those living with HIV and AIDS. He suggests that rather than allowing individuals more autonomy in the experience and management of their health, these were actual subtle governmental strategies for producing responsible, self-managing subjects.

I think this study emphasises the value of attending to situated practices, and exploring the ways in which, in this example, responsibility as a possible strategy of governance is constructed in different spaces and sites. Again, it is a nominal term, which needs exploring for the ways in which it is made intelligible in different contexts, and makes possible specific practices based on these understandings. For example, if one examines the 'Cancer Journals', writings by the black, lesbian poet, Audre Lorde (1996) about her experiences of breast cancer, one could argue that she is deploying 'healthism' as a strategy for managing her illness. These journal entries are moving descriptions of her experience of living with cancer, her treatment by the medical profession as a black lesbian, and her rejection of prosthetics following a mastectomy. However, if we explore these practices as embodied and situated, her strategies for living, which emphasised her own control and autonomy in the management of her health, were articulated through 'discourses of survival' in a world structured by inequalities and oppressions, rather than discourses of public health and medicine. Again, we need to pay attention to the forms of subjectivity created within the interstices between scientific discourses and the myriad of other discourses, which articulate the body and subjectivity in radically different ways.

This attention to situated embodied practices must explore not only all those practices, knowledges, problems and concepts which

Foucault (1973) so cogently described in his archaeologies of the human sciences. We must also explore the emotional, biological and psychological economies – themselves discursively produced – which frame and articulate our different understandings of aspects of selfhood. We are now getting to the crux of the kind of approach I am beginning to develop in relation to embodiment, and how to understand a phenomenon such as voice-hearing which crosses the boundaries between particular understandings of the biological, psychological and social. I want to begin by thinking about the realm of the 'psychological', and will compare some of the practices of the HVN with particular 'self-help' practices popular as ways of thinking about problems, conflicts and miseries in our everyday lives.

You have the power to change!

Much has been written about the cultural significance of the rise of self-help practices, which currently circulate within many cultural spaces, including chatshows (Michaelidou 2000), women's magazines and so forth (Rimke 2000). Media scholars have been quick to comment on their social significance, arguing that they reproduce sexist and oppressive forms of femininity. McRobbie (1996) for example, argues that these practices align women's fears and desires with a consumer culture offered to them as a compensatory device for their bodily and emotional dissatisfactions and inadequacies. What is given less attention is the role these practices may play at an emotional and psychological level. This psychological realm and emotional economy is neither interior, if that implies outside discourse, nor private if that implies it is not socially shared. The view I wish to develop is one that argues that these practices, and their embodiment, must be analysed in relation to the difficulties of living the 'psy' image of personhood, what Rose (1990) terms the 'fiction of autonomous selfhood'. We must begin to explore how an economy of pain, fear, anxiety and distress is part of the apparatus through which this fictional identity is produced, lived and kept in place. Walkerdine (1996) has made similar arguments in the need to develop a 'psychology of survival' to explore the ways in which people 'live' and struggle with the competing ways in which they are addressed as subjects.

For example, practices of self-help identify particular experiences – the mundane psychopathology of everyday life – as potential transformative experiences. We are probably all familiar with the incitement and injunction of change constantly beckoning us from adverts, holiday brochures, new age practices, chatshows and so forth – 'You Have the Power to Change'. Conflicts and problems in relationships, the world of work, health, beauty and friendships are offered as the site or stimulus for change and self-improvement. In relation to this injunction to change a certain emotional economy is promoted as a power chain of signifiers of failure – unconfidence, unhappiness, unease, distress, lack of control, anxiety, guilt and frustration for example. The first step in change or transformation is recognising or identifying these experiences as signifiers of personal inadequacy and failure and believing that you can be in control, you can choose, you can be independent and autonomous. Ironically then, the 'psy' image of selfhood – the independent, freely choosing individual – is maintained as normative through the way the very difficulties of living this fictional identity are produced within these practices as signs of personal failure and inadequacy. What is more important, is that these practices identify personal bodily and psychological distress and articulate and make them intelligible in particular ways. This is not simply about language and concepts, but the ways in which psychological and bodily experiences (produced in relation to particular ways of living and being) are an important part of this discursive apparatus.

This is where I want to raise problems and possibilities for this kind of work into the new millennium, especially in considering and analysing new forms of subjectivity. In the last chapter, we explored how telepathic practices are one of the most popular and successful ways of managing voices within the groups – those who through hard work, effort and struggle have come to embody their voices as a key site for spiritual development and transformation. I argued that one factor may be that the spiritual church offers guidance, compassion and understanding, as well as actual techniques and practices, such as development circles, where voice-hearers can attend to and transform their relationships to their voices. I would also argue that what these practices do is engage with an emotional and biological economy, itself produced through 'psy' relations to the voices, such as fear, distress, dread, terror, shame, confusion and anxiety. This emotional economy many have argued, as we saw in Chapter 6, is itself generated by the psychiatric definition of hallucination. This definition is seen to produce a negative societal response, and anxiety, fear, shame and self-doubt rather than the more positive emotional responses within other cultural settings (Wallace 1959). Within telepathic practices and understandings, disintegration and states of mind not usually associated with waking rationality are viewed as conducive to a state of psychic mindfulness. Thus, those very bodily experiences of distress and anxiety viewed as further symptoms of psychopathology within the 'psy' disciplines, become the object of practices which attempt to achieve relaxation through more meditative and visualisation techniques. In other words, they are worked on and transformed at the level of sensuous, bodily awareness. Bodily distress is recognised and identified as the potential for psychic reverie, rather than failure and inadequacy.

Embodiment and biology

This example highlights the importance of exploring biological and psychological processes as generative potentialities, which can be transformed through the strategies and practices we develop to identify and act upon these processes. These processes are also not static, constant categories, but are produced in relation to different ways of understanding what it means to be human, across a range of practices which 'make up' the social. The kind of practice and engagement with the 'psychological' and 'biological' I wish to develop, has affinities with a tradition of work being produced within a sub-discipline of anthropology – medical anthropology. Thomas Csordas (1994, 1997) has developed what he terms a 'cultural phenomenological' approach to the study of the relationship between embodiment and biology. He wants to attend to some of the problems with 'biologism' by starting from a methodological standpoint of 'an experiential understanding of being in the world' (1994:269). This approach is a move away from understanding experience as located within a 'pre-objective world' or pre-social body (a view which focuses upon experience prior to language and the social, i.e. Merleau-Ponty 1962).

Cultural phenomenology argues that 'cultural meaning is intrinsic to embodied experience on the level of being in the world' (Csordas 1994:270). Let us explore how Csordas develops this work, by taking an example from a study he carried out with Dan, a 30-year-old Navajo Indian who is suffering from a left-lobe cancerous lesion on his brain. The lesion and its post-operative treatment and removal creates particular kinds of neurological symptomatology, such as memory loss, seizures, auditory hallucinations, mild retardation and loss of verbal and written ability. In the clinical literature the experiential and behavioural symptoms of post-operative treatments for lesions and tumours include what is constituted as a psychiatric profile. It is termed 'hyperreligiousity' – a schizophrenic-like experience with repeated experiences of religious conversion. What Csordas is interested in, is what he terms Dan's dialogue with his biological experience. How does Dan integrate and incorporate these kinds of experiences into his life?

Dan decided that much of the experience was a 'calling' to follow the Navajo way – to become a healer and medicine man who would help others. This was a kind of cultural validation for his experience, the most important factor being that the elders of the community recognised this calling as genuine and authentic. Within Navajo traditions, peyote-inspired prayer meetings take place where these callings are validated. Through prayer, and the ingestion of peyote (a hallucinogenic), the healer is seen to hear voices, from the Holy Gods, instructing them in healing ways. One of the problems for Dan was because of the loss of his verbal ability a lot of the voices he heard and repeated did not make much sense to the elders. He validated this by saying that the voices he heard were speaking to the contemporary situation of younger Navajo Indians who were acculturated, and that he had not become sick when ingesting the peyote. The understanding was, that if peyote made one sick, it was a punishment from the gods for bad words.

One could argue that these experiences were purely biological or neurological, brought on by post-operative symptoms and the ingestion of peyote, which were then interpreted and given a religious significance by Dan. This is a popular way, as we have already seen that biology or psychology is seen to interact with culture. This view assumes the universality and causality of biology, where biology is a constant category used to explain the aetiology of certain experiences. What is missing from these analyses, Csordas argues, is the space 'in-between' where both become transformed. For example, in many of the studies of LSD in the Sixties, it was argued that there was no such thing as an 'LSD experience'. The drug itself was simply a potentiality where the actual psychedelic experience was informed by the 'setting', an environment which could positively, or negatively, shape the experience, and the guide – a person who could stimulate trust, stability and emotional serenity (Masters and Houston 1966). Similarly, Csordas argues that the strategies and understandings that people use to engage with bodily experiences transform the bodily experience itself. Neither one, nor the other can be disentangled, rather there is a synthesis of bodily experience with a deep sociality. Csordas is arguing that biological processes are an important part of embodiment, but that they are not reducible to biology. Going beyond a preoccupation with causality, he argues that the body is an agent, not a resource, and that biology is always situated, a dynamic process. This is not simply an 'interaction' between biology and the social, but that we carry the social in our bodies; it is an inseparable process.

> Here we rejoin Heidegger and Merleau-Ponty; one condemning the error of biologism that consists in merely adding a mind or soul to the human body considered as an animal organism, the other condemning the error of treating the social as an object instead of recognising that our bodies carry the social about inseparably with us before any objectification. The errors are symmetrical; in one instance biology is treated as objective (the biological substrate), in the other the social is treated as objective, and in both instances the body is diminished and the preobjective bodily synthesis is missed. For biologism, the body is the mute, objective biological substrate upon which meaning is superimposed. For sociologism, the body is a blank slate upon which meaning is inscribed, a physical token to be moved about in a pre-structured symbolic environment, or the raw material from which natural symbols can be generated for social discourse. (Csordas 1994: 287)

Csordas thus argues that a phenomenological grounding of both 'biology' and 'culture', rather than a biological substratum overlaid by culture, should be the starting point for analysis. This work seems crucial for finding and developing ways of bringing the body and biology back into our cultural analyses. We need to find ways of engaging with biological and psychological processes, and reopening a dialogue with those disciplines, such as the human and life sciences, who deploy reductionist and causal ways of understanding biological processes. We also must avoid the kinds of social and discourse determinism which we have inadvertently developed through the rejection of biology in processes of subject formation. These concerns, as we have already seen in this chapter, have been voiced by many. Donna Haraway (1991, 1997), a biologist by training, has argued quite cogently for the materiality of bodies, as have other feminists in different ways (Butler 1993, Grosz 1995). Linda Birke (1998, 1999), a cardiologist by training, has begun to explore the kinds of metaphors and ways of imagining biological processes which underpin clinical medicine. This work is hugely important and signals future directions for research, and dialogue with those currently working in these disciplines. In the final concluding chapter I wish to draw together some of the different aspects we have explored, in the 'problem of hallucination', and begin to think about how this work can be developed in critical psychology and cultural analysis more generally. I have not provided a blueprint for the future in this chapter, but merely drawn out some of the themes which need urgent attention, if we are to approach biology, psychology and the social as embodied practices.

9
Conclusion: 'Imagining the Future'

My starting point for the themes which have been raised in this book was how we might begin to rethink the 'problem of hallucination' in a radically revised way. Although I align my work with the tradition of critical psychology, the 'turn to language' characteristic of this burgeoning discipline does not allow us to talk about 'psychology' or 'biology' other than as complicated effects of discursive processes. I hope that some of the arguments in the previous chapter go some way to drawing out why urgent attention is needed to revisit biological and psychological processes as generative potentialities, rather than static entities which can be rejected and relocated within language. I will develop some of these lines of argument as I offer some new directions for research for 'cultural critics' confronting science and those working in the professions who may be seeking some new and novel ways of engaging with the 'problem of hallucination'.

In this concluding chapter I want to draw together some of the arguments and connections made throughout the book, and particularly think about the current context in which particular claims are being made about the role of psychological understandings and techniques in the treatment of the psychoses. A recent article in the British newspaper, the *Guardian* Weekend magazine supplement, started with the headline, 'Talking Heads. A few sceptics survive, but it is now generally accepted that therapy can alleviate all manner of mental health problems, from schizophrenia to depression to phobia. But how to choose among the 400 kinds of treatment on offer?' (e.g. Miller and Rose 1994, 1997, for historical research on the emergence of the Tavistock Clinic as a site for managing the neuroses). This heralding of psychology as having a more prominent role in treating symptoms most associated with strictly biochemical or biological processes is important to examine. A recent BPS (British Psychological Society) report titled: *Recent Advances in the Understanding of Mental Illness and Psychotic Experience*[1] also champions the 'psychological' in the treatment of psychosis (again those experiences which historically have been associated with the bio-chemical and neurological, as opposed to the neurotic and hence psychological). This report ties together recent understandings and use of psychological techniques with psychosis (i.e., CBT) and the campaigns of service users calling for the social isolation and stigma to be challenged, which further discriminates against and disadvantages those with mental health problems in society.

Rather than understand this as a linear shift towards the 'softer' side of 'psy' practice, I want to underline how there has always been an alliance and connection between the 'harder' biologically oriented studies and those which evaluate and advocate more psychologically oriented techniques (Miller 1986). It is the nature of the shifting connections between the 'biological', 'psychological' and 'social', throughout the transformation of both disciplines (psychology and psychiatry), that alerts us to the error of seeing the present as a time of rapid innovation and progress, which has moved psychology more centre-stage. As I argued in the introduction to the book, psychological understandings are not simply unproblematic alternatives and have their own conditions of emergence. Scientific progress and innovation certainly cannot account for why specific forms of psychological technique are now being increasingly used in the management of voices for example. It is also important to recognise the effects that the campaigns of service users are having on the treatment and understanding of phenomena such as voice-hearing. The BPS report was written in consultation with service users and promulgates one of the main conclusions to come out of various user campaigns, including those of the Hearing Voices Network. That is, that service users are the experts on their own experience, and that professionals should listen and learn, rather than simply diagnose symptoms according to a biomedical framework of explanation. Romme and Escher (2000), two psychiatrists who have been instrumental in the development of the Hearing Voices Network, both here and in the Netherlands, argue that this reverse in the professional/client relationship was one of the biggest challenges to their own practice. As they state (ibid.:136):

> From our own research and work with voice hearers it is clear to us that thinking in terms of specific diseases, typified by the DSM, does no good when it comes to psychiatric illnesses. We need a paradigm shift if psychiatry really is to make progress in the treatment of psychosis. This shift is quite simple: we need to

accentuate the complaints and analyse their relationship in relation to the person's life history and in relation to each other. This is the usual medical way of working, from which only psychiatry deviates in jumping from complaint to diagnosis instead of back to causational factors.

Let us explore some of the contexts, problems and questions which psychological techniques are beginning to address and frame in particular kinds of ways. We explored in the beginning of the book, how two key problems have emerged which are linked to psychiatry's perceived role to provide the kinds of 'techniques of cure' to allow people to safely return to and live within the community. I do not want to get into a debate about what kind of community people are entering upon leaving hospital for example, but want to think about how 'failure' within the community is predominantly understood. Within the profession itself, one key problem, as we have seen, is the issue of compliance. Again and again, when the broadsheets choose to represent mental health issues there are key signifiers, such as 'risk', danger and often violence or death which structure how the issue is presented to the public (cf. Philo 1994, Blackman and Walkerdine 2001). People with mental health problems are presented as time-bombs waiting to go off, and the safety valve or cushion is the medication, which many cannot or choose not to take. In the case of Christopher Clunis, upon release from hospital he had stopped taking his drugs, although his psychiatrists had considered him well and able to live outside the hospital prior to this point. He had then gone on to stab and kill Jonathon Zito.

The issue of non-compliance, as well as becoming a governmental and legal issue, is also a concern for pharmaceutical companies. We saw in Chapter 2, how one of the key issues surrounding compliance is that of patients feeling as if they can exert some kind of control over the illness (Drury et al. 2000). One role for psychological techniques, and CBT in particular has been to facilitate these kinds of beliefs. However, pharmaceutical companies and psychiatrists also realise that in order for people to manage their own symptoms, through self-administered medication, they also need to believe in the efficacy of the drugs. We saw some of the responses from pharmaceutical companies to this problem, such as experimenting with soluble drugs and so forth.

Compliance then is a problem which connects across a nexus of agencies, sites and ways of managing mental distress, all of which are concerned with what are constituted as the 'psycho-social' factors which influence the on-going management of symptoms. This is certainly opening up a space for psychological techniques, but as we have seen, these are usually seen as a useful adjunct to the more biomedical interventions, and usually only in relation to non-compliance or 'treatment-resistant' symptoms. 'Treatment-resistant' symptoms challenge the legitimacy of many of the diagnostic categories and concepts which psychiatry uses to differentiate the pseudo-hallucination from the hallucination. We saw the way that psychiatric theories and definitions of hallucination deploy a number of key concepts, such as duration, control, vividness, source, location and severity to make this distinction. These concepts are combined with particular judgements made about social and work functioning used to measure how well a person is adjusted to 'reality'. 'Treatment-resistant' symptoms are those which have been deemed 'psychiatric' as opposed to 'psychological' in origin, and yet do not respond to medication. The categories which overlay these distinctions, such as the psychotic and neurotic, biological/environmental and natural/social are all being challenged by the practice of psychiatry which does not easily respond to such diagnostic practices and classifications.

Griggers (1998) focuses her critique of the practices of 'bio-psychiatry' on another disorder, which first began to emerge in the 1990s. Post-traumatic stress disorder, as we explored in Chapter 1, is a disorder which is seen to produce symptoms, including hallucinations, which are constituted as a normal reaction to a severe and calamitous event. The concepts articulated within psychiatric practice to make the distinction between the pseudo- and the pathological hallucination are also challenged by symptoms usually characterised as signs of psychosis. Citing an expert in the field she argues that what can be agreed on by practitioners, is that many of the usual assumptions about symptoms do not apply. 'For example, the presence of hallucinations may not indicate psychosis, depression may not be major affective disorder, episodic overwhelming anxiety may not be panic, and hypomanic agitation may not be bipolar disorder' (Dominiak 1992 in Griggers 1998:136).

This may not be such a surprise given the implications of the historical investigation carried out in Chapters 4, 5 and 6. The concepts and categories embedded in the theories psychiatry deploys in its diagnostic measures are not simply the accumulation of knowledge and 'truths' built up through scientific experimentation. We have begun to see the ways in which the current psychiatric and psycho-logical landscape, and the terms which map and identify these realms are made possible by a complex interweaving of shifts within the discipline and particular events and historical circumstances which played a part in these mutations. They are neither entirely 'internal' nor 'external' but combine and relate in complex ways. What is certain is that the current terms and categories through which we recognise the psychiatric and the psychological are not simply the expression of the steady march of scientific progress. As I argued in these chapters, the terms 'psychiatric' and 'psychologi-cal' are not continuous terms which are simply evolving as we discover more about these areas, but are articulated through allied concepts and explanatory structures, such that their meaning is always contingent. Indeed, the psychological and the terms, which identify this realm, bear little relationship to those which mapped the 'moral' in the nineteenth century. This was a space which could be termed psychological, but was articulated through concepts which actually unsettle the image of psychological normality and health so prevalent in the present (cf. Blackman 2001).

If we remain sceptical about the 'steady march of science', as a trope for understanding some of the shifts we may be witnessing across the 'psy' disciplines as I conclude this book, how can we evaluate and diagnose the present? In Chapter 3 we explored some ways in which critical psychologists have responded to the 'crisis' within the discipline by redefining the subject-matter and methods of psychological inquiry. The focus is on language and the methods used are for the most part interpretative, providing what are seen as 'social' rather than 'psychological' or 'biological' explanations. Latour (2000) warns of opposing the natural and the social in such a way. We have explored this move in many guises, where the natural or the essential are rejected and appeals to social explana-tions for behaviour, thought and conduct are provided (Riley 1983, Fuss 1989). The appeal to the social as a constructive force is often made, but there is little sense of where this process occurs, and indeed quite what the 'social' is.

> 'Society' has to be composed, made up, constructed, established, maintained and assembled. It is no longer to be taken as the hidden source of causality which could be mobilised so as to account for the existence and stability of some other action or both. (Latour 2000:113)

Latour (ibid.) suggests the trope of 'translation' rather than 'social construction' as a way of thinking about the 'making up' of the present. Rather than reject the realm of the biological or psychological as essentialist, we could begin to explore the ways in which these realms are translated into particular kinds of 'entities', which other concepts are then used to describe, categorise, classify and so forth. This was the basis of the kind of discursive analysis developed in Chapters 1 and 2, where we explored the boundaries, alliances and tapestry of the modern 'psy' architecture in relation to the phenomenon of hearing voices. This kind of detailed analysis goes beyond the theme of 'social constructionism' with its echoes of social or discourse determinism. The focus is on the ways in which, particular concepts and explanatory structures combine and recombine with ways of thinking about the biological, psychological and psychiatric to frame and articulate the 'problem of hallucination'. These may be specific problems encountered within clinical practice, the parameters of which may also have been set in advance, by those authoritative institutions such as the legal system or even the media, who pronounce particular experiences as troublesome or pathological in some way (i.e., non-compliance and the 'risk' that may ensue).

This kind of discursive analysis maps the kinds of concepts and explanatory structures which underpin the protocols of modern psychiatric practice, and also structure encounters between most 'psy' professionals and voice-hearers. These protocols are summed up by Romme and Escher (2000) in a recent article in *Mental Health Care*, and were analysed using Foucault's approach to 'practices and techniques of the self' in Chapter 7. These include paying little attention to the content of voices, getting the voice-hearer to deny their reality and view them as signs of disease and illness, deciding on their psychiatric or psychological status and reaching for the prescription pad for the former. The legitimacy of these distinctions is increasingly blurred as we have seen, but this kind of diagnostic practice and intervention is still the *raison d'être* of biomedical psychiatry. This continues even when there are still no unified explanations and much dissent and controversy over the exact mechanisms seen to produce the possibility of the experience.

As we have seen then, one way of evaluating those concepts, which map the psychiatric and psychological terrain, is to explore the kinds of practices and interventions made possible in relation to the 'problem of hallucination'. It has been argued, in different ways, that 'psy' practices help to produce a particular emotional economy, such as fear, anxiety, omnipotence and paranoia for example, which are then read as further signs of psychopathology within much psychiatric practice. The emotional responses to the voices are produced out of the lived relations to the voices, rather than the voices per se. These responses also incorporate particular imagined and materialised experiences of bodily processes, which are often used as the basis for differentiation and classification. In such an evaluation it is important to pay attention to the synthesis of bodily experience with a deep sociality (Csordas 1994), such that we do not approach either the biological or psychological as separate, constant categories, which we can untangle and view as causally determining such an experience.

Let us take an example from Chapter 4 to develop this theme further. In this chapter we explored how the terms 'moral', 'physical' and the 'biological' shift and change in meaning through their location within allied fields of concepts and explanatory structures. Thus, the term 'moral' that underpinned the practices and understandings at the York Retreat in 1792, were rather different from the notion of 'moral insanity' which was part of the psychiatric classificatory system in the mid-nineteenth century (Esquirol 1845). These different understandings, which combined particular ways of specifying the 'physical' and 'biological', made possible very different self-understandings and practices. Hack Tuke (1872), the grandson of Samuel Tuke, the founder of the Retreat, revisited some of these practices and advocated a particular way of understanding the 'psychological' which he argued underpinned their efficacy. This mapping of the psychological constituted the imagination as the principle through which particular experiences were produced, such as mesmerism, hypnotism, the effects of emotion in producing disease and so forth. This way of understanding the psychological was very different from some of the terms and concepts which mapped the psychiatric and the psychological within evolutionary understandings, which were incorporated into psychiatry at the time of his writings. Particular terms mapped Tuke's 'psycho-physical' space, including the will, the notion of sympathetic action, expectant-attention and so forth, which relied on very different ways of imagining biological processes and their relationship to aspects of the body, which for Tuke were located within the mind. Mind–body relations within this way of specifying the 'moral' were in an inseparable union.

This way of imagining the biological is very different from some of the more fixed and mechanistic models which were incorporated into clinical medicine in the nineteenth century. The biological was conceived as an interior space, which one could dissect, look inside and reveal the diseased organs to the gaze of the clinician (Foucault 1973). The focus within clinical medicine, as we saw in Chapter 5, was on mapping the location of disease within the brain structures of the individual, which were seen to produce sensory disturbances echoing the physical and psychic degeneration. Tuke imagined biological processes in very different ways, which were more fluid and less fixed in organs as seats of disease and pathology. The notion of 'sympathy' was central to Tuke's theories, which saw the body and mind as fluid, interconnecting systems, which could affect each other. His focus was on explaining 'spiritual phenomena' for example, rather than focusing upon materialist conceptions of the body, which could only understand particular experiences as markers of illness and disease.

I am not a trained biologist so feel hesitant in expanding further on the very different ways of mapping the 'interior' which underpin the above contrasting examples. However, as I argued in the last chapter, this would seem a fruitful direction for further research and development. Linda Birke (1999) has produced a cogent and illuminating account of some of the different ways in which the 'interior' of the body is mapped both within clinical medicine and lay-discourse. She shows how the term 'biology' is slippery and does not have a fixed meaning throughout the life sciences, and yet also how the predominant narratives of biology are mechanistic or even militaristic (Haraway 1991). She also explores how new understandings of the body are emerging from the disciplines of cybernetics where the notion of 'information' in terms of the genetic code, is creating new and novel ways of thinking about what makes us human (cf. Gilroy 2000). She explores how the various metaphors for mapping the interior always have an intimate relationship to wider cultural ways of thinking about individuality and sociality.

We have seen the ways in Chapter 7, in which the 'body' within social and cultural theory, even though making a fashionable comeback in the last decade or so, is one which is posited as endlessly transformable through discursive and social processes. As Birke (1999) highlights, it is the surface of the body which is paid most attention within these accounts, focusing upon the ways in which the surface of the body is changed and defined through practices of consumption, leisure and advertising (cf. Blackman 2000). The 'interior' of the body is left for the biological sciences to theorise alongside the cultural accusations of its biological determinism. We saw in Chapter 7, how social and cultural theory has increasingly turned to consumption as a topography of the social (Drotner 1994, Fiske 1992, Shirato 1993, Wolf 1993). Arguments concerning the diversification and commodification of the market are said to have produced concomitant changes in identity and its formation (Featherstone 1991). The more postmodern accounts suggest that culture is made up of a collection of packaged styles organised around taste and aesthetics in the arenas of fashion, music, relationships and so forth. The subject is now a consumer; free to choose, fashion and style their own identities from the cultural resources on offer (Chamber 1986, Crook et al. 1992, Kellner 1995, Polhemus 1994, Shields 1992, Strinati 1995)

This focus upon the 'socially constructed' body, as we saw in the last chapter, actually denies or negates the issue of biology altogether. The body is written upon by cultural discourses, to the point where biology is either conceived of as a fixed entity, which is interpreted in different ways, or is silenced and given little analytic attention. As Birke (ibid.:137) argues,

> The biological body thus disappears, constructed in such work only as and through discourse and not the reverse. This discursive body might be contrasted in social theory to concepts based on the agency of the body, while the biological body remains a silence shadow.

One of the questions raised in relation to the 'social constructionist' thesis is whether there is a residue, which lies beyond discourse or can we only speak the body through the very ways it has been made to signify within discourse? What are conceived of as particular bodily and psychological experiences are then viewed in a more romantic fashion as the recalcitrant material that normative power relations fail to regulate (Pizzorno 1992). Thus particular acts, gestures, states of mind and body have become the 'outside', resistant, material from which to critique the regulatory functioning of the practices producing modern, disciplined 'man'.

Birke (1999) suggests a way of engaging with biology, which focuses upon potentiality and possibility, rather than fixity, which as we have seen easily reduces to essentialism and determinism (Fuss 1989, Riley 1983). She also raises a point which has been a key issue throughout the writing of this book. That is that many scientists are equally dismissive of our work as deterministic and argue that they are always looking at the 'interaction' between the social and nature. We saw in Chapter 1 how this notion of 'interaction' is equally problematic (Riley 1983:28), viewing biology as a set of invariant characteristics, which set limits on how a person is able to interact with the social, and also the levels to which the social can impact or impinge upon the individual. The notion of potentiality has much to offer, allowing us to explore how biological processes are a key condition of possibility for particular kinds of embodied experiences which always enter and are lived and transformed by individuals through a nexus of social and historical relations. The following quote from Burkitt (1999:1) illustrates to a certain extent, this notion of biology as a transformative potentiality:

> it is also common for individuals who have undergone surgery which has radically altered their physical features (also) to feel that their self-image has changed as well. There is obviously a complex process going on around the body, in which the body itself can create a symbolic image and understanding of itself, yet changes in the body can also radically alter its symbolization.

Thomas Csordas (1994) has sketched out some of the key foci, which might be key concerns in the development of this kind of approach. In his cultural phenomenological study of charismatic healing (1997), he explores the kinds of 'self-processes', biological, cultural and what we might term psychological or even psychiatric, which underpin particular ways of understanding and acting upon the embodied self. This is the basis of the kind of approach to voice-hearing as an embodied practice I developed in Chapter 7, exploring the different embodied experiences of voices made possible through different problematisations and interventions in relation to aspects of existence and how they were articulated and made salient. Even though some of the practices the voice-hearers engage in can be found within psychological approaches to voices, such as CBT, their work is not simply a move to the psychological. Within the diverse practices encouraged within the network, are very different ways of imagining and specifying the psychological and its relationship to the biological, different models of personhood, different ways of

understanding the body (mind–body relations), different authoritative institutions, different 'ethical substances' and very different aims
and strategies.

The kind of analysis we encountered in Chapter 7 also prob-
lematises the notion that particular practices of the self are a key link
point between the ways in which authorities seek to govern individuals and how individuals understand and act upon themselves
(Rimke 2000, Rose 1990). As I argue with Walkerdine in *Mass
Hysteria: Critical Psychology and Media Studies* (2001), the painful
necessity of self-invention and self-transformation, central to the
practices of liberal democracies and those knowledges which
underpin them, also creates the possibility of new forms of subjectivity, sociality and new ways of coping. It is not that the 'psy'
discourses determine how individuals relate to and act upon themselves, but that the injunction to relate to and act upon oneself,
through the fiction of autonomous selfhood, in the gaps, silences
and contradictions creates the possibility of its own transformation.
It is the new kinds of psychology and subjectivity made possible in
these embodied practices which also needs analytic attention.

As I conclude this book, I am left thinking about some of the contradictions which surround the 'problem of hallucination'. We are
witnessing attacks on the theoretical codes of psychiatric practice,
both by allied professionals such as psychologists, but also from
service users who are finding more help, guidance, encouragement,
support and new ways of coping from other survivors. These survivors have turned to organisations such as the HVN, partly because
of the very failure of psychiatry to help them cope with their voices.
More attention is being paid to the way in which media reports of
mental health help to maintain and reinforce the stigma and social
isolation felt by people with mental health problems. This runs
alongside governmental and legal calls for 'detainment' of those
who constitute a 'risk', even when no criminal act has been committed. A thorough shake-up of the mental health system has been
called for, and it is important to remind the reader that mental
health charities such as MIND have successfully campaigned against
stricter juridical measures as the 'knee-jerk' solution to the problem
of compliance and treatment-resistant symptoms. It is clear that
professionals need to challenge their own practice, both in terms of
the theoretical codes and professional relationships they maintain
and reproduce with their clients. Many service users do not want
partnership, others maintain that this will only be possible if pro-

fessionals are truly able to listen to them, rather than objectify and transform them into medical objects.

What is clear, is that unless those who wish to critique science from cultural perspectives are able to work more closely and create dialogues with those working in the biological sciences, there will be more and more of a gap between theory (including theoretical critique), and the partnering of biomedical psychiatry with the biomedical industry. The alliance between 'hard' and 'soft' approaches to phenomena such as hearing voices will be more finely distributed across different sites and agencies. The 'hard' edge of psychiatric practice, particularly with the rise of genetic science and the human genome project, linked as it is with commerce, the commodification of knowledge and vast sums of money, will carry on with its investment in human misery and suffering. In order to close down the boundary likely to open up further between 'the molecular' and the practice of clinical psychiatry and psychology, we need to find ways of working more closely with those trained in biology and its related disciplines to find ways of re-imagining biological processes as potentialities.

I hope that the study this book presents is an example of the value of approaching phenomena as both situated (historically and socially for example) and embodied. As a critical psychologist and cultural theorist I hope I have convinced you of the value of not simply moving to text and discourse as a way of understanding the constitution of the psychological. I have taken what some might argue to be a small, socially marginal aspect of being and explored the central role its articulation plays in the current boundaries and understandings of what it means to be human. I hope I have also convinced you of the value of historical investigation, detailed discursive analysis of the language and concepts of the 'psy' disciplines themselves and the issue of embodiment. This is an important shift to explore how these processes are translated and embodied by those struggling with the very real materialities of those psychological, psychiatric and biological objects which 'make up' some of the ways in which we experience the exigencies of our lives. I hope that this book can open up the debate further and bring together all those professionals and academics who are interested in supporting service users in their struggles. I do not believe that service users necessarily need 'us' in their struggles, but that attacks on the various levels and functioning of 'psy' practice is important in what could be the transformation and modernisation of both disciplines.

Notes

Introduction

1. Psychology and psychiatry.
2. Miller and Rose 1986:3 suggest that critiques of psychiatry since its inception have played a crucial role in the transformation and modernisation of the practice.
3. Those symptoms which anti-psychotic drugs fail to suppress or lessen.
4. Cf. Blackman and Walkerdine (2001) for a more detailed discussion.
5. What Rose (1990) terms the 'fiction of autonomous selfhood'.

Chapter 1

1. 'The person may "see" a group of people hovering over the bed when no one is actually there' (*DSM III R*, p. 101). 'Most common are auditory hallucinations which frequently involve many voices the person perceives as coming from outside his or her head' (*DSM III R*, p. 187).
2. *Guardian*, 22 February 1994, p. 17.
3. Or to use a term adopted by the psychiatric user movement, the 'psychiatrised personality'.
4. Neurological, biochemical, gnomic and so forth.
5. 'In their elegant study Baron and Gruen (1988) found a greater familial risk for schizophrenia and schizophrenic spectrum disorders using probands born in the winter and spring, than among those born during the remainder of the year. This finding is not in line with the major part of the pre-existing literature, which primarily indicates an opposite trend' (Sacchetti 1989:266).

Chapter 2

1. *Guardian*, 5 February 1992, p. 19.
2. August 2000, volume 177.
3. Often referred to as the black box theory of perception.
4. See Blackman and Walkerdine 2001 for a fuller discussion of these points, and the possibility of developing a critical psychology along these lines.
5. 'The content of people's beliefs, be they mentally healthy or sick, stems directly from their life experience and hence is inevitably influenced by their culture' (Leff 1981:7).

6. Often termed a 'hermeneutic circle'.
7. 'It is important to note, however, that a person cannot maintain his position in a full-fledged fantasy community while landing a jet-plane on an aircraft carrier' (ibid.:134).

Chapter 3

1. A label which dismisses biological explanations as reductionist and deterministic.
2. A conception of truth used as an independent means to evaluate discourse, that is, that is true and that is false.
3. For example, a concern with food manufacturing processes, the use of additives, genetically modified food, the danger of interspecies disease and so on and so forth.
4. The recent book by bell hooks (2000) 'all about love' is a good example of the ways in which the concept of 'self-help' can be a 'practice of survival' for marginalised and oppressed groups.

Chapter 9

1. Available from the BPS; it can be downloaded free from <www.understandingpsychosis.com>

Bibliography

Adlam, D., Henriques, J., Rose, N., Salfield, A., Venn, C. and Walkerdine, V. (1977) 'Psychology, Ideology and the Human Subject'. *Ideology and Consciousness*. 1, 5–56.

Al-Issa, I. (1977) 'Social and Cultural Aspects of Hallucinations'. *Psychology Bulletin*. 84, 570–87.

Al-Issa, I. (1978) 'Sociocultural Factors in Hallucinations'. *International Journal of Social Psychiatry*. 24, 167–76.

Alexander, F.G. and Selesnick, S.T. (1966) *The History of Psychiatry*. Harper and Row: New York.

Alpert, M. (1985) 'The Signs and Symptoms of Schizophrenia'. *Comprehensive Psychiatry*. 26, 103–12.

American Psychiatric Association (1980) *DSM 3: Diagnostic and Statistical Manual of Mental Disorders*. American Psychiatric Association: Washington, DC.

Ardener, E. (1971) *Introductory Essay in Social Anthropology and Language*. Tavistock: London.

Armistead, N. (ed.) (1974) *Reconstructing Social Psychology*. Penguin: Harmondsworth.

Armstrong, D. (1983) *Political Anatomy of the Body*. Cambridge University Press: Cambridge.

Barber, T.X. and Calverley, D.S. (1964) 'An Experimental Study of "Hypnotic" (Auditory and Visual) Hallucinations'. *Journal of Abnormal and Social Psychology*. 63, 13–20.

Barnes, M. and Berke, J. (1971) *Two Accounts of a Journey Through Madness*. MacGibbon and Kee: London.

Barnes, T.R.E. and McPhilips, M.A. (1999) 'Critical Analysis and Comparison of the Side-effects of Anti-Psychotic Drugs'. *British Journal of Psychiatry*. 174 (Supplement 38), 34–43.

Baron, M. and Gruen, R. (1988) 'Risk Factors of Schizophrenia: Season of Birth and Family History'. *British Journal of Psychiatry*. 152, 460–5.

Beau Travail (1998) Directed by Claire Denis. Artificial Eye Productions.

Belensky, G.L. (1979) 'Unusual Visual Experiences Reported by Subjects in the British Army Study of Sustained Operations, Exercise Early Call'. *Military Medicine*, 144, 695–6.

Bentall, R.P. (1990) 'The Illusion of Reality; A Review and Integration of Psychological Research on Hallucinations'. *Psychological Bulletin*. 107, 82–95.

Bentall, R.P. (1996) 'From Cognitive Studies of Psychosis to Cognitive-Behavioural Techniques for Psychotic Symptoms' in Haddock, G. and

Slade, P.D. (eds) *Cognitive-Behavioural Interventions and Psychotic Disorders*. Routledge: London and New York.

Bentall, R.P. and Slade, P.D. (1985) 'Reality Testing and Auditory Hallucinations: A Signal Detection Analysis'. *British Journal of Clinical Psychology*. 24, 159–69.

Beveridge, W.H. (1905) 'The Problems of the Unemployed'. *Sociological Papers*. 3, 324–31.

Bhabha, H. (1994) *The Location of Culture*. Routledge: London.

Birke, L. (1998) 'The Broken Heart' in Shildrick, M. and Price, J. (eds) *Vital Signs. Feminist Reconfigurations of the Bio/logical Body*. Edinburgh University Press: Edinburgh.

Birke, L. (1999) *Feminism and the Biological Body*. Edinburgh University Press: Edinburgh.

Blackman, L. (1994) 'What is Doing History? The Use of History to Understand the Constitution of Contemporary Psychological Objects'. *Theory and Psychology*. 4(4), 485–504.

Blackman, L. (1996) 'The Dangerous Classes: Retelling the Psychiatric Story'. *Feminism and Psychology*. 6(3) August, 361–79.

Blackman, L. (1998) 'Culture, Technology and Subjectivity' in J. Wood (ed.) *The Virtual Embodied. Presence/Practice/Technology*. Routledge: London and New York.

Blackman, L. (1999a) 'An Extraordinary Life: the Legacy of an Ambivalence'. *New Formations* 'Diana and Democracy' (Special Issue). 36, 111–24.

Blackman, L. (1999b) 'Beyond the Fragile Chains We Call Democracy: Ethics, Embodiment and Experience' in Maiers, W. et al. (eds) *Challenges to Theoretical Psychology*. Captus Press: Toronto.

Blackman, L. (2000) 'Ethics, Embodiment and the Voice Hearing Experience'. *Theory, Culture and Society*. 17(5) October, 55–74.

Blackman, L. (2001) 'A Psychophysics of the Imagination' in V. Walkerdine (ed.) *Millennium Psychology*. Palgrave: Basingstoke and New York.

Blackman, L. and Walkerdine, V. (2001) *Mass Hysteria: Critical Psychology and Media Studies*. Palgrave: Basingstoke and New York.

Blackwood, D.R., Glabus, M., Duncan, J., O'Carroll, R., Muir, W.J. and Ebmeier, K. (1999) 'Altered Cerebral Perfusion Measured by SPECT in Relations of Patients with Schizophrenia'. *British Journal of Psychiatry*. 175, 357–66.

Bleuler, E. (1923) *Textbook of Psychiatry*. Allen and Unwin: London.

Bloor, M. and McIntosh, J. (1990) 'Surveillance and Concealment: A Comparison of Techniques of Client Resistance in Therapeutic Communities and Health Visiting' in S. Cunningham-Burley and N. McKeganey (eds) *Readings in Medical Sociology*. Routledge: London.

Booth, C. (1892) 'Inaugural Address'. *Journal of the Royal Statistical Society*. 60(52), 1–57.

Bourguignon, E. (1970) 'Hallucinations and Trance: An Anthropologist's Perspective' in W. Keup (ed.) *Origins and Mechanisms of Hallucinations*. Plenum Press: New York.

Boyd, H.J., Pulver, A.E. and Stewart, W. (1986) 'Season of Birth: Schizophrenia and Bipolar Disorder'. *Schizophrenia Bulletin*. 12, 173–86.

Boyle, M.E. (1990) *Schizophrenia, a Scientific Delusion?* Routledge: London.

Bradbury, T.N. and Miller, G.A. (1985) 'Season of Birth in Schizophrenia: A Review of Evidence, Methodology and Aetiology'. *Psychological Bulletin*. 98, 589–94.

Bucher, B. and Fabricatore, J. (1970) quoted in I. Al-Issa (1977) 'Social and Cultural Aspects of Hallucinations'. *Psychology Bulletin*. 84, 570–87.

Buckes (1901) in Shortt, S.E.D. (1986) *Richard M. Bucke and the Practice of Late Nineteenth Century Psychiatry*. Cambridge University Press: London, New York, New Rochelle, Melbourne, Sydney.

Buckley, P.F. and Friedman, L. (2000) 'Magnetic Resonance Spectroscopy. Bridging the Neurochemical and Neuroanatomy of Schizophrenia'. *British Journal of Psychiatry*. 176, 203–5.

Bucknill, C. and Tuke, D.H. (1858) (1968) *A Manual of Psychological Medicine*. Hayner Publishing Company: New York and London.

Bugelski, B.R. (1971) quoted in I. Al-Issa (1977) 'Social and Cultural Aspects of Hallucinations'. *Psychology Bulletin*. 84, 570–87.

Burchell, C. (1993) 'Liberal Government and Techniques of the Self'. *Economy and Society*. 22(3), 267–83.

Burchell, C., Gordan, C. and Miller, P. (eds) (1991) *The Foucault Effect*. Harvester Wheatsheaf: Brighton.

Burkitt, I. (1999) *Bodies of Thought: Embodiment, Identity and Modernity*. Sage: London.

Burman, E. (1990) 'Differing with Deconstruction: A Feminist Critique' in I. Parker and J. Shotter (eds) *Deconstructing Social Psychology*. Routledge: London.

Burman, E. (1992) 'What Discourse is Not'. *Philosophical Psychology*. 4(3), 325–42.

Butler, J. (1993) *Bodies That Matter: On the Discourse Limits of 'Sex'*. Routledge: London.

Buxton, C.E. (1985) *Points of View in the Modern History of Psychology*. Academic Press Incorporated: London.

Byrne, P. (1999) Editorial: 'Stigma of Mental Illness. Changing Minds, Changing Behaviour'. *British Journal of Psychiatry*. 174, 1–2.

Carlsson, A., Harisson, L.O., Waters, N. and Carlsson, M.L. (1999) 'A Glutamatergic Deficiency Model of Schizophrenia'. *British Journal of Psychiatry*. 174 (supplement 37), 2–6.

Carpenter, E. (1805) *Who Are the Deluded?* W. Marchmont: London.

Castel, R. (1988) *The Regulation of Madness: The Origins of Incarceration in France*. Polity Press: Cambridge.

Castel, R. (1991) 'From Dangerousness to Risk', in C. Burchill, C. Cordan and P. Miller (eds) *The Foucault Effect*. Harvester Wheatsheaf: Brighton.

Casterton, J. (1997) 'In the Yellow Room'. *Psychoanalysis, Groups, Politics, Culture*. 6(40), 493–512.

Chamber, I. (1986) *Popular Culture. The Metropolitan Experience*. Routledge: London and New York.

Clement, C. (1994) *Syncope. The Philosophy of Rapture*. University of Minnesota Press: Minneapolis, London.

Cochrane, R. (1977) 'Mental Illness in Immigrants to England and Wales. An Analysis of Mental Hospital Admissions'. *Social Psychiatry*. 12, 23–35.

Coleman, R. and Smith, M. (1997) *Working with Voices: Victim to Victor*. Handsell Publishing: Gloucester.

Comer, N.L., Madow, L. and Dixon, J.J. (1967) 'Observation of Sensory Deprivation in a Life-Threatening Situation'. *American Journal of Psychiatry*. 124, 164–9.

Condillac, E.B.A. de (1754) (1930) *Treatise on the Sensations*. Favil Press: London.

Coulter, J. (1973) *Approaches to Insanity*. The Pitman Press: Bath.

Coulter, J. (1979) *The Social Construction of Mind*. Macmillan: London.

Coulter, J. (1989) *Mind in Action*. Macmillan: London, Basingstoke.

Coward, R. (1989) *The Whole Truth: The Myth of Alternative Health*. Faber and Faber: London.

Crook, S., Pakulski, J. and Waters, M. (1992) *Postmodernisation: Changes in Advanced Society*. Sage: London, Newbury Park and New Delhi.

Crow, T.J. (1989) 'A Current View of the Type 2 Syndrome: Age of Onset, Intellectual Impairment and the Meaning of Structural Changes in the Brain'. *British Journal of Psychiatry*. 155 (Supplement 7), 15–20.

Crown, S. (1970) *Essential Principles of Psychiatry*. Pitman Medical and Scientific Publishing Co. Ltd: London.

Csordas, T. (1994) 'Words from the Holy People: A Case Study in Cultural Phenomenology' in T. Csordas (ed.) *Embodiment and Experience. The Existential Ground of Culture and Self*. Cambridge University Press: Cambridge, New York, Melbourne and Madrid.

Csordas, T. (1997) *The Sacred Self. A Cultural Phenomenology of Charismatic Healing*. University of California Press: Berkeley, Los Angeles and London.

Curt, B.C. (1994) *Textuality and Tectonics: Troubling Social and Psychological Science*. Open University Press: Buckingham, Philadelphia.

Danziger, K. (1990) *Constructing the Subject*. Cambridge University Press: Cambridge.

Darwin, C. (1871) *The Descent of Man Vol.1*. John Murray: London.

Darwin, C. (1909) *Foundations of the Origins of Species*. Cambridge University Press: London.

Davies, P. (1974) 'Conditioned Visual Afterimages 1'. *British Journal of Psychology*. 65, 191–204.

Davies, P. (1976) 'Conditioned Visual Afterimages 3'. *British Journal of Psychology*. 67, 181–9.

Davies, P., Davies, C.L. and Bennett, S. (1982) 'An Affective Paradigm for Conditioning Visual Perception in Human Subjects'. *Perception*. 2, 663–9.

Davis, J.M. and Casper, R. (1997) 'Antipsychotic Drugs: Clinical Pharmacology and Therapeutic Use'. *Drugs*. 1977(14) 260–82.

Dean, M. (1994) *Critical and Effective Histories. Foucault's Methods and Historical Sociology*. Routledge: London and New York.

Defendorf, H. (1902) *Clinical Psychiatry* (Abstracted and adapted from the sixth German edition of E. Kraepelin's *Lehrbuch der Psychiatrie*). Macmillan: New York.

Dominiak, G. (1992) 'Psychopharmacology of the Abused' in G. Dominiak and S. Shapiro (eds) *Sexual Trauma and Psychopathology: Clinical Intervention with Adult Survivors*. Lexington Books: New York.

Donnelly, M. (1983) *Managing the Mind*. Tavistock: London.

Drotner, K (1994) 'Ethnographic Enigma's: The Everyday in Recent Media Studies'. *Cultural Studies*. 8(2), 341–57.

Drury, V., Birchwood, M. and Cochrane, R. (2000) 'Cognitive Therapy and Recovery from Acute Psychosis: A Controlled Trial'. *British Journal of Psychiatry*. 177, 8–14.

Du Gay, P. (1991) 'Enterprise Culture and the Ideology of Excellence'. *New Formations* 13, Spring, 45–63. Routledge: London.

Eagleton, T. (1983) *Literary Theory: An Introduction*. Basil Blackwell: Oxford.

Ebbinghaus, H. (1913) in K. Danziger (1990) *Constructing the Subject*. Cambridge University Press: Cambridge.

Edwards, D. and Potter, J. (1992) *Discursive Psychology*. Sage: London.

Eisenburg, L. (2000) Editorial. 'Is Psychiatry More Mindful or Brainier than it Was a Decade Ago?' *British Journal of Psychiatry*. 176, 1–5.

Esquirol, J.E. (1845) *Mental Maladies: A Treatise on Insanity*. Lea and Blanehard: Philadelphia.

Eysenck, M. (1976) 'Arousal, Learning and Memory'. *Psychology Bulletin*. 83, 389–404.

Fanon, F. (1967) *Black Skins, White Masks*. Grove Weidenfeld: New York.

Featherstone, M. (1991) *Consumer Culture and Postmodernism*. Sage: London.

Feinburg, I. and Guazzelli, M. (1999) 'Schizophrenia – A Disorder of the Corollary Discharge Systems that Integrate the Motor Systems of Thought with the Sensory Systems of Consciousness'. *British Journal of Psychiatry*. 174, 196–204.

Fiske, J. (1992) 'Cultural Studies and the Culture of Everyday Life' in Grossberg, L. et al. (eds) *Cultural Studies*. Routledge: London and New York.

Flugel, J.C. and West, D.J. (1964) *A Hundred Years of Psychology. 1833–1933*. Gerald Duckworth and Co. Ltd: London.

Fombonne, E. (1989) 'Season of Birth and Childhood Psychosis'. *British Journal of Psychiatry*. 155, 655–61.

Foucault, M. (1971) *Madness and Civilisation: A History of Insanity in the Age of Reason*. Routledge: London.

Foucault, M. (1972) *The Archaeology of Knowledge*. Routledge: London and New York.

Foucault, M. (1973) *The Birth of the Clinic*. Tavistock: London.

Foucault, M. (1977) *Discipline and Punish*. Allen Lane: London.

Foucault, M. (1980) *Power/Knowledge. Selected Interviews and Other Writings 1972–1977*. Edited by Gordan, C. Harvester Wheatsheaf: London and New York.

Foucault, M. (1985) *A History of Sexuality, 1*. Penguin: London.

Foucault, M. (1987a) *The Use of Pleasure. The History of Sexuality, 2*. Peregrine: London.

Foucault, M. (1987b) (Foreword by Hubert Dreyfus). *Mental Illness and Psychology*. University of California Press: Berkeley, Los Angeles and London.

Foucault, M. (1988) 'Technologies of the Self' in Martin et al. (eds) *Technologies of the Self*. Tavistock: London.

Foucault, M. (1989) *Foucault Live*. Semiotext(e): New York.

Foucault, M. (1990) *The Care of the Self. The History of Sexuality, 3*. Penguin: London.

Foucault, M. (1991a) 'Remarks on Marx. Conversations with D. Tranbadori' in J. Fleming and S. Lothringer (eds) *Semiotext(e)*. Semiotext(e): New York.

Foucault, M. (1991b) 'The Ethic of Care for the Self as a Practice of Freedom' in J. Bernauer and D. Rasmussen (eds) *The Final Foucault*. The MIT Press: London and Cambridge.

Fox, D.R. (1985) 'Psychology, Ideology, Utopia and the Commons'. *American Psychologist*. 40(2) 48–58.

Freud, S. (1900) (1932) *The Interpretation of Dreams*. 3rd edn. Allen and Unwin: London.

Freud, S. (1922) *Introductory Lectures on Psycho-Analysis*. Allen and Unwin: London.

Frith, C.D. (1979) 'Consciousness, Information Processing and Schizophrenia'. *British Journal of Psychiatry*. 134, 224–35.

Fuss, D. (1989) *Essentially Speaking: Feminism, Nature and Difference*. Routledge: London.

Garfinkel, H. (1974) 'On the Origins of the Term "Ethnomethodology"' in R. Turner (ed.) *Ethnomethodology*. Penguin: Harmondsworth.

Gatens, M. (1996) *Imaginary Bodies. Ethics, Power and Corporeality*. Routledge: London and New York.

Gergen, K.J. (1973) 'Social Psychology as History'. *Journal of Personality and Social Psychology*. 8, 507–27.

Gergen, K.J. (1985) 'The Social Constructionist Movement in Modem Psychology'. *American Psychologist*. 40, 266–75.

Gergen, K.J. (1989) 'Warranting Voice and Elaboration of Self' in J. Shorter and K.J. Gergen (eds) *Texts of Identity*. Sage: London.

Gergen, K.J. (1991) *The Saturated Self: Dilemmas of Identity in Contemporary Life*. Basic Books: New York.

Gergen, K.J. (1992) 'Toward a Postmodern Psychology' in S. Kvale (ed.) *Psychology and Postmodernism*. Sage: London, Newbury Park and New Delhi.

Gilbert, C.N. and Mulkay, M. (1984) *Opening Pandora's Box: A Sociological Analysis of Scientist's Discourse*. Cambridge University Press: Cambridge.

Gilroy, P. (2000) *Between Camps. Race, Identity and Nationalism at the End of the Colour Line*. The Penguin Press, Allen Lane: London, New York, Victoria, Ontario and Auckland.

Gjerde, P.F. (1983) 'Attentional Capacity Dysfunction and Arousal in Schizophrenia'. *Psychological Bulletin*. 93(1) 57–72.

Goater, N., King, M., Cole, E., Leavey, G., Johnson-Sabine, E., Bilizard, R. and Hoar, A. (1999) 'Ethnicity and the Outcome of Psychosis'. *British Journal of Psychiatry*. 175, 34–42.

Gordan, C. (1992) 'Histoire de la Folie' in A. Still and I. Velody (eds) *Rewriting the History of Madness. Studies in Foucault's Histoire de la Folie*. Routledge: London and New York.

Gowan, J.C. (1975) *Trance, Art and Creativity*. California State University: San Francisco.

Greeley, A.M. (1974) *Ecstasy: A Way of Knowing*. Prentice-Hall: New Jersey.

Griggers, C. (1998) 'The Micropolitics of Biopsychiatry' in Shildrick, M. and Price, J. (eds) *Vital Signs. Feminist Reconfigurations of the Bio/logical Body*. Edinburgh University Press: Edinburgh.

Grosz, E. (1995) *Space Time and Perversion*. Routledge: London and New York.

Gunderson, J.G., Siever, L.J. and Spaunding, E. (1983) 'The Search for the Schizotype'. *Archives of General Psychiatry*. 40, 15–22.

Haddock, G. and Slade, P.D. (1996) *Cognitive-Behavioural Interventions and Psychotic Disorders*. Routledge: London and New York.

Hall, S. (1981) 'Cultural Studies: Two Paradigms' in T. Bennett et al. (eds) *Culture, Ideology and Social Processes*. Open University Press: Milton Keynes.

Hall, S. and Du Gay, P. (1996) (eds) *Questions of Cultural Identity*. Sage: London, New York and New Delhi.

Haraway, D. (1991) *Simians, Cyborgs and Women. The Reinvention of Nature*. Free Association Books: London.

Haraway, D. (1997) *Modest Witness@Second Millennium.FemaleMan Meets OncoMouse: Feminism and Technoscience*. Routledge: New York and London.

Harré, R. (1974) 'Blueprint for a New Science' in N. Armistead (ed.) *Reconstructing Social Psychology*. Penguin: Harmondsworth.

Harré, R. (1981) 'The Positivist-Empiricist Approach and its Alternative'. In P. Reason and J. Rowan (eds) *Human Inquiry: A Sourcebook of New Paradigm Research*. Wiley: New York.

Harré, R. (1983) *Personal Being: A Theory for Individual Psychology.* Basil Blackwell: Oxford.

Harré, R. (1985) 'Review of Social Representations'. *British Journal of Psychology.* 76, 136–40.

Harré, R. (1986) 'An Outline of Social Constructionist Viewpoint' in R. Harré (ed.) *The Social Construction of Emotions.* Basil Blackwell: Oxford.

Harré, R. (1989) 'Problems of Self-Reference and the Expression of Selfhood' in J. Shorter and K.J. Gergen (eds) *Texts of Identity.* Sage: London.

Harré, R. (1992) 'What is Real in Psychology: A Plea for Persons'. *Theory and Psychology.* 2(2), 153–8.

Harré, R. and Secord, P. (1972) *The Explanation of Social Behaviour.* Basil Blackwell: Oxford.

Harrison, G., Amin, S., Singh, S.P., Croudace, T. and Jones, P. (1999) 'An Increased Incidence of Psychiatric Disorders Repeatedly Reported among African-Caribbeans in the UK'. *British Journal of Psychiatry.* 175, 127–34.

Hefferline, R.F., Bruno, L.J. and Camp, J.A. (1972) 'Hallucinations: An Experimental Approach' in F.J. McCuigan and R.A. Schoonover (eds) *The Psychophysiology of Thinking: Studies of Covert Processes.* Academic Press: New York.

Heidegger, M. (1962) *Being and Time.* Blackwell: Oxford.

Henderson, D.R. and Gillespie, R.D. (1927) *A Text-Book of Psychiatry for Students and Practitioners.* Humphrey Milford Oxford University Press: Oxford.

Henriques, J., Hollway, W., Urwin, C., Venn, C. and Walkerdine, V. (1984) *Changing the Subject: Psychology, Social Regulation and Subjectivity.* Methuen: London. 2nd edn Routledge: London, 1998.

Hickling, F.W., McKenzie, K., Mullen, R. and Murray, R. (1999) 'A Jamaican Psychiatrist Evaluates Diagnoses at a London Psychiatric Hospital'. *British Journal of Psychiatry.* 175, 283–5.

Hinshelwood, D. (1999) 'The Difficult Patient. The Role of "Scientific Psychiatry" in Understanding Patients with Chronic Schizophrenia or Severe Personality Disorder'. *British Journal of Psychiatry.* 174, 187–90.

Hochschild, A. (1983) *The Managed Heart. The Commercialisation of Human Feeling.* University of California Press: Berkeley, California and London.

Hollingshead, A.B. and Redlich, F.C. (1958) quoted in I. Al-Issa (1977) 'Social and Cultural Aspects of Hallucinations'. *Psychology Bulletin.* 84, 570–87.

hooks, bell (2000) *all about love.* The Women's Press Ltd: London and New York.

Howard, C.S. (1985) 'The Role of Values in The Science of Psychology'. *American Psychologist.* 40, 255–65.

Howells, J.G. (1968) *Modern Perspectives in World Psychiatry.* Oliver and Boyd: Edinburgh and London.

Hoy, D.C. (1999) 'Critical Resistance: Foucault and Bourdieu' in Weiss, G. and Haber, H.F. (eds) *Perspectives on Embodiment. The Intersection of Nature and Culture.* Routledge: London and New York.

Huxley, A. (1961) *The Doors of Perception and Heaven and Hell*. Penguin: London.

Hwa Yol Yung (1996) 'Phenomenology and Body Politics'. *Body and Society*. 2(2), 1–22.

Inouye, T. and Shimizu, A. (1970) 'The Electromyographic Study of Verbal Hallucinations'. *Journal of Nervous and Mental Disease*. 151, 415–22.

Itill T.M. (1969) 'Changes in Digital Computer Analyzed EEG During "Dreams" and Experimentally Induced Hallucinations' in W. Keup (ed.) *Origins and Mechanisms of Hallucinations*. Plenum Press: New York and London.

James, W. (1902) *Varieties of Religious Experience: A Study in Human Nature*. Longmans, Green and Co.: London.

Jenkins, J.H. and Schumacher, J.G. (1999) 'Family Burden of Schizophrenia and Depressive Illness. Specifying the Effects of Ethnicity, Gender and Social Ecology'. *British Journal of Psychiatry*. 174, 31–8.

Jones, C., Cormac, I., Mota, J. and Campbell, C. (1998) 'Cognitive Behaviour Therapy for Schizophrenia'. *The Cochrane Library*. Issue 4, 1–20.

Juhasz, J.B. (1972) 'An Experimental Study of Imagining'. *Journal of Personality*. 40, 588–600.

Jung, C.G. (ed.) (1978) *Man and His Symbols*. Pan Books: London.

Kantor, J.R. (1963) *The Scientific Evolution of Psychology. Vol. 1*. The Principia Press Inc.: Chicago.

Kay, S.R., Opler, L. and Lindenmayer, J.-P. (1989) 'The Positive and Negative Syndrome Scale (PANSS): Rationale and Standardisation'. *British Journal of Psychiatry*. 155 (Supplement 7), 59–65.

Kellner, D. (1995) *Media Culture: Cultural Studies, Identity and Politics between the Modern and the Postmodern*. Routledge: London and New York.

Kelly, G.A. (1955) *The Psychology of Personal Constructs*. Norton: New York.

Kendall, R. (2000) 'The Next 25 Years'. *British Journal of Psychiatry*. 176, 6–9.

Kerwin, R. and Owen, M. (1999) 'Genetics of Novel Therapeutic Targets in Schizophrenia'. *British Journal of Psychiatry*. 174 (supplement 38), 1–4.

Kinsman, G (1996) 'Responsibility as a Strategy of Governance: Regulating People Living with AIDS and Lesbians and Gay Men in Ontario'. *Economy and Society*. 25(3), August, 393–409.

Kitzinger, C. (1987) *The Social Construction of Lesbianism*. Sage: London, Newbury Park, Beverly Hills and New Delhi.

Kitzinger, C. (1990) 'The Rhetoric of Pseudoscience' in I. Parker and J. Shorter (eds) *Deconstructing Social Psychology*. Routledge: London.

Kraepelin, Dr E. (1913) *Clinical Psychiatry: Lectures and Clinical Psychiatry*. Bailliere, Trindall and Cox: London.

Kraepelin, E. (1919) *Dementia Praecox and Paraphrenia*. E. and S. Livingstone: Edinburgh.

Krafft Ebing, Dr R. von (1904) *Text-Book of Insanity*. F.A. Davis and Co.: Philadelphia.

Kraviecka, M., Goldberg, D. and Vaughan, M. (1989) 'The Manchester Scale'. *British Journal of Psychology*. 155 (supplement 7), 46–8.

Kuhn, T.S. (1962) *The Structure of Scientific Revolutions*. University of Chicago Press: Chicago.

Kvale, S. (ed.) (1992) *Psychology and Postmodernism*. Sage: London, Newbury Park and New Delhi.

Laing, R.D. (1960) *The Divided Self: A Study of Sanity and Madness*. Tavistock: London.

Laing, R.D. (1967) *The Politics of Experience*. Penguin: Harmondsworth.

Laski, M. (1961) *Ecstasy*. The Cresset Press: London.

Latour, B. (1986) 'The Power of Association' in J. Law (ed.) *Power, Action, Belief*. Routledge, Kegan Paul: London.

Latour, B. (1987) *Science in Action*. Open University Press: Milton Keynes.

Latour, B. (2000) 'When Things Strike Back: A Possible Contribution of "Science Studies" to the Social Sciences'. *British Journal of Sociology*. 51(1), 107–23.

Leary, T. (1968) *High Priest*. World Publishing Company: Cleveland.

Leary, T. (1973) *The Politics of Ecstasy*. Granada Publishing: London.

Leff, J.P. (1981) *Psychiatry Around the Globe: A Transcultural View*. Marcel Dekker, American Psychiatric Press Corporated: North America.

Lewis, I.M. (1971) *Ecstatic Religion: A Study of Shamanism and Spirit Possession*. Routledge: London, New York.

Lindsley, O.R. (1959) quoted in I. Al-Issa (1977) 'Social and Cultural Aspects of Hallucinations'. *Psychology Bulletin*. 84, 570–87.

Littlewood, R. (1980) 'Anthropology and Psychiatry – An Alternative View'. *British Journal of Medical Psychology*. 53, 213–25.

Littlewood, R. and Lipsedge, M. (1989) *Aliens and Alienists: Ethnic Minorities and Psychiatry*. Unwin Hyman: London, Boston, Sydney and Wellington.

Locke, J. (1689) (1929) *An Essay Concerning Human Understanding*. Clarendon Press: Oxford.

Lorde, A. (1996) *The Audre Lorde Compendium: Essays, Speeches and Journals*. Pandora: London.

Lucey, H. and Reay, D. (2000) 'Social Class and the Psyche'. *Soundings*. 139–54.

Lupton, D. (1997) 'Foucault and the Medicalisation Critique' in A. Petersen and R. Bunton (eds) *Foucault. Health and Medicine*. Routledge: London and New York.

Lury, C. (1996) *Consumer Culture*. Polity Press: Cambridge.

McCarthy, B., Hansley, D., Schrank-Fernandez, C., et al. (1989) 'Unpredictability as a Correlate of Expressed Emotion in the Relatives of Schizophrenics'. *British Journal of Psychiatry*. 148, 727–31.

McDermot, V. (1971) *The Cult of the Seer in the Ancient Middle East. A Contribution to Current Research on Hallucinations Drawn from Coptic Texts*. Wellcome Institute of the History of Medicine: London.

MacDonald, M. (1981) *Mystical Bedlam: Madness, Anxiety and Healing in Seventeenth-Century England*. Cambridge University Press: Cambridge.

McKellar, P. (1968) *Experience and Behaviour*. Penguin Press: Harmondsworth.

McKellar, P. (1968) quoted in I. Al-Issa (1977) 'Social and Cultural Aspects of Hallucinations'. *Psychology Bulletin*. 84, 570–87.

McLemore, C.W. (1972) quoted in I. Al-Issa (1977) 'Social and Cultural Aspects of Hallucinations'. *Psychology Bulletin*. 84, 570–87.

McNamee, S. and Gergen, K.J. (1992) (eds) *Therapy as Social Construction*. Sage: London, Thousand Oaks and Delhi.

McNay, L. (1992) *Foucault and Feminism*. Polity Press: Cambridge.

McRobbie, A. (1996) 'More! New Sexualities in Girls' and Women's Magazines' in J. Curran, D. Morley and V. Walkerdine (eds) *Cultural Studies and Communications*. Edward Arnold: London.

McRobbie, A. (1998) *British Fashion Design. Rag Trade or Image Industry?* Routledge: London and New York.

Mani, L. (1992) quoted in Ross (1992) 'New Age Technoculture' in L. Grossberg, C. Nelson and P. Treichler (eds) *Cultural Studies*. Routledge: London and New York.

Margo, A., Hemsley, D.R. and Slade, P.D. (1981) 'The Effects of Varying Input on Subjects Hallucination'. *British Journal of Psychology*. 139, 122–7.

Martin, L., Gutman, H. and Hutton, P. (1988) *Technologies of the Self*. University of Massachusetts Press: Amherst.

Maslow, A.H. (1954) *Motivation and Personality*. Harper & Row: New York.

Maslow, A.H. (1968) *Towards a Psychology of Being*. 2nd edn. Van Nostrand: Princeton.

Masters, R.E.L. and Houston, J. (1966) *The Varieties of Psychedelic Experience*. Holt, Rinehart and Winston: New York.

Maudsley, H. (1874) *Responsibility in Mental Disease*. Harry S. King and Co: London.

Maudsley, H. (1879) *Pathology of the Mind*. Macmillan and Co: London.

Mayer-Gross, W., Slater, E. and Roth, M. (1969) 3rd edn. *Clinical Psychiatry*. Bailliere, Tindall and Cassell: London.

Mayo, T. (1817) *Remarks on Insanity: Founded on the Practice of John Mayo*. M.D. Thomas and George Underwood: Fleet Street.

Mayo, T. (1838) *Human Elements of the Pathology of the Mind*. John Murray, Albemarle Street.

Mead, G.H. (1934) *Mind, Self and Society*. University of Chicago Press: Chicago.

Mercer, K. (1986) 'Racism and Transcultural Psychiatry' in P. Miller and N. Rose (eds) *The Power of Psychiatry*. Polity Press: Cambridge.

Merleau-Ponty, M. (1962) *The Phenomenology of Perception*. Routledge and Kegan Paul: London and New York.

Merskey, H. and Tonge, W. (1965) *Psychiatric Illness*. Bailliere, Tindall and Cox: London.

Michael, M. (1992) 'Postmodern Subjects: Towards a Transgressive Social Psychology' in S. Kvale (ed.) *Psychology and Postmodernism*. Sage: London, Newbury Park and New Delhi.

Michailidou, M. (2000) 'Femininity Confessed: The Transformation of Feminine Experience from Postwar Women's Magazines'. Unpublished PhD thesis. University of London.

Middleton, D. and Edwards, D. (eds) (1990) *Collective Remembering*. Sage: London, New York.

Miller, P. (1986) 'Critiques of Psychiatry and Critical Sociologies of Madness' in P. Miller and N. Rose (eds) *The Power of Psychiatry*. Polity Press: Cambridge.

Miller, T. (1998) *Technologies of Truth*. Routledge: London and New York.

Miller, P. and Rose, N. (1986) *The Power of Psychiatry*. Polity Press: Cambridge.

Miller, P. and Rose, N. (1994) 'On Therapeutic Authority: Psychoanalytical Expertise Under Advanced Liberalism'. *History of the Human Sciences*. 7(3), 29–64.

Miller, P. and Rose, N. (1997) 'Mobilising the Consumer. Assembling the Subject of Consumption'. *Theory, Culture and Society*. 14(1), February, 1–36.

Mintz, S. and Alpert, M. (1972) 'Imagery Vividness, Reality Testing and Schizophrenic Hallucinations'. *Journal of Abnormal Psychology*, 79, 310–6.

Morss, J.R. (1990) *The Biologising of Childhood*. Lawrence Erlbaum: Brighton.

Mort, F. (1996) *Cultures of Consumption. Masculinities and Social Space in Late Twentieth Century Britain*. Routledge: London and New York.

Neisser U. (1967) *Cognitive Psychology*. Appleton Century Croft: New York.

Neisser, U. (1976) *Cognition and Reality: Principles and Implications of Cognitive Psychology*. W.H. Freeman and Company: San Francisco.

Nettleton, S. (1992) *Power, Pain and Dentistry*. Open University Press: Buckingham and Philadelphia.

Nightingale, D. (1999) '(Re)Theorising Constructionism'. 417–25 in W. Maiers, et al. (eds) *Challenges to Theoretical Psychology*. Captus Press: Toronto.

Nixon, S. (1996) *Hard Looks: Masculinities, the Visuals and Practices of Consumption*. University of London Press: London.

Osbourne, T. and Rose, N. (1999) 'Do the Social Sciences Create Phenomena?: The Example of Public Opinion Research'. *British Journal of Sociology*. 50(3), 367–96.

Ouspensky, P.D. (1968) *The Psychology of Man's Possible Evolution*. Bantam: New York.

Owen, R. (1813) *A New View of Society, or Essays on the Principles of the Formation of the Human Character*.

Owen, R. (1836) *The Book of the New Moral World*.

Paivio, A. (1971) quoted in T.R. Sarbin and J.B. Juhasz (1978) 'The Social Psychology of Hallucinations'. *Journal of Mental Imagery*. 2, 117–44.

Parish, E. (1897) *Hallucinations and Illusions: A Study of the Fallacies of Perception*. Walter Scott Ltd: London.

Parker, G., Mahendran, R., Koh, E. and Machin, D. (2000) 'Season of Birth in Schizophrenics. No Latitude at the Equator'. *British Journal of Psychiatry*. 176, 68–71.

Parker, I. (1989) *The Crisis in Modern Psychology – and How to End It.* Routledge: London and New York.

Parker, I. (1990a) 'Discourse: Definitions and Contradictions'. *Philosophical Psychology.* 3(2), 189–204.

Parker, I. (1990b) 'The Abstraction and Representation of Social Psychology' in I. Parker and J. Shorter (eds) *Deconstructing Social Psychology.* Routledge: London.

Parker, I. (1992) *Discourse Dynamics: Critical Analysis for Social and Individual Psychology.* Routledge: London and New York.

Parker, I. and Shotter, J. (1990) (eds) *Deconstructing Social Psychology.* Routledge: London.

Parnas, J. and Jorgensen, A. (1989) 'Pre-Morbid Psychopathology in Schizophrenia Spectrum'. *British Journal of Psychiatry.* 155, 623–7.

Paul, S. (1999) 'CNS Drug Discovery in the 21st Century'. *British Journal of Psychiatry.* 174 (supplement 37), 23–5.

Pavlov, I. (1927) *Conditioned Reflexes.* Oxford University Press: Oxford.

Peralta, V. and Cuesta, M. (1999) 'Diagnostic Significance of Schneider's First Rank Symptoms in Schizophrenia'. *British Journal of Psychiatry.* 174, 243–8.

Perky, C.W. (1910) quoted in I. Al-Issa (1977) 'Social and Cultural Aspects of Hallucinations'. *Psychology Bulletin.* 84, 570–87.

Peters, R.S. (1953) *Brett's History of Psychology.* George Allen and Unwin Ltd: London.

Petersen, A. and Bunton, R. (1997) (eds) *Foucault. Health and Medicine.* Routledge: London and New York.

Pfister, J. and Schnog, N. (1997) (eds) *Inventing the Psychological. Toward a Cultural History of Emotional Life in America.* Yale University Press: New Haven and London.

Philips, L., Broverman, I.K. and Zigler, E. (1956) quoted in I. Al-Issa (1977) 'Social and Cultural Aspects of Hallucinations'. *Psychology Bulletin.* 84, 570–87.

Philo, G. (1994) 'Media Images and Popular Belief'. *Psychiatric Bulletin.* 18, 173–4.

Philo, G. (1996) 'The Media and Public Belief' in G. Philo (ed.) *Media and Mental Distress.* Longman: London.

Piaget, J. and Inhelder, B. (1971) quoted in T.R. Sarbin and J.B. Juhasz (1978) 'The Social Psychology of Hallucinations'. *Journal of Mental Imagery.* 2, 117–44.

Pile, S. and Thrift, N. (1995) (eds) *Mapping the Subject. Geographies of Cultural Transformation.* Routledge: London and New York.

Pizzorno, A. (1992) 'Foucault and the Liberal View of the Individual' in T. Armstrong (ed.) *Michel Foucault. Philosopher.* Harvester Wheatsheaf: New York, London, Toronto, Sydney, Tokyo and Singapore.

Polhemus, T. (1994) *Streetstyle. From Sidewalk to Catwalk.* Thames and Hudson: London.

Popper, K.R. (1969) *Conjectures and Refutations: The Growth of Scientific Knowledge*. Routledge: London.

Porter, R. (1987b) *Mind-Forg'd Manacles: A History of Madness in England from the Restoration to the Regency*. The Athlone Press: London.

Posey, T.B. and Losch, M.E. (1983) 'Auditory Hallucinations of Voice Hearers in 375 Normal Subjects'. *Imagery, Cognition and Personality*. 2, 99–113.

Potter, J. and Edwards, D. (1990) 'Nigel Lawson's Tent: Discourse Analysis, Attribution Theory and the Social Psychology of Fact'. *European Journal of Social Psychology*. 20, 24–40.

Potter, J. and Wetherell, M. (1987) *Discourse and Social Psychology: Beyond Attitudes and Behaviour*. Sage: London.

Potter, J., Wetherell, M., Gill, R. and Edwards, D. (1990) 'Discourse: Noun, Verb or Social Practice'. *Philosophical Psychology*. 3(2), 205–17.

Price, J. and Shildrick, M. (1998) 'Uncertain Thoughts and the Dis/abled Body' in Shildrick, M. and Price, J. (eds) *Vital Signs. Feminist Reconfigurations of the Bio/logical Body*. Edinburgh University Press: Edinburgh.

Prior, L. (1991) 'Mind, Body and Behaviour: Theorisations of Madness and the Organisation of Therapy'. *Journal of the British Sociological Association*. 25, (3), 403–21.

Rabinow, P. (1991) *The Foucault Reader. An Introduction to Foucault's Thought*. Penguin: London.

Rabinow, P. (2000) (ed.) *Michel Foucault. Ethics. Essential Works of Foucault 1954–1984. Volume 1*. Penguin Books: London, New York, Victoria, Ontario and Auckland.

Rabkin, R.M.D. (1970) 'Do You See Things that Aren't There? – Construct Validity of the Concept "Hallucinations"' in W. Keup (ed.) *Origins and Mechanisms of Hallucinations*. Plenum Press: London and New York.

Reason, P., and Rowan, J. (eds) (1981) *Human Inquiry. A Sourcebook of New Paradigm Research*. John Wiley and Sons: Chichester.

Reese, W.D. (1971) 'The Hallucinations of Widowhood'. *British Medical Journal*. 210, 37–41.

Richards, C. (1987) 'Of What is History of Psychology a History?' *British Journal of the History of Science*. 20, 201–11.

Richardson, A. (1969) *Mental Imagery*. Routledge and Kegan Paul: London.

Riley, D. (1983) *War in the Nursery*. Virago Press: London.

Rimke, H. (2000) 'Governing Citizens Through Self-Help Literature'. *Cultural Studies*. 14(1), 61–78.

Rogers, C. (1961) *On Becoming a Person*. Houghton Mifflin: Boston.

Romme, M. and Escher, A. (1993) (eds) *Accepting Voices*. Mind: London.

Romme, M. and Escher, S. (1996) 'Empowering People Who Hear Voices' in G. Haddock and P.D. Slade (eds) *Cognitive-Behavioural Interventions and Psychotic Disorders*. Routledge: London and New York.

Romme, M. and Escher, S. (2000) 'We Hear What They Say'. *Mental Health Care*. 1(4), 134–7.

Rose, N. (1984) 'Child Psychology and Social Regulation'. Paper presented at the annual conference of the Developmental Psychology section of the BPS, held in Lancaster. September.

Rose, N. (1985) *The Psychological Complex. Psychology, Politics and Society in England. 1869–1939.* Routledge and Kegan Paul: London, Boston, Melbourne and Henley.

Rose, N. (1986a) 'Psychiatry: The Discipline of Mental Health' in P. Miller and N. Rose (eds) *The Power of Psychiatry.* Polity Press: Cambridge.

Rose, N. (1986b) 'Law, Right and Psychiatry' in P. Miller and N. Rose (eds) *The Power of Psychiatry.* Polity Press: Cambridge.

Rose, N. (1987) 'Beyond the Public/Private Division: Law, Power and the Family'. *Journal of Law and Society.* 14(1), 61–76.

Rose, N. (1988) 'Calculable Minds and Manageable Individuals', *History of the Human Sciences.* 1, 179–200.

Rose, N. (1989) 'Individualising Psychology' in J. Shotter and K. Gergen (eds) *Texts of Identity.* Sage: London, Newbury Park and New Delhi.

Rose, N. (1990) *Governing the Soul: The Shaping of the Private Self.* Routledge: London. 2nd edn Free Association Books, 1999.

Rose, N. (1996a) *Inventing Ourselves. Psychology, Power and Personhood.* Cambridge University Press: Cambridge, New York and Melbourne.

Rose, N. (1996b) 'Psychiatry as a Political Science: Advanced Liberalism and the Administration of Risk'. *History of the Human Sciences.* 9(2), 1–23.

Rose, N. (forthcoming) 'The Politics of Life Itself: Biosociality, Genetics and the Government of the Human "Vital Order"'. *Theory, Culture and Society.*

Rose, N. and Miller, P. (1992) 'Political Power Beyond the State: Problematics of Government'. *British Journal of Sociology.* 43(2), 173–205.

Ross, A. (1992)) 'New Age Technoculture' in L. Grossberg, C. Nelson and P. Treichler (eds) *Cultural Studies.* Routledge: London and New York.

Ryle, C. (1949) *The Concept of Mind.* Harmondsworth: Penguin.

Sacchetti, E. (1989) 'Risk factors in Schizophrenia', correspondence in the *British Journal of Psychiatry.* 155, 266.

Sampson, E.E. (1977) 'Psychology and the American Ideal'. *Journal of Personality and Social Psychology.* 35, 767–82.

Sampson, E.E. (1981) 'Cognitive Psychology as Ideology'. *American Psychologist.* July 1981, 730–43.

Sampson, E.E. (1989) 'The Deconstruction of the Self' in J. Shotter and K.J. Gergen (eds) *Texts of Identity.* Sage: London.

Sampson, E.E. (1990) 'Social Psychology and Social Control' in I. Parker and J. Shotter (eds) *Deconstructing Social Psychology.* Routledge: London and New York.

Sarbin, T.R. (1967) 'The Concept of Hallucination'. *Journal of Personality.* 35, 359–80.

Sarbin, T.R. and Coe, W.C. (1972) *Hypnotism: The Social Psychology of Influence Communications.* Holt, Rinehart and Winston: New York.

Sarbin, T.R. and Juhasz, J.B. (1967) 'The Historical Background of the Concept of Hallucination'. *Journal of the Behavioural Sciences.* 3(4), 339–58.

Sarbin, T.R. and Juhasz, J.B. (1970) 'Toward a Theory of Imagination'. *Journal of Personality.* 38, 52–78.

Sarbin, T.R. and Juhasz, J.B. (1978) 'The Social Psychology of Hallucinations'. *Journal of Mental Imagery.* 2, 117–144.

Sargeant, W. (1967) *The Unquiet Mind.* Pan Books: London.

Sargeant, W. (1973) *The Mind Possessed: A Physiology of Possession, Mysticism and Faith Healing.* Cox and Wegeinan: London.

Sawicki, J. (1991) *Disciplining Foucault, Feminism, Power and the Body.* Routledge: London.

Schaefer, H.H. and Martin, P.L. (1969) quoted in I. Al-Issa (1977) 'Social and Cultural Aspects of Hallucinations'. *Psychology Bulletin.* 84, 570–87.

Schneider, K. (1959) *Clinical Psychology.* Grune and Stratton: New York.

Schwartz, S. (1975) 'Individual Differences in Cognition: Some Relationships between Personality and Memory'. *Journal of Research in Personality.* 9, 217–25.

Seashore, L.E. (1895) 'Measurements of Illusions and Hallucinations in Normal Life'. *Studies of the Yale Psychology Laboratory.* 3, 1–67.

Seitz, P.F. and Molholm, H.B. (1947) 'Relation of Mental Imagery to Hallucinations'. *Archives of Neurology and Psychiatry.* 57, 469–80.

Shallice, T. (1972) 'Dual Functions of Consciousness'. *Psychological Review.* 79, 383–93.

Shean, C. (1973) quoted in I. Al-Issa (1977) 'Social and Cultural Aspects of Hallucinations'. *Psychology Bulletin.* 84, 570–87.

Shepard, R.N. and Metzler, J. (1971) 'Mental Rotation of Three Dimensional Objects'. *Science.* 171, 701–3.

Shepard, M. (1983) *The Psychosocial Matrix of Psychiatry.* Tavistock: London and New York.

Shields, R. (1992) *Lifestyle Shopping. The Subject of Consumption.* Routledge: London and New York.

Shildrick, M. and Price, J. (1998) *Vital Signs. Feminist Reconfigurations of the Bio/logical Body.* Edinburgh University Press: Edinburgh.

Shirato, T. (1993) 'My space or Yours? De Certeau, Frow and the Meanings of Popular Culture'. *Cultural Studies.* 7(2).

Shortt, S.E.D. (1986) *Richard M. Bucke and the Practice of Late Nineteenth-Century Psychiatry.* Cambridge University Press: Cambridge, London, New York, New Rochelle, Melbourne and Sydney.

Shotter, J. (1974) 'What Is It to Be Human' in N. Armistead (ed.) *Reconstructing Social Psychology.* Penguin: Harmondsworth.

Shotter, J. (1984) *Social Accountability and Selfhood.* Basil Blackwell: Oxford.

Shotter, J. (1986) 'A Sense of Place: Vico and the Social Production of Social Identities'. *British Journal of Psychology.* 25, 199–211.

Shotter, J. (1987) 'Cognitive Psychology, Taylorism and the Manufacture of Employment' in A. Costall and A. Still (eds) *Cognitive Psychology in Question*. Harvester Press: Brighton.

Shotter, J. (1989) 'Rhetoric and the Recovery of Civil Society'. *Economy and Society*. 18(2), 149–66.

Shotter, J. (1990) 'Social Individuality versus Possessive Individualism: The Sounds of Silence' in I. Parker and J. Shotter (eds) *Deconstructing Social Psychology*. Routledge: London.

Shotter, J. (1993) *Conversational Realities: Constructing Life through Language*. Sage: London, New Delhi and Thousand Oaks.

Shotter, J. and Gergen, K. (1989) *Texts of Identity*. Sage: London.

Showalter, E. (1987) *The Female Malady. Women Madness and the English Culture, 1830–1980*. Virago: London.

Sidgewick, H.A. et al. (1894) 'Report of the Census of Hallucinations'. *Science*. 171, 701–3.

Singer, J.L. (1966) *Daydreaming*. Random House: New York.

Singer, J.L. (1970) 'Drives, Affects and Daydreams: The Adaptive Role of Spontaneous Imagery or Stimulus-Independent Mentation' in J.S. Antrobus (ed.) *Cognition and Affect*. Little, Brown: Boston.

Slade, P.D. and Bentall, R.P. (1988) *Sensory Deception: A Scientific Analysis of Hallucination*. Croom Helm: London and Sydney.

Slade, P.D. and Bentall, R.P. (1989) 'Psychological Treatments for Negative Symptoms'. *British Journal of Psychiatry*. 155 (supplement 7), 133–5.

Spence, J. (1995) *Cultural Sniping: The Art of Transgression*. Routledge: London and New York.

Stein, K.B. (1968) quoted in I. Al-Issa (1977) 'Social and Cultural Aspects of Hallucinations'. *Psychology Bulletin*. 84, 570–87.

Stenner, P. (1993) 'Discoursing Jealousy' in E. Burinan and I. Parker (eds) *Discourse Analytic Research*. Routledge: London and New York.

Stenner, P. and Eccleston, C. (1994) 'On the Textuality of Being. Towards an Invigorated Social Constructionism'. *Theory and Psychology*. 4(1), 85–103.

Stevens, J. (1993) *Storming Heaven. LSD and the American Dream*. Flamingo: London.

Still, A. and Velody, I. (eds) (1992) *Rewriting the History of Madness. Studies in Foucault's Histoire de la Folie*. Routledge: London and New York.

Stoyva, J. (1973) quoted in I. Al-Issa (1977) 'Social and Cultural Aspects of Hallucinations'. *Psychology Bulletin*. 84, 570–87.

Strinati, D. (1995) *An Introduction to Theories of Popular Culture*. Routledge: London and New York.

Stroemgren, E. (1989) 'The Development of the Concept of Reactive Psychoses'. *British Journal of Psychiatry*. 154 (supplement 4), 47–50.

Tarnier, N., Wittkowski, A., Kinney, C., McCarthy, E., Morris, J. and Humphreys, L. (1999) 'Durability of the Effects of Cognitive-behavioural Therapy in the Treatment of Chronic Schizophrenia: 12 Month Follow Up'. *British Journal of Psychiatry*. 174, 500–4.

Tarrier, N., Barrowclough, C., Porceddu, K. et al. (1988) 'The Assessment of Physiological Reactivity to the Expressed Emotion of the Relatives of Schizophrenic Patients'. *British Journal of Psychiatry*. 152(6), 18–624.

Tarrier, N., Barrowclough, C., Vaughn, C., Bamrah, J.S., Porceddu, K., Watts, S. and Freeman, H. (1989) 'Community Management of Schizophrenia: A Two-year Follow-Up of a Behavioural Intervention with Families'. *British Journal of Psychiatry*. 154, 625–8.

Taylor, S.F. and Liberzon, I. (1999) 'Paying Attention to Emotion in Schizophrenia'. *British Journal of Psychiatry*. 174, 24–6.

Thomson, R. (1968) *The Pelican History of Psychology*. Penguin: Middlesex.

Torgenson, S. (1985) 'Relationship of Schizotypical Personality Disorders to Schizophrenia'. *Genetics. Schizophrenia Bulletin*. 11, 554–63.

Tuke, D.H. (1872) *Illustrations of Influence of the Mind Upon the Body: In Health and Disease*. Churchill: London.

Tuke, D.H. (1878) *Insanity in Ancient and Modern Life with Chapters on Its Prevention*. Macmillan and Co.: London.

Tuke, D.H. (ed.) (1892) *Dictionary of Psychological Medicine. Vol. 1, A–H.* Churchill: London.

Turkington, D. and Kingdon, D. (2000) 'CBT for General Psychiatrists in the Management of Patients with Psychosis'. *British Journal of Psychiatry*. 177, 101–5.

Turner, B. (1992) *Regulating Bodies. Essays in Medical Sociology*. Routledge: London and New York.

Turner, B. (1997) 'From Governmentality to Risk' in A. Petersen and R. Bunton (eds). *Foucault. Health and Medicine*. Routledge: London and New York.

Underhill, E. (1911) *Mysticism: A Study in the Development of Man's Spiritual Consciousness*. Methuen: London.

Vasseleu, C. (1998) 'The Mouth and the Clinical Gaze' in M. Shildrick and J. Price (eds) *Vital Signs. Feminist Reconfigurations of the Bio/logical Body*. Edinburgh University Press: Edinburgh.

Wagstaff, G. (1983) *Hypnosis: Compliance and Belief*. Harvester Press: Brighton.

Walker, N.P., Fox, H.C. and Whalley, L.J. (1999) 'Lipids and Schizophrenia'. *British Journal of Psychiatry*. 174, 37–41.

Walkerdine, V. (1984) 'Developmental Psychology and the Child-centred Pedagogy: The Insertion of Piaget into Early Education' in J. Henriques et al. (eds) *Changing the Subject: Psychology, Social Regulation and Subjectivity*. Methuen Press: London.

Walkerdine, V. (1990) *Schoolgirl Fictions*. Verso: London.

Walkerdine, V. (1996) 'Psychological and Social Aspects of Survival' in S. Wilkinson (ed.) *Feminist Social Psychologies*. Open University Press: Buckingham and Philadelphia.

Walkerdine, V. (1997) *Daddy's Girl. Young Girls and Popular Culture*. Macmillan: Basingstoke.

Walkerdine, V. (1999) 'The Crowd in the Age of Diana: Ordinary Inventiveness and the Popular Imagination' in Kear, A. and Steinberg, D.L. (eds). *Mourning Diana: Nation, Culture and the Performance of Grief.* Routledge: London.

Walkerdine, V. (2001) Editorial. 'Critical Psychology'. *International Journal of Critical Psychology.* Launch Issue. Lawrence and Wishart: London.

Wallace, A.F.C. (1959) 'Cultural Determinations of Response to Hallucinatory Experience'. *Archives of General Psychiatry.* 1959, 1.

Weil, A. (1973) *The Natural Mind.* Jonathan Cape: London.

Weiss, G. and Haber, H.F. (1999) *Perspectives on Embodiment. The Intersection of Nature and Culture.* Routledge: London and New York.

West, D.J. (1948) 'A Mass Observation Questionnaire on Hallucinations'. *Journal of Psychiatric Treatment and Evaluation.* 5, 259–61.

West, L.J. (1962) 'A General Theory of Hallucinations and Dreams'. In L.J. West (ed.) *Hallucinations.* Grune and Stratton: New York.

West, L.J. (1975) 'A Clinical and Theoretical Overview of Hallucinatory Phenomena'. In R.K. Siegel and L.J. West (eds) *Hallucinations: Behaviour, Experience and Theory.* Wiley: New York.

Wetherell, M. and Potter, J. (1992) *Mapping the Language of Racism.* Harvester Wheatsheaf: Hemel Hempstead.

Whitman, J.R. (1961) quoted in I. Al-Issa (1977) 'Social and Cultural Aspects of Hallucinations'. *Psychology Bulletin.* 84, 570–87.

Whitwell, J.R. (1936) *Historical Notes in Psychiatry.* Lewis: London.

Wittgenstein, L. (1963) *Philosophical Investigations.* Blackwell: Oxford.

Wolf, J (1993) 'On the Road Again: Metaphors of Travel in Cultural Criticism'. *Cultural Studies.* 7(2), May, 224.

Wolpe, J. (1958) quoted in I. Al-Issa (1977) 'Social and Cultural Aspects of Hallucinations'. *Psychology Bulletin.* 84, 570–87.

Woodward, K. (1997) (ed.) *Identity and Difference.* Sage: London, Thousand Oaks and New Delhi.

Wright, E. (1984) *Psychoanalytic Criticism: Theory in Practice.* Methuen: London.

Wykes, T., Parr, A. and Landon, S. (1999) 'Group Treatment of Auditory Hallucinations. Exploratory Study of Effectiveness'. *British Journal of Psychiatry.* 175, 180–5.

Zilboorg, C. (1941) *History of Medical Psychology.* Norton: New York.

Index